Dunkirk

Dunkirk

From Disaster to Deliverance
Testimonies of the Last Survivors

SINCLAIR McKAY

Aurum Press

First published in Great Britain
2014 by Aurum Press Ltd
74–77 White Lion Street
Islington
London N1 9PF
www.aurumpress.co.uk

This paperback edition first published in 2015 by Aurum Press Ltd

Illustration by Richard Beacham

A catalogue record for this book is available from the British Library.

ISBN 978 1 78131 294 0
eISBN 978 1 78131 384 8

1 3 5 7 9 10 8 6 4 2
2015 2017 2019 2018 2016

Typeset in ITC New Baskerville by SX Composing DTP, Rayleigh Essex
Printed and bound by CPI Group (UK) Ltd, Croydon, CR0 4YY

Contents

Prologue

The small elegant boats bob and curtsey, dipping daintily as the fresh river water ripples over their bows. A silent September Sunday morning, early and pale blue, the sun warming, although the breeze brings news of autumn. There is a labyrinth of narrow wooden jetties, and moored beside them a polished mass of smart 1930s vintage Thames motor yachts. We are upstream of Hampton Court Bridge; the great palace lies beyond. And here, on the grassy bank of the River Thames, under attentive oaks, a convocation of old men and their families is taking place.

For the moment, they are still. A prayer is being said, a lone voice rising above the silence. But the atmosphere is celebratory. In attendance is HRH Prince Michael of Kent. Also present are a great number of young naval cadets, girls and boys, alongside a multitude of jolly women in smart frocks, and wind-burned men in boating blazers and white trousers. There is a pleasing incongruity about their presence next to the very elderly soldiers in berets, with full medals on show. The mix of people is fitting: the story they are commemorating, one which they celebrate here annually, is a brilliant and perhaps unique instance of the military, the navy and enthusiastic sea-going civilians all joining together in one courageous enterprise.

Now the mingling has begun. Some of these veterans, in their mid-nineties, have been brought from across the country in coaches with their families and friends and associates. This is their chance to catch up with some of those faces familiar from so many years ago. Their families know one another too. There is always much to discuss. But the day is only just beginning. With unobtrusive help from the smiling young naval cadets, the old soldiers are helped from that grassy shore, along the slightly slippery wooden jetties, and thence aboard the Thames pleasure boats. Each veteran has been allocated a space. The boats have an emotional resonance that for these men can never fade. They are just a few of the 'little ships' – the boats that, in May 1940, were among a great fleet of varied vessels that sailed back and forth across the English Channel to rescue a host of Allied soldiers and in so doing, forged a national legend that is now invoked more than any misty myth like Excalibur or Camelot. This particular legend encapsulates how the British still like to define themselves. The core image is of a sea-going island people with a genius for improvisation; it also incorporates the giftedness of untrained amateurs, the extraordinary courage of ordinary men, and the life-affirming eccentricity of taking on a technologically ruthless foe with an armada of tiny boats intended for Sunday afternoon river jaunts.

Some now refer to the myth of Dunkirk and seek to point out that the evacuation of some 338,000 troops, British, French and Belgian, in the space of nine days, from an encircled, bombed-out harbour and beaches, was not all about ordinary civilians. No, of course it wasn't; it was about the Royal Navy and the RAF, and about young untested soldiers finding within themselves depths of endurance that their scanty training alone could not have helped summon. But the word 'myth' has another meaning, that of allegory. So the myth of Dunkirk can also be taken as an allegory for Britain as it then was; a fleeting but crucial historical moment in which the character of the people – civilian and military – was suddenly illuminated, as though in a lightning flash.

These pleasure boats – which were among some 700 vessels that wove between Dover, Ramsgate, Margate and Dunkirk, in routes that steered past lethal hazards like mines, and obstacles such as submerged destroyers and paddle steamers and the Goodwin Sands, and through the harrowing dangers of bombs and machine guns – now, on this early Sunday morning, look so gleaming and smart and creamy in their leather furnishings that it is difficult to believe that they have been sailing for over seventy-five years. This community of vessels – though owned by all sorts of different people – is watched over lovingly by the Association of Dunkirk Little Ships, which also organises the annual reunions. The Dunkirk veterans – some army, some navy – take their seats on board, in the open, under the strengthening sun, listening to the Thames slurping at the hulls. The proud owners of the boats understood, when they bought these vessels, that they were buying history, and that they would have to take care that the past was honoured. What finer way to fulfil that task than a Sunday morning jaunt with such distinguished veterans on board?

Other naval traditions are carefully observed. The enthusiastic juvenile naval cadets ask the aged veterans if they would care for a warming tot; rum, perhaps, but there is whisky too. The wind on the water is brisk; the veterans do not refuse. This was also the case on that splendid – if utterly soaking – summer day in 2012 when, to mark the Queen's Diamond Jubilee, the little ships took part in a great Thames pageant. These veterans were there, sailing through the City of London under those swags of icy rain, sipping whisky. Those of us who witnessed the ships passing – I watched from the balcony of my flat in Limehouse, in the east – found the spectacle inexplicably moving. After all, they were just boats; and it was all a very long time ago. How could it possibly stir any feeling now? Yet as they sailed by, I felt my eyes prickle. Others who watched the spectacle that day found the same, again without truly understanding why.

Today, the veterans' destination is a grand lunch, to be held a few miles upstream. On this stretch of the river, the charming villas of suburbia gradually give way to a world that is more redolent of *The Wind in the Willows*; a quiet idyll of swirling water and lush waterside trees. It is quite difficult to imagine a greater contrast between this and the cacophony and fear and the smell of slaughter on those wide French beaches in May 1940.

'You got used to the scream of the bombers,' says RAF veteran Arthur Taylor, gently. He was there in France as a signalsman and got caught up in the maelstrom. 'You knew that noise couldn't hurt you. But the bombs. You could see the bombs being released, and you would think, please God . . .'

These veterans were obviously very young men then and as some point out, they were in some ways less mature than today's teenagers. To us, it seems as though they must have all grown up anticipating an inevitable war. The veterans remember differently: how would it have been possible for them to anticipate, years beforehand, exactly what was coming? The 1930s Britain they grew up in was emerging from the darkness of depression; for many parts of the country, though, poverty remained profound and stubborn. The city skies were under permanent industrial clouds. Housing was crowded, and comforts such as hot water and proper bathrooms were scarce. An affluent new world of refrigerators and central heating existed side by side with regions that still had one foot in the nineteenth century. When looking back at this period, our own generation tends only to see material misery; but for some of the veterans and their contemporaries, such considerations were of secondary importance when they were young. Some remember instead their youthful passions for football; others recall the immense freedom they gained when they were able to afford their first bicycles. Similarly, when we listen to the music of the period now – all those pawky songs from George Formby and Gracie Fields – we are not listening to the music that the young people of the time really favoured. Even by the 1930s, the cultural influence of America was enormous. This young generation dressed sharp, fussed over its hair, and danced to swing.

And it was this generation that was to grow up very suddenly on the bloody beaches of Dunkirk. 'Inside, you were terrified,' says naval veteran Vic Viner, who was there for six days and six nights. 'But you had to keep calm. You had to show everyone else that things would be all right.'

By 1939, Britain was still haunted by the echoes of the Great War, which had ended only twenty-one years before. Indeed, it seemed – from the fascist predations on Abyssinia and Spain, from Austria to the Sudetenland to Czechoslovakia – that the drums of war had never really fallen silent. Appeasement – the foreign policy pursued by Neville Chamberlain's government towards Hitler in 1938 – is now universally used as a stinging insult, an accusation of cowardice and dishonour. During that time, for many members of the public, it didn't hold those meanings at all; rather, it was seen as a measured response to a foaming dictator who wanted to unleash more of the carnage that within recent memory had already damaged the lives of almost every family in Britain.

For these Dunkirk veterans, now sitting smiling on an array of boats, as they sail upriver past little islands and lagoons, life was simply something to get on with when they were teenagers. In 1938, when many of them were eighteen or nineteen (or even younger) they were not sitting around brooding about the geopolitical situation. Instead, they acted impulsively. Some had signed up for the Territorial Army in 1938; not out of bellicosity, or anti-German passion, or even anxiety to get fully trained – but simply because it was something to do with your mates.

Similarly, in the days and months between the declaration of war and the extraordinary rescue of the British Expeditionary Force from the harbour and beaches of that small northern French port town and pleasure resort, there was something quite unstoppable about everyday British life, and also about the everyday quirks of the nation. In the period now known as 'the Phoney War' (an American term – the more widely used British phrase was 'the Bore War'), everyone from Mass Observation volunteers, who kept diaries of their everyday lives the better that those lives could be understood by the state, to literary figures like Virginia Woolf and George Orwell, recorded and examined it all. Orwell was fascinated by the popular press, and by extension, by the advertising in those newspapers; in some ways, one could almost read the psychology of the nation between the lines of all those ads for indigestion tablets, denture cleaners and whisky and Guinness.

The veterans on this cruise to Shepperton ask, rhetorically, why the moment of Dunkirk should be remembered at all; indeed, the commemorative medal for veterans was only instituted in 1948. Yet what happened throughout those days and nights involved staggering bravery. And there is more. 'The miracle of Dunkirk' is actually about miraculous transformation, a moment when national certainty crystallised for the world to see. Just as the soldiers and sailors found their characters being forged in these fires, so the people back home took stock of this sudden, volcanic crisis; and then in the midst of the spontaneous exultation that welled up from nowhere as the troops came home, determined that no matter what, everyone would fight on. This is where the People's War began.

Many veterans – as we will see – have stories that make you wonder how they can now smile so serenely on the world. 'That night you could see the glow of Dunkirk,' says Gareth Wright, a young Territorial who had signed up in his small Devon village just two weeks before war was declared, musing on his company's desperate retreat to the Channel coast. 'The roads were choc-a-bloc with refugees. The German pilots were taking advantage of the chaos. They would go along the roads. Machine gunning, bombing, absolute chaos, havoc, no communication. Everything just collapsed.'

Others see greater depth in the term 'miracle'. 'How did that sea stay so flat and calm during the evacuation?' muses one veteran. 'It hasn't been like that in the seventy-five years since. There is only one answer. Some power above. You don't have to say it's God if you don't want to – but some power did that.'

Of course, their war stories don't end at Dunkirk; rather, Dunkirk was merely the beginning. After this, they would go on to fight in the desert, in the Mediterranean, on the beaches of Normandy in 1944. But they are insistent that Dunkirk should be remembered properly. It is not too much to say that those nine days in May and June 1940 decisively changed the course of a war that had only just begun.

But in order to fully grasp the impact of that defeat and subsequent escape, it is also important to understand the weeks and months that came beforehand; the period during which these young men were drawn away from their everyday lives, sent to France, and gradually fell in love with a different, rural world far removed from the dark coal smogs of their home towns. It is also important to understand what was happening back in Britain, politically and culturally. There is a sense of a new, sharper, younger world struggling to emerge from beneath the suffocating weight of a Victorian heritage: the old aristocratic establishment was in its final ebbs. The increasingly confident trade unions had found their voice. Some time before the Beveridge Report and the inception of the welfare state, there was already a powerful feeling that things had to be done differently. The declaration of war – and the later shock of Dunkirk – seemed to work as catalysts, bringing this new world closer. This was reflected in the military too: at the start of the war, the old class hierarchies – public-school educated officers with independent means, working-class Tommies – were as rigid as they had been fifty years beforehand. After Dunkirk came the first inklings of a more meritocratic structure.

There are shades of anti-establishment Ealing comedy too: this is the period in which the population undertook mass evacuations, was issued with millions of gas masks – and then promptly forgot all about the emergency that had engendered them. The children were brought home, the gas masks were left neglected in cupboards. It is important to understand that in some ways, there was nothing inevitable about the war; even up to the last desperate days of Dunkirk, some high up in Cabinet continued to argue for 'making terms' with Hitler. Churchill, who by that stage had only been Prime Minister for some three weeks, was obliged to go outside Cabinet to muster support for his position that the fight had to go on.

The little ships on the Thames have reached their destination, an assembly hall on the leafy riverbank, outside which a piper greets their arrival in sluicing rain. As the boats are tied up one by one, the veterans are helped indoors, where they are given a splendid lunch. They must think back, not only to their own experiences, but to what they saw others going through. The sight of thousands of soaked, exhausted men, desperately hungry and thirsty, wading out far into the shallow sandy sea, that seemingly endless shelf of sand, to reach motor yachts such as these; the effort of hauling themselves up on board, weak after days without proper rations. The sensation of being crammed in, shoulder to shoulder, and an uneasy feeling that the vessel was either about to capsize or sink. The feeling of exposure as the Stukas fell from the sky, firing red-hot bullets through wood and glass. For some veterans, the after-effects remained unacknowledged in later years – in medical terms, there was still only the most basic understanding of what is now termed post-traumatic stress disorder. A few veterans, even twenty years afterwards, would find themselves catapulting out of bed in the middle of the night, colliding with the wall in their dream panics. For one or two veterans, even now the nights are only guaranteed ease with the help of one or two whiskies.

Yet this moment of Dunkirk was not simply about the military; it was also about the women and men back in Britain who – quite unbidden – defied Churchill and turned an outright military humiliation into an occasion for celebration. It is often asserted that

Churchill inspired the people. On this crucial occasion, it seems to have been the other way around.

The other important way to fully appreciate what is also termed 'the Dunkirk spirit' is to examine the sheer oddness of the weeks and months that came before it: civilians and soldiers alike braced for a war that never quite seemed to come. During that time we see an effusion of both radicalism and unselfconscious good humour, as well as apprehension and foreboding. From new military recruits finding themselves being billeted in brightly coloured seaside holiday camps to occasionally crazed civilian plans to foil fifth-columnist spies, ordinary life went on at a distinctly odd slant. London was blacked-out but people went dancing all the same. They couldn't be stopped. Later, exhausted soldiers rescued from those hellish beaches recalled the dazzling strangeness of arriving back in England and seeing rural cricket matches being played under the same warm sky from which, just a few miles away, Stukas had dived.

The story of Dunkirk, as we shall see, is fundamentally about metamorphosis; days in which ordinary civilian men turned into soldiers and people back home readied themselves for total war. Dunkirk is woven into the tapestry of national identity. This is the story of the people, the events, and the little ships, that make the tapestry so moving and vivid.

PART ONE

1

'Would You Like to Join the Army?'

September 1939

The gathering storm had been heard some distance off. During the summer of 1939, even small children felt the foreboding. In London, on the night of 10 August, all the lights went out. The city's population was not accustomed to pure darkness; in the 1930s, bursts of new American-style neon, glowing from cinemas and restaurants, radiating from advertising hoardings on Piccadilly and the Great West Road, had cast auroras of deep red and green and pink into the city's thick night fogs. But on that warm summer night, the blackened streets felt clammily dead. It was a dummy run for the blackouts to come. And already, these streets – and those of other cities around Britain – were beginning to echo with a wider absence: between June 1939 and the declaration of war on Sunday 3 September, it was reckoned that an extraordinary three million people – mothers and children – had moved from the nation's large industrial cities to other areas, other regions, that were perceived to be safer. 'Glad they've gone,' one young woman in east London was reported as saying. 'They were a damned nuisance.'[1] There were also reports of family pets across the country being destroyed.

But there was no sense, in September 1939, of catharsis, of relief, of the storm finally arriving; the hollow booms had been heard for too long. Men in their late twenties and thirties gathering after a day's work for quick pints in nicotine-slicked pubs discussed the call-up; they wondered when they would receive those official papers, or whether they should expedite the process and report immediately to the local recruiting office. The pubs were doing brisk business. 'The wife . . . said that when she went up town last night,' wrote one Huddersfield diarist, 'she saw more drunk people than she had seen for a long time.'[2]

Almost exactly a year beforehand, it had seemed as though that mighty storm was about to break when Hitler demanded secession of the Sudetenland, and Prime Minister Neville Chamberlain flew out to Germany to try to fathom the Führer's future aims and seek a guarantee that no further aggression would take place. While he did so, thousands in Britain volunteered for Air Raid Precautions (ARP) duties. On top of this, thousands more young men – some very young indeed – blithely signed up with their local Territorial Army units. For lads of sixteen and seventeen (some lying about their ages) this was quite often not to do with any terrific patriotic fervour, or indeed with a desire to see battle; it was more to do with finding ways to pass the long evenings. They would sometimes join simply because their friends had done so. And the idea of gaining that military training, of spending weekends in rough country learning to shoot, was attractive to boys not yet old enough to spend their time in the pub. But they were not daft; they also knew that their newly acquired skills might be tested at any moment.

Since April 1939, and after the full scale invasion of Czechoslovakia, there had been conscription in Britain, as there had been during the Great War. The left-wing *Daily Mirror* newspaper was initially outraged. 'What, another big army of fine young men for idiotic and dud generals to drive to death and destruction?' it shouted. Senior Labour politician Ernest Bevin was, according to Alan Bullock, 'angry that the government had brought in conscription by the back door and tried to put it over on the working class'.[3] But Bevin was equally enraged by far-left demands for industrial action to oppose the call-up. The Tory establishment sang a more compelling tune. 'Conscription is the cry that leaps to all men's mouths,' wrote Duff Cooper in the *Evening Standard*; soon he was to be appointed Minister of Information. By August 1939, the call-up was accelerated, though at this stage, the very youngest were not summoned. In any case, it seemed to be widely understood that this would be a new kind of war.

For civilians, around thirty-eight million gas masks were manufactured, and distributed around the country. These masks, however, were not available for very small infants. This was not the only reason that they inspired horror; nor was the uncanny skull-like effect they evoked when worn. It was more to do with that shuddering echo of what had gone before. The thin victims of mustard gas attacks in the trenches, their lungs beyond repair, still limped Britain's streets with haunted faces. Very few families up and down the land had not been touched by the damage – physical and psychological – wrought on the Great War battlefields of France. The issuing of gas masks had been interpreted as a chilly official declaration that in this new age of warfare, no one would be spared the horrors that the previous generation of soldiers had seen.

In September 1938, when Chamberlain held in his hand the piece of paper that signalled 'peace in our time', it seemed to be widely understood and accepted among the public that the state of affairs in Europe was quite the opposite; that the Nazi threat to Britain was growing. Like a patient who feels distinctly the onset of fever – the temperature, the giddiness – so too the British people seemed aware that the crisis was at hand. Even before the 1938 Munich conference – the point at which many members of the public gloomily expected an instant declaration of hostilities – Sir

Thomas Inskip, Minister for Co-ordination of Defence, had stated: 'the plain fact which cannot be obscured is that it is beyond the resources of this country to make proper provision in peace for the defence of the British Empire against three major powers in three different theatres of war.' In other words, any conflict that involved the Germans, Italians and Japanese would be unwinnable.

Senior Foreign Office diplomat – and furious anti-appeaser – Sir Robert Vansittart had been crisper about it: there was simply too much territory for the over-stretched British to defend. 'We're over-landed,' he said. None the less, Vansittart believed the British could not afford to close their ears to the increasingly ugly news from the continent or take comfort from their island status. He was particularly angry with the equivalent of today's chattering classes, 'people here, who, in smug insularity, refused to credit, or even to hear, those horrors . . . the Channel has screened the modern Pharisees from horrors'.

However, it is instructive to remember that for a long time, polls showed that the majority of British people, despite their pessimism, considered that careful diplomacy might somehow calm Hitler and keep Britain out of the war. In February 1939, a few months after the Munich agreement was signed, 74 per cent of those questioned thought it would help keep conflict at bay; only 24 per cent thought it would bring it closer.

Opinion polls are but a snapshot; they don't measure deeper currents of unease. Yet against the thick darkness sweeping across Europe, the growing feeling of approaching menace from a German war machine that seemed pitiless and ineluctable, quotidian life in Britain continued. How could it not? The sound of those distant hollow booms had to be blocked out somehow. In the spring of 1939, courting couples trooped along in vast numbers to see the lavish (and slightly sugary) Hollywood version of *Wuthering Heights* with Laurence Olivier. The phenomenally popular Technicolor epic *Gone with the Wind* would open in the nation's cinemas some months later; but in the meantime, Margaret Mitchell's novel, upon which the film was based, was devoured throughout that year. Books were still an expensive commodity; they were borrowed from lending libraries in vast quantities rather than bought. This, though, was one of the rare exceptions.

But cinema was the truly popular art form. Other terrific hits in the weeks before the war included Alfred Hitchcock's adaptation of Daphne du Maurier's *Jamaica Inn*, Alexander Korda's richly colourful imperial adventure *The Four Feathers*, Robert Donat and Greer Garson in the shamelessly sentimental *Goodbye Mr Chips* and George Formby in the comedy *Trouble Brewing*, in which the hapless ukulele player is up against a gang of counterfeiters. Children meanwhile smuggled themselves into cinemas for the Hollywood horror *Son of Frankenstein*, Boris Karloff's final turn as the Monster. Film would remain immensely popular over the next few years. In the weeks before the war, there had been seething debate about the closure of theatres and music halls, out of fear of bombing raids. The closure of cinemas, though implemented very briefly for a few days as the war began, seems never to have been seriously considered as a long-term option – for even that brief withdrawal of entertainment drew piercing yelps of protest.

One unexpected contributor to the art of the silver screen at that time was none other than the aforementioned diplomat in chief and anti-appeaser Sir Robert Vansittart. When he was not raging about the laid-back attitude of Berlin ambassador Sir Neville Henderson towards Hitler, Vansittart was co-writing a screenplay for producer Alexander Korda: *The Thief of Baghdad*. In pre-war Britain, it was not unusual for politicians to have wide and rewarding hinterlands. The Korda film went into production in the summer of 1939. Interviewed by C.A. Lejeune at that time – when everyone from the Cabinet down was tensing themselves for the coming conflict – Vansittart explained his Baghdad epic quite cheerfully: 'I was at our legation in Persia for some time,' he said. 'I loved the life there and I learned to speak the language . . . In the pre-war world,' he added of his diplomatic career before the Great War, 'even people in fairly busy posts had a certain amount of leisure.' The film – a colourful tapestry of escapism – was released the following year. It is still regarded as a classic, partly because of its energetic wartime provenance.

The only other leisure activity to have commanded such a fanatical following at the time was dancing. Londoners still flocked to see the musical *Me and My Girl*, featuring the Lambeth Walk, in such numbers that extra buses to the Victoria Palace Theatre had been laid on. The King and Queen went to see it (and the Queen enjoyed herself so much that she went again). A year previously, a *Times* editorial had declared: 'While dictators rage and statesmen talk, all Europe dances – to The Lambeth Walk.' It was indeed a continent-wide hit. Throughout 1939, people everywhere were affecting the wide, swaggering gait of the dance, set to Noel Gay's catchy song. In the south London district of Lambeth itself ('the sky ain't blue, the grass ain't green'), locals were blithely adjusting to this international fame. In the native (and drunken) version of the dance, the tougher men sometimes wore women's clothing.

In fact, dance halls around the country in 1939 were consistently and solidly booked, while an outdoor dance held in London's Finsbury Park attracted so many people that 'the official arrangements broke down' and the stomping could be heard in several districts around. The young people – including young men preparing themselves for conscription – lived for their dancing. In the West End, on Friday 31 August 1939, the owners of an illegal dancing and drinking venue, the wonderful sounding 'Maryland Bottle Party', were prosecuted for not holding licences either for drinking or for dancing. The undercover inspectors were especially aggrieved at having been charged eight shillings for a sandwich.

Throughout those days before the conflict, women and men also sought escape in light reading. One of the bestselling – and most borrowed – books on the weekend that war came was the latest Agatha Christie thriller, *Murder Is Easy*. The story featured as protagonist retired policeman Luke Fitzwilliam, a character felt by a few reviewers to be lacking the essential little grey cells of Christie's more popular creation Hercule Poirot. There was also the new P.G. Wodehouse novel, *Uncle Fred in the Springtime*, the latest chapter in the saga of Blandings Castle. On the day that war was declared, the *Sunday Times* reviewer wrote: 'Is this not the right moment to renew our acquaintance with Lord Emsworth . . . and the fifth earl of Ickenham . . . and their various nephews and nieces?' Yes: this was the exact moment for such escapism. Sadly, Wodehouse's conduct in the conflict to follow was to prove that his sunny comedy was strictly for the page, and couldn't survive the reality of the Nazis.

The serious hit thriller of the day was Geoffrey Household's *Rogue Male* – a story that could not have been timed better. The British hero takes it upon himself to travel to a Germany-style mittel-European country to assassinate a brutal dictator (who bears a strong resemblance to Hitler). Indeed, the hero reaches the monster's country residence and almost gets him within his sights. But he is foiled by a sentry, and what follows is a nightmare of torture, and then pursuit, as Nazi-esque agents remorselessly pursue the hero back to England and hunt him through Dorset. It very quickly became essential reading in the Territorial Army. For these young men, the passages where the hero seeks ingenious means of escape in the thorn thickets and 'hollow ways' of the Dorset landscape would have ignited their imaginations about their own roles in the coming fight. Could they learn such quick-thinking self-reliance? The novel's fame spread further when war broke out.

The week before war was declared, on Monday 28 August 1939, the government announced that it was implementing Emergency Regulations, the list of which was so long – there were 104 of them – that they were not all reported. These ranged from compulsory evacuations of vulnerable people, to the close monitoring of homing pigeons, which could conceivably be used by enemy agents for conveying vital information. It also assumed the power to requisition large properties for war use; and the Admiralty assumed control of certain areas of merchant shipping.

In the town of Coventry, in the Midlands' industrial heartland, there were still simmering tensions in the wake of a terrorist bomb – the 'bicycle bomb' – that had killed five and injured 100 the previous week. The device had been planted in the front basket of a bicycle, and it was widely assumed that the Irish Republican Army (IRA) was to blame. Consequently there were many who protested at having to work alongside Irishmen. Petitions were presented to the Mayor and the Chief Constable of Coventry.

In London, meanwhile, the blackout claimed its first victim before it had even properly started: Henry Godfrey, who worked for Marylebone Borough Council, was killed by a car at Marble Arch as he painted the kerbstones white in preparation for the darkness to come.

By the middle of that last week in August – as the population of Poland put itself on a war footing – Britons followed the twists of high diplomacy between the Foreign Office and 'Herr Hitler' via BBC broadcasts. The streets of east London grew a little quieter; this was the start of hop season, where by way of a holiday, workers and their families would head off to Kent to take part in the hop harvest, living in corrugated iron shanty towns while they did so. Despite the electrical charge of tension in the air, these families were not to be deterred. Elsewhere saw the genesis of a new institution called the 'Citizens Advice Bureau'. Its original purpose was to advise families in situations of war crisis; if, say, they had found themselves homeless after a bombing raid.

There appeared to be a certain amount of unofficial evacuation going on as well, particularly among those with the financial wherewithal. Some country house hotels in the greener shires came to be termed – perhaps unfairly – as 'funk-holes', while certain smart women from the more rarefied strata of society deemed it prudent to quit London. A few others departed the country's shores entirely, embarking on voyages to the United States. The upmarket newspapers carried advertisements for cruise liners offering passage to America. For those who had no choice but to stay, however, officially, Britain had already been divided into three zones: 'evacuation', 'reception' and 'neutral'.

It was easier for the young to be blithe, or offhand, or even cheerful; but their parents were filled with the dread engendered by the previous war. A year earlier, for young Arthur Taylor, living at the time in the south-west London suburb of Wimbledon, there had been the pre-war impatience to join up and get started. Out cycling one afternoon, he and his friends spotted an impromptu recruitment drive going on in the street. Mr Taylor says now, with a laugh, 'There was an army group and they were stopping people and they stopped us and said "Would you like to join the Territorial Army?" So we said yes. The soldier asked how old we were. First of all, I said, "Sixteen." But I was too young. So, I thought very quickly for a second then said, "Seventeen, I mean." We were all signed up and I joined 306 Company London Electrical Engineers, Royal Engineers. Joined up that afternoon.' During that time, the Territorial Army had quietly increased in size from thirteen divisions to twenty. A year later, though, Mr Taylor made the switch to the Royal Air Force. 'I wanted to join as a photographer,' he says. 'But they gave me a job as wireless operator.' There was a certain level of military tradition running in Mr Taylor's family; but for other similar teenage recruits, their parents' reaction was sometimes angry. Only twenty years before, family members had been mutilated in foul trenches; there was the pervasive fear of another generation being sent into that hell.

Perhaps this is why so very few people admitted out loud to believing that the coming conflict was inevitable. There is a great deal of denial to be heard in Mass Observation (MO) reports; a refusal to believe that political leaders could allow this to happen again. But among the young men – the Territorial reservists who by September 1939 had already been called up, and the labourers and clerks and junior managers who expected to be conscripted – one can hear in their later accounts how they had settled in their own minds what was approaching.

The startling tide of romance that washed over the nation in those hours before the war tells its own story of what people deep down were anticipating. 'Hundreds of young couples flocked to the principal register offices in London on Saturday to give notice of marriage,' went one report of 2 September, 'and to try and arrange the earliest possible date for the ceremony.'

There was also an understanding, however, that war this time would not be conducted in a distant land; it would be fought in the skies directly above. The immediate assumption – from the War Office to the saloon bar of the Anchor and Crown – was that as soon as war was declared, the Germans would unleash a terrible blitzkrieg against British cities. All had seen the cinema newsreel footage of the Spanish Civil War, and the nightmare rained down upon the people of Guernica. All had seen that there was virtually nothing that could be done to stop a mighty squadron of bombers. One of the most prominent newspaper advertisements in that last week before the war was for the disinfectant brand Dettol; the strapline of the artwork read starkly: 'Air Raid Precautions: Be prepared for any emergency and keep Dettol, the modern anti-septic, in your First Aid Kit. No matter how small the wound, it is essential to apply an anti-septic . . . buy a bottle from your chemist now.'

There were other, slightly more neurotic preparations. At London Zoo, for instance, the snakes and spiders and various rare insects with potentially dangerous bites were destroyed, for fear that the bombs would allow them to escape and make their way unhindered into London homes. Larger animals, such as the giraffes, were evacuated to the Hertfordshire zoo at Whipsnade, which was felt to be far enough to keep them from harm.

On the morning of Friday 1 September came the news that Germany had invaded Poland, unleashing massive bombing on Warsaw. In an unprecedented reversal of protocol, King George VI visited the Prime Minister at Downing Street; Chamberlain was too busy to make the usual journey across Horseguards Parade to the Palace.

This was a tiny metonym for the wider social reversals to come. The government was still notionally a 'National Government'; it had been formed all the way back in 1931, under Labour leader Ramsay MacDonald, in the wake of the vast crisis caused by the Depression, as a government of all parties, the best men to try and guide the country through. MacDonald had been succeeded by Conservative Stanley Baldwin, who won a huge majority in 1935 for the continuation of this coalition government. Stepping down in 1937, he in turn had been succeeded by fellow Conservative Neville Chamberlain. By 1939, though, Chamberlain was getting no support from the Labour benches, and it would become clear that support was falling away sharply among some of his own party.

Like a canary chirruping in a coal mine, the incredibly popular entertainer Gracie Fields contrived to underline the seriousness of the days; she announced that she was curtailing her six-month sojourn on the island of Capri and returning to Britain for the duration. For the wealthier classes – specifically, the very rich 20,000 or so people in London who owned recently invented television sets – this would be their last chance to enjoy them for a while. On 1 September, the BBC Television service, which had been broadcasting from the north London suburb of Alexandra Palace for about three years, was suspended. The last programme put out before the cathode ray tubes went dead was a Mickey Mouse cartoon.

The weather was fine in the hours before war came. Boats that would soon acquire much greater significance were navigating quiet waterways. Near Ipswich, an Edwardian sailing barge called the *Tollesbury* was skippered by a man called Lemon Webb. His vessel carried a variety of cargos, from Canadian oats to stone. Months later, its capacity would be tested to an extraordinary degree. Elsewhere, on the sun-dappled waters of the Dart estuary in Devon, a 40ft motor launch called *Lady Cable* was running boat trips to Torquay. None of its passengers would have envisaged the vessel crammed with soldiers, some hanging on to the sides. In London, sailing back and forth past the Houses of Parliament was a fine daytrippers' motor boat called the *Hurlingham*, which was destined to see distinguished service (and indeed still ploughs the Thames today, playing host to thumping late night 'disco cruises'). Conversely, a little further up the Thames, another civilian summer pleasure cruiser, *Tigris 1*, had actually been constructed during the Great War as a submarine chaser; it would not be long before it saw military service again.

In east London, that weekend, the fascists were shouting frantically. In a hall in Hackney, Sir Oswald Mosley, leader of the British Union, declared that the entire war crisis was the result of British political leaders betraying the people for the sake of an alliance with Russia, while simultaneously kow-towing to interests thinly disguised as 'financiers'. 'Let us end the shame of a British government,' he roared, 'trotting like a tame dog at the heel of Poland ready at the Polish command to attack anyone who threatened the interests of the financiers who rule their country.'

There was, as novelist Virginia Woolf had observed several years previously, a quiet pervasiveness about the British Union of Fascists in some districts that was somehow even more disquieting than the shouting. She and her husband Leonard were driving through the East End one foggy night; they had a small accident, the fog became impossible to negotiate and Virginia had to get out of the car in order to help direct it. 'Figures suddenly emerged,' she wrote. 'The kind man with a paper. I walked by his side leading the car . . . Another man led us; offered me a rest. In the car I looked and found the paper was "The Blackshirt".'[4]

Present a few years later at another of Sir Oswald's fevered and thuggish meetings, in Richmond, Surrey, was a teenage lad called Reg Vine. Just months later, Mr Vine would be among the youngest people – a sea cadet – to find himself wading through the corpses in the Dunkirk surf in his effort to help rescue British troops. But in those days before the conflict began, the likes of Mosley held a certain fascination for young minds. 'When I was a lad, I joined Mosley's crowd, the fascist movement,' Mr Vine says now. The spell was swiftly broken. 'They made a lot of promises. I went up, signed up, at Richmond and funnily enough, that's where I met the wife, in a side turning. Every Friday night, Mosley used to be there.'

Mr Vine was only fifteen, and at an impressionable age, although he soon gathered what Mosley was really about. 'Now, Oswald Mosley – people could listen to him down there at Richmond, his speeches were fantastic and the promises . . . He never mentioned the Jews, though, funnily enough, when I was there. There were just the promises and the stories.' But young Vine soon sensed the insidious undercurrent of all those promises and stories, and he swiftly disengaged: 'When I found out what Hitler was doing with the Jews – even before the war – I never turned up to those meetings any more. I could see where it was going. And I thought, if we have a war, Hitler will be over here.'

Long before the war, there was a broad understanding of the increasing physical, as well as psychological, menace to the Jews in Germany. The *Manchester Guardian* produced on its front page a precise chronology, since Hitler came to power, of the methods used to oppress and intimidate and terrorise, the seizure and theft of money and goods, the barring from trades, the horror of 'Kristallnacht' and the burning of synagogues. There was no secret about what was happening; which was why, for instance, mathematical genius and Bletchley Park codebreaker-to-be Alan Turing sponsored the education of two Jewish boys who had been bundled out of Germany, and why prospective foster parents gathered in the darkness of London's Liverpool Street station to meet hundreds more children who had come over with the *Kindertransport*.

Some sophisticates scoffed at what they saw as crude propaganda. The novelist Henry Green, an Old Etonian who had taken himself off to a Midlands foundry to live among working-class people, mused as the war began of the terrible things that were being heard about the Germans. 'As I write, there are tales of concentration camps as bad as any told when Belgium was invaded in 1914,' he wrote, adding that the 'wild hysteria' was reminiscent of the material in old

Great War editions of Punch.[5] Similarly sniffy was the writer Mollie Panter-Downes, who confided to her American readers in *The New Yorker* that 'atrocity stories that everyone . . . remembers from the last war have turned up again, as good as new, but with different details'. Yet there was real, terrifying ugliness, which the broader public seemed to understand very well.

There was, moreover, at the other extreme of the political spectrum, a pervasive suggestion of revolution in certain circles. A few of George Orwell's friends, for instance, felt that Britain stood on the edge of a socialist uprising. Perhaps it is more accurate to say that they wished it did so. In fact, the British people were already experiencing a different form of social earthquake without any suggestion of Bolshevism. Even the outbreak of this war was shaking the established order of things. The trick, not merely for the government, but for everyone, was to make it seem as if it was still somehow possible to maintain the familiar way of life.

That very weekend, in the hours before Chamberlain's declaration, life for everyone in Britain, and in particular for its young men, was shifting fast. The forces were being mobilised. Territorial reserves clocking off their shifts found themselves, mere hours later, standing in uniform; indeed some, like Gareth Wright from a small village near Dartmoor, found themselves being taken straight away to the docks, there to embark immediately for France, having undergone little in the way of real training. In Manchester, there were reports of mothers crying in the streets as their newly uniformed sons marched off, their faces 'a mix of bravado and fear'.

Indeed, for Mr Wright, the war had crashed in upon his life with unexpected speed just a few weeks after he had joined the Territorial Army at the age of nineteen. 'We were in what was just a little small hamlet really – Horndon, on the edge of Dartmoor,' he says. 'Loved it up there. And the boys in the village around my age, just about all of us joined what was the 153 Battery Anti-Aircraft. There was a Territorial Army unit in Tavistock.' Their reasons for joining were less to do with fighting zeal than with a sense of escapism. 'It was for something to do of a weekend,' says Mr Wright now with a laugh. 'We got a pair of boots and a uniform, we joined this unit – and we were all boys together. Ken Stevens, Roger Palmer, Peter Dodd, Harry Anderson . . . we all joined up.

'When it looked pretty obvious there was going to be a war,' Mr Wright continues, 'they called us up a week before the outbreak. We went into Tavistock. On the Sunday morning, we had a church service in the Guildhall with the Salvation Army. I remember it as though it was yesterday. At 11 a.m. they put the old wireless on, and Chamberlain came on. Incidentally we should have gone on a fortnight's firing camp training, starting on that very day, 3 September. But on the Monday morning we were right away, then made our way to Avonmouth and got on board an old Channel steamer, the *Lady of Man* – a blooming cockleshell of a thing – and we went across to St Nazaire.'

For Arthur Taylor, who had himself so eagerly signed up with the Territorials, the darkening skies over Europe did not impinge on his job with Harrods for a while. Indeed, when it came to fancy goods and groceries for the well-to-do, life after Munich continued very much as normal throughout 1938 and into much of 1939. Young Mr Taylor was engaged in complex organisational work in the deliveries department. 'I did all round London within a thirty-mile radius,' he says. 'I was still working there when I was in the Territorials.'

After he joined the RAF, Mr Taylor adds, 'All of a sudden I was in Swindon for an unofficial [reserve] weekend. And we were listening to the wireless when Chamberlain announced, "we are now at war". And so the Bristol Bus Company provided a coach, we were all rounded up and taken back to camp. The coach was there within an hour of his speech. I was still training as a wireless operator. Virtually confined to camp from then on.'

For Bob Halliday, a young Glaswegian who worked in the Clydeside shipyards, the terrible prospect of coming war was alleviated a little by a wider use of his technical skills: he was to be drafted, for a while, into the highly skilled map-making team. He was acutely aware of the matter of class, and of the limitations that it could throw around life. Just a couple of years previously, as a lad, he had joined up with a volunteer scheme for young men run by the Duke of York: 'I went to the King's Camp down at Southwold in Suffolk. It was 250 public schoolboys with 250 apprentices from the shipyards . . . and I was picked to go down. So we went down and competed. Runs, jumps, cricket and football. Against the public schoolboys. And there was I, as a young apprentice with a secondary education.

'The public schoolboys were the masters – they went down the pub and they drank cider and they were going to win this and they were going to win that and they were so self-assured that they gave us an inferiority complex. We were running in this two and a half mile cross-country and they had already decided who was going to win it. I was running behind this guy and I wouldn't run past him. Because I thought if I did, he would run past me again. So I came second. I could have passed him easily.'

In the weeks and the days of August 1939, it did start to occur to a very few within the army that this kind of schism was about to be played out on a grander scale, and at a time of national crisis: the officer class, educated to believe in their entitlements, and then the ordinary soldiers, for the most part urban boys from rough, industrial backgrounds and some with an angry sense of inferiority. Although membership of organisations like the Communist Party was, in 1939, relatively low and weak, there was none the less a strong socialist undertow in the larger cities. Mr Halliday now tells his story of superior young men being allowed to win races to illustrate how quickly he managed to shake himself free of that particular attitude. The wise few in the army understood that conscription would bring many recruits who would not be easy to mould into the old class-based regime, where superiority was automatically assumed.

This sense of class friction in the forces was also underscored a little later in a broadcast by the then extremely popular author and playwright J.B. Priestley, who said that the war would not be won 'by the England the films are so fond of showing us: the old Hall, the hunt breakfast, the hunt ball, the villagers touching their caps, all the old bag of tricks', but by 'machines and the men who make and drive those machines'.

The historian Alfred Sauvy observed that France gingerly tiptoed into the new war with Germany like a reluctant swimmer shiveringly moving step by step into the icy sea of mid-December. Given the sacrifices made just over twenty years before, this might not be altogether surprising. In Britain, Whitehall looked with great enthusiasm upon the conscription programme. In July 1939, attending the Bastille Day parade in Paris, Lord of the Admiralty Winston Churchill had remarked to an aide: 'Thank God we've got conscription or we wouldn't be able to look these people in the face.' The French high command regarded their own forces as being greatly superior to the army that the British were assembling. And even among the British, there was a sense that the French had terrific technical proficiency. Intriguingly though, right at the start were foreshadowings of events to come, among which was the British reluctance to deploy much in the way of air power to France. Even in the final days before war broke out, military chiefs and senior politicians alike sensed that Britain would have to rely too heavily on its fighter planes at home to see them being put at unnecessary risk elsewhere.

On 3 September 1939, when Britain went to war over the invasion of Poland, no one – not the newly called-up men, nor their officers, nor their wives and girlfriends and mothers, nor the politicians – appeared to imagine that the armed forces would be sent over to Poland to join battle with the German foe. There was no suggestion of troops being flown in to help grab back Warsaw and repulse the invaders. Obviously, given Poland's accutely vulnerable location between Germany and Russia, those newly minted allies of the Molotov/Ribbentrop pact, such an idea would never have been given even fleeting consideration. It seemed to be widely understood up and down the land; Poland was simply the crossed line in the sand, the pretext, the trigger. And though we would be standing shoulder to shoulder with France and Belgium, British thoughts tended towards the insular. How soon – how many hours or minutes – before Hitler launched an attack on this island? This reflex, this mass holding of breath, was to characterise the next few curious weeks. This was the background against which young – and older – men, were now trooping into the army, the air force and the Royal Navy. And it was the navy – better staffed, more experienced – that would be the first to taste this new war. For many young inexperienced soldiers, though, there was instead the prospect of being shipped to France without having had quite the full training that they expected.

2

'Their Tax in Blood'

September–December 1939

As soon as they were mobilised, the young soldiers of Britain – along with those of France, Belgium and other European countries – found themselves gazing out across a hazily unknowable prospect. This was also true of the apprehensive civilians back at home. While some older people dreaded that the coming conflict would repeat the nightmares of the last – the faces shot off, the mutilations, the organs burned by silvery gas – others feared that it would be fought on new and even more terrible terms. The British codebreakers who had worked in Broadway Buildings, just off St James's Park near Westminster, had already been evacuated from London. Admiral Sir Hugh Sinclair, head of the Secret Intelligence Service, thought it likely that a massive aerial bombardment from Germany would begin at once.

The struggle to assemble a fully trained military force, which had begun with conscription in April 1939, was stepped up massively as war broke out. Several years before, General Montgomery-Massingberd had remarked acidly that 'it is more than a five minute job to create an army'. The French top brass might have all too readily agreed. At around that same time, in the mid-1930s, France's General Maxime Weygand had come to Britain for talks with senior military commanders, and in the course of doing so had dropped in on some armoured exercises being carried out near Sandhurst. 'He shook his head and went away,' said General Sir John Burnett Stuart, 'hoping that we really had something better than what he was shown.'[1]

The soldier who was to command these men up to and during the ordeal of Dunkirk was General Viscount Gort, who had been appointed Chief of the Imperial General Staff in 1937. His full name was John Standish Surtees Prendergast Vereker, a name that seemed to have strutted forth from some nineteenth-century operetta. But there was rather more to 53-year-old Lord Gort than that. When he was young, he had gained the ironic nickname of 'Fat Boy' (he was big, but not fat). He had an enduringly boyish sense of humour, setting off water hoses under the doors of men who had retired early from drinking in the mess. But he was acutely aware of the threat Britain faced, and he argued consistently in Whitehall for the extra forces and equipment he knew would be needed.

The Secretary of State for War was the man who had invented the orange safety beacon for pedestrian road crossings. Leslie Hore-Belisha had started in his new role in 1937 by setting out to modernise barracks and uniforms, bringing in Joe Lyons (of Corner House fame) to improve army catering, and also by lowering the retirement age for senior officers. He had a knack for thinking in terms of newspaper headlines. There were those in the army hierarchy who despised him for it. Hore-Belisha's initial judgement, in his new role, was that the British Army would not have to fight again in Europe; and he considered the Maginot Line quite secure. But by the time war broke out, his views had completely changed. By autumn 1939, Hore-Belisha was a very anxious man.

The expectation among other politicians and public alike was that because Britain had a mighty empire, then surely its standing forces would be equally formidable; moreover, surely Britain's superior armed technology meant that sheer numbers weren't as important as they used to be? But Lord Gort knew that it was less simple. Certainly there were many highly trained professional British soldiers dotted around the different territories, but their attentions were fixed on other matters. For instance, there was the Arab revolt in Palestine in 1936–7 which, as one historian noted, 'served to underline how imperial defence priorities still weighed more heavily in London than a continental commitment'.[2]

Even then, if such a commitment were to be made, what really would it have amounted to? In the late 1930s, the British army was relatively poorly equipped. 'The available Regular force was only two thirds the size of the [First World War] Expeditionary Force and would arrive in France more slowly,' wrote one historian, 'while [the] Territorial Army was in no state to take the field.'[3]

For the young men either in the Territorials or freshly conscripted, training quite often consisted of blank ammunition and thunder-flashes, by means of simulation. Some young men remembered that they were asked to 'imagine' the enemy in their manoeuvres. Nor, at the start, was the organisation as efficient as it was later to become. Among the civilians drafted in were skilled electricians, cooks, salesmen, plumbers. Efforts were made to ensure that they were found suitable positions in regiments where their skills might be used. But often this was not the case. Added to this was the culture clash whereby young, independent men were required to defer to public-school officers who in civilian life would have drawn their scornful mirth.

It was a little easier for the experienced soldiers; even if their experience was, in terms of warfare, outdated. One such soldier was Harry Malpas, who had lied about his age to sign up with the Royal Warwickshire Regiment in 1936. Malpas had come from a desperate background; he and his siblings were orphans, their father having died very young and their mother – who worked in a Wolsey car factory – having been killed in an extraordinary industrial accident on a day when Gandhi (of all people) was being shown around the premises. Young Harry tried several times to run away and join up with the military, despite being under age. After several attempts, he succeeded in joining up as an officer's groomsman. The new position saw him set sail in 1936 for India, which still had a few years left to go as the flashing jewel in the crown of the British Empire. Then, says his widow Jean, he was swept north, and into Afghanistan and Kabul. The borders between the countries were then – as now – fraught with hideous danger for soldiers; the local people resisted them with zeal. 'Harry was photographed on a mule train,' says Jean. 'Instead of tanks and armoured cars, they had mules. Harry told me all about the Khyber Pass. They had concrete sentry boxes. The night-time guard procedure was that they would shine a torch to one another to say they were all right. They also had wind-up phones in there connected to HQ. And if a soldier didn't shine a torch at a specified time, they had to send men out to see what had happened. On one occasion, Harry said that they went out into the night and the sentries had been crucified on the doors of the sentry boxes. And it was the women that did it, and cut their private parts off. Harry said it was terrible, they were terrible. But,' she added, 'he liked India.' And the gruelling conditions that he found in some aspects of his work were to set him up perfectly for the ordeal that lay ahead in France 1940.

The point was that men like Harry Malpas – experienced and seasoned – would be needed to add a proper sense of weight to the forces being sent across the Channel (referred to as the British Expeditionary Force or BEF), even if the warfare they had seen so far had been the sort that involved mule trains. This question of modernity was important. The Spanish Civil War had demonstrated that this was a new age of technology, of blitzkrieg. The novelist George Orwell, in his 1937 account of the conflict, *Homage to Catalonia,* had outlined to his readers the pitiless nature of modern firepower directed against those armed with ancient shotguns, and the total war of blanket bombing; streets and squares reduced to ash in minutes, the faceless aggressors flying away unharmed and ready to return.

Back in Britain itself, before conscription, there were other questions of modernisation: the army was run on lines that to some eyes seemed more suited to the nineteenth century than the twentieth. There was still, to begin with, the all-pervasive element of class: those in the officer class were largely expected to have some form of private means. Like Lord Gort (an Old Harrovian), they were certainly funnelled through the most traditional of educations, from Eton, Westminster and Winchester. The social gulf between officers and 'Tommies' was notably wide. There was a perception, particularly among the left, that the military hierarchy was a hermetically sealed world, accountable only to itself and its own antediluvian rules and regulations. A popular newspaper cartoon figure of the time was David Low's 'Colonel Blimp', a roaring old reactionary with a walrus moustache who seemed rooted in the Boer War.

Despite the joint declaration of hostilities by the UK and France, Britain did not enter into a formal military alliance with its neighbour; but it was understood on both sides that she would immediately begin sending reinforcements – men and materiel – across the Channel. As a result, having only recently joined up, young Gareth Wright from rural Devon found himself in that very first week sailing across the sea. He had never left Britain's shores before.

Prime Minister Neville Chamberlain had quietly intimated to colleagues that in terms of standing shoulder to shoulder with their French counterparts, the British should only accept 'limited liability'. His First Lord of the Admiralty, Winston Churchill, saw it a little differently, as illustrated by his chilling remark: 'The English, too, will have to pay their tax in blood.'

If the start of the war seemed relatively quiet for the army, it was quite a different matter for the navy. Expectations were dramatically different too. The Royal Navy was widely regarded by the British public as being the finest in the world, almost impregnably superior. These were the proud fleets that patrolled and protected the wildest corners of the British Empire. And it was true: if the army was unprepared and in some senses ramshackle, the navy was a vast and sleek operation, manned with recruits who had joined for their love of the ocean and a thirst to see lands more colourful than their own. In the 1930s, young men also had strong economic reasons to want to sign up; with large regions of the country still crushed under the dead weight of depression, and unemployment remaining stubbornly high, the navy, for some, made for an alternative career that could have its own rewards.

Vic Viner – who was to play a crucial role on the beaches at Dunkirk – had signed up for his naval service for family, as well as economic reasons. His parents had recently moved to Surrey and young Mr Viner found himself being edged out of home. He joined the navy in 1933. 'I was fifteen years and nine months old. I joined as a boy seaman. My father was navy, and he retired in 1922. My elder brother had already gone in, two years before me. And the simple fact was that round Dorking, where we had moved, there wasn't any work, other than being on a farm.

'The other thing was that my father had had to bring his parents to live with him, and there wasn't room for me in the house. There were three boys and my younger brother was three years younger than me. So he was able to stay at home but I was off to the navy. Which I didn't mind at all.

'I'd left school, so from fourteen, I went to Redhill Technical and had eighteen months there. What I should have done of course – I did try for it – was the Artificer Apprenticeship in the navy.' This was a highly sought-after training course, a rare route to great things in the otherwise rigid naval establishment. 'There were only seventy-five places, two competitions a year – seventy-five places and if you are right down low . . . So the only answer for me was to go into the navy in the lower deck as a boy.

'I was sixteen on 21 March. I went to HMS *Ganges*, off Harwich, the main naval base for seaman boys then.' Indeed, the establishment for boy entrants into the navy continued operating until 1976. 'You can imagine what it was like to arrive there – what have we let ourselves in for?' laughs Mr Viner. 'Our training was eighteen months. We went to sea in August 1934. I was still a boy. You didn't become an adult until you were seventeen, eighteen.'

But for Mr Viner, the experience opened up much wider horizons than those he had seen before. 'We were very lucky,' he says. 'If you had had this sort of education, you didn't have to go to school when you joined the navy.

'In the first six years, we went to Australia and New Zealand. We joined the Australian squadron. The ship was designated to take the Duke of Gloucester – George V's son – to Victoria, which was celebrating its centenary as a state. So we came on the royal ship, took him from Marseilles, and took him all the way to Australia, calling in at Colombo, places like that.'

The navy then was almost – though not quite – as sclerotic as the army when it came to class inflexibility. When Mr Viner was there as a boy, the prospect of promotion to certain ranks, such as midshipman, would depend as much on one's family and upbringing as on ability. Mr Viner himself was wryly aware that 'daddy would have to be a lord' for certain posts to be accessible. But perhaps because the navy recruited so young, there was a compensating sense that those on the lower deck were properly looked after. They were mentored by slightly older seamen on other decks, and the technical education was excellent, particularly in the esoteric and highly skilled art of wireless telegraphy and interception. 'You'd be surprised at how well the boys were looked after in the navy,' he says. 'They really were.'

There was also a question of physical health; compared to life in Britain's densely populated, polluted industrial northern cities in the 1930s, these young recruits, out on the oceans, were getting sunshine and air and proper food and proper exercise. This was not an oppressive Jack Tar life. Indeed, they were in far better shape than many of the later young conscripts into army regiments.

One pre-war anxiety of the government – and a fully justified one – had been the physical condition of men of fighting age; even with a full army assembled, would they be any match for a sleeker, fitter, stronger enemy? British government officials and dignitaries had seen at close hand in 1936 at the Berlin Olympics the impressive specimens produced by a fascist regime. In 1937, Prime Minister Neville Chamberlain declared that

> we shall have to raise the general standard of fitness and physical development . . . we have no desire to exchange our form of government for that of a totalitarian state but in this matter of attention to physical development, we surely may learn something from others. Nothing made a stronger impression upon visitors to the Olympic Games . . . than the splendid condition of the German youth, and though our methods were different from theirs, in accordance with our national character and traditions, I see no reason why we shouldn't be equally successful in our results.

Actually there was every reason; not least that government ministers had for the last few years been refusing to acknowledge any causal link between poverty or unemployment and malnutrition. They had closed their ears to the relatively new branch of science that dealt with food and public health issues, and insisted that if there were deficiencies in the diet of the poor, then these were the result of ignorance as opposed to lack of money; a simple want of common sense in what to cook. After all, certain vegetables were inexpensive, so why could they not be used more as part of a wider diet? Why did poorer families instead seem to rely so much on bread and tea? What was needed was better education of mothers, not simply handing the poor and the feckless more taxpayers' money. Professor E.P. Cathcart was among the first to express polite scepticism – and some diplomacy – about this rigorous view. After a study, he concluded that 'no doubt . . . generally people in institutions were much better fed than many persons outside . . . poor people . . . at present lived in many cases on bread and ready-cooked foods. They suffered not only from lack of money but lack of cooking facilities . . . and the knowledge and ability to use to best advantage the materials they were able to secure.'[4]

In those families dwelling in conditions of the harshest urban blight were the young boys who would soon grow up to be of fighting age. Yet how many of them would really be of any use to the military? Although the debate touched jangling political nerves – then, as now, there was a belief among many that unemployment assistance was perfectly adequate for the prudent to live upon – it stretched rather wider, and came to involve establishment figures such as Lord Dawson of Penn, personal doctor to the King and head of the Royal College of Physicians. In the large industrial cities in the north, it was found that rickets was spreading. In unemployment black spots such as Tyneside, South Wales and County Durham, tuberculosis in young men was on the increase.

Curiously, at the same time, there was a growing middle-class craze for the body beautiful; a new popular enthusiasm among the better-off for long country walks, for callisthenic exercises, for gymnastics and weight work. The Nazis may have made a cult of physical perfection but they were by no means alone in their fascination for, in particular, the sculptured musculature of the male form. This was an age of eugenics, a Darwinian belief in natural selection, and evolution, and the breeding out of certain weaknesses. Such ideas were not solely the province of the fascists. And as anxiety in Europe grew, so Britain's doctors, generals and politicians started almost subconsciously assessing the state of the national 'stock'. Even by 1934, the National Association of Boys' Clubs was describing the average British youth as 'shadowy and shiftless', bearing sorry comparison to the young 'men of heroic mould' that were being turned out under totalitarian regimes.

A government white paper of 1937 set out a new national scheme of fitness training, which would have a budget of £2 million to be spent over the next three years. The money would go to local authorities and councils and would be used to set up physical fitness clubs, which would especially be aimed at young men, though women were very much encouraged too. The hope was that every urban district, every town, every village, would start such a club and enrol as many young people as possible. At the time, Oliver Stanley, then of the Board of Education, was forced to deny an accusation that the new scheme was 'militaristic'. Quite the reverse, he averred. In every one of these clubs up and down the country, there was not a hint of compulsion; rather, it was all purely voluntary, predicated on the hope that word would get around about how glorious real fitness and physical well-being felt.

There were unsubtle poster campaigns as well. 'Fitness wins!' shouted one poster, while another stridently declared: 'England expects every man and woman to be healthy and fit!' Quite how this could be interpreted as anything but militaristic is anybody's guess. But there was success too; by 1939, some 540 physical fitness clubs had been established up and down the country. The movement had been helped in part by a strong endorsement from King George VI. It was, he said, 'A cause of the first importance. We have a duty to ourselves and our generation . . . nothing adds more to the pleasure of life.'

Crucially, it was the army that had noticed just how sickly so many of its potential recruits were. In the mid-1930s, the Adjutant General had reported that 'over 52% of the men who went to the recruiting office did not come up to the physical standard laid down and in the big industrial areas of the north, the percentage of rejection rose to 68%'. Several years later, when anxiety in military circles about the issue was clearly rising, the recruiting officers in Aldershot tried an experiment. Taking on a batch of young men who were

– at that moment – medically unfit, they paid them a little extra, exhorting that the money should be spent on good, nutritious food. The young recruits did as they were told, gratefully; a few months later, they were tested again. Now they were found to be in much more satisfactory condition. Technology was also starting to help; by the end of the 1930s, techniques for canning food had led to a rise in the availability of slightly less expensive meat and fruit products. Meanwhile the spread of refrigeration meant that it was now possible to store milk for longer, and this in turn led to a rise in consumption. At the end of 1939, in the first three months of the war, the government quietly conceded that it might be able to help boost the health of the poor; it started a scheme to make free or cheap milk available to all children, plus pregnant women, and women who had just given birth. As historian Madeleine Mayhew noted, 'the National Milk Scheme was followed by a scheme to supply the same vulnerable groups with orange juice, cod liver oil and vitamin tablets.'[5]

So, in 1939, great numbers of young army recruits were being drawn away from lives of hard physical work – from smelting furnaces to mines to factories – and from cramped homes. Is it any wonder that there are so many accounts of these young men heading quite cheerfully for the recruitment offices, and happily queuing around the block to sign up for the conflict?

As well as a perception of physical incapacity, there was a cultural distrust of this new young generation among the military high command. Young men who went about using American sounding expressions that they had copied from the cinema, who spent good money on gangster trilbies and oily hair products and frittered so much time in dance halls, were assumed to lack discipline. According to the military, how could these shiftless, shifty young articles measure up to the greatness of the generation that had come before them, with all the extraordinary sacrifices that had been made? 'By comparison with the French or the Germans, for that matter,' said

General Auchinleck in the War Cabinet not long after the conflict started, 'our men for the most part seem distressingly young, not so much in years as in self-reliance and manliness generally . . . they give an impression of being callow and undeveloped.'

Yet to a middle-aged soldier, what younger generation has not looked callow? And for their part, a great many of these 'undeveloped' youths were just as willing as their forebears to sign up for life-threatening jeopardy.

One such was Charles Searle, together with his brothers Alfred and William. Charles, the youngest, was also interestingly an illustration of how much healthier life down south could be. He was – and indeed is – a proud cockney, having been brought up in the East End district of Bow. And that life, he says, was very active and absorbing. 'I was cycling round all over the place,' he says now. 'The life we lived, we were quite all right.' Mr Searle was born in 1918; and even though the old East End had a reputation for squalor and poverty every bit as fearsome as the decayed industrial north, Mr Searle insists that, for his family anyway, it really wasn't so. Part of the reason, intriguingly, was the increasingly widespread availability of bicycles. When a young man acquired one, he not only gained mobility, but also a certain level of fitness. This was helped by the huge local enthusiasm for football; Mr Searle and his friends would play teams from all over London on the vast expanses of the Hackney Marshes.

'I left school aged fourteen in 1932,' says Mr Searle. 'And I became a shop boy working for a tailor in Bow. I used to travel all over London, taking coats and picking stuff up. And he taught me as well.' It was not only a good trade to be in; it was thriving, thanks to the advent of Burton's Fifty Shilling Suits, and the fashion among young middle-class and working-class men for dressing smartly in public. And Mr Searle had a talent for it; much later after the war, in the 1960s, he was on Savile Row, winning awards.

'In the 1930s, I used to travel all over picking up work, Highbury Corner, Finchley, all those places. And along the Strand. Cleavers of the Strand, near the Gaiety Theatre. My life was quite interesting. And of course I was learning the trade in tailoring.' Eventually, Mr Searle's ambitions sharpened into focus. 'I thought, I'll go to the City, get to the better class tailors. I started looking for a job in Cheapside because there were about fifty tailoring shops in Cheapside before the war.'

Having secured a new and valuable position with a City tailoring firm, Mr Searle – aged twenty-one – received his call-up papers. If there was any sense of frustration, he kept it to himself. And indeed his brothers were very keen to see action. Mr Searle's older brother William had in fact 'dreamt of being a Spitfire pilot'. Working for the gas firm Presseys, he was in a reserved occupation, but, says Mr Searle, 'joined up as a volunteer reserve'. This was to lead to tragedy very early on in the war. 'They made him a rear gunner. That's more like committing suicide. The plane he was on crashed in the Firth of Forth on a volunteer raid. They just couldn't make the landing, and he got killed. We got him home. He was all in one piece. His neck was broken, all swollen. We opened the coffin and had a look because of my mother, she wanted to see him. We thought he might have been smashed up but he wasn't, his body was OK. So we buried him in the normal way.'

Mr Searle's own army career – which would come into sharp focus at the time of Dunkirk – was angled in quite a different direction. Because he had St John's Ambulance training – with the accompanying certificate to prove it – he was drafted into the Royal Army Medical Corps.

While Charles Searle learnt the tailoring trade, young naval recruit Vic Viner – who had a comfortable upbringing compared to many others – was gazing out on to waters bluer than he would ever have imagined. Having been part of the Australian squadron, patrolling that bright ocean, when Mussolini launched his assault on Abyssinia in 1935, Mr Viner and his crewmates set sail for the Mediterranean. 'When you went abroad,' he says, 'it was a three-year commission, not three months or three weeks.

'My six years in the navy before the war was one of the most glorious times of my life. I saw the world as God made it, before the concrete jungles arrived. The island of Bali – when I first saw it – was just a gem. Unspoiled. We were there because my last posting was to the China fleet. March 1938. And of course, 3 September 1939, we turned, made our way back to this country. I came ashore to do extra training in underwater weapons. Mine disposal, sabotage, all sorts of things. By 1939, I was twenty-three. Then my career all started.'

Dunkirk, for Vic Viner, was to prove more than just a formative experience. Yet it is also true that Mr Viner was superbly prepared for the almost inhuman demands that were to be put upon him in those days and nights of 1940.

Another young lad who received valuable naval training was London boy Reg Vine, who came about his pre-Dunkirk experience in a rather less conventional way. 'In the spring of 1940, I was fifteen,' he says now. 'I left school at thirteen. My father used to do moonlight flits. Every month when the rent was due, we'd all have to shift to another place because he had no money. And we had no benefits either because he was a self-employed sweep.' Home life was precarious. It was made all the more so when Mr Vine's mother died at the age of only forty-two.

'I became a sea cadet,' says Mr Vine. 'I went down to Park Road, Twickenham – we lived not far away – met this young navy bloke and he said: "Want to join the sea cadets?" And I said to him: "Oh that's an idea, because I don't want to be a boy scout." And he said "This is nothing to do with scouts – this is being a sea cadet." So I said yes.

'And then I did all my training, rifle training and that.' Having finished his training, Reg said to the recruiting officer: 'I'm leaving home.' The officer asked why. 'I said: "Well, mum's died." Actually, I had been thinking of joining the navy earlier and I think it broke her heart. But anyway – she was gone.' And meanwhile, he adds, 'my old man ran off with a couple of birds.' Sea cadets offered a semblance of stable routine, even if, as Mr Vine suspected, the 'touchy-feely' recruiting officer 'was a bit gay'.

'With this sea cadet thing, I thought, at least it was somewhere to go at night and to meet the lads,' he says. 'And I liked the rifle shooting and all that.' Mr Vine's experience at Dunkirk was to be one that no amount of rifle training – nor sailing down the tranquil Thames near Eel Pie Island – could prepare him for.

In the opening weeks of the war, the RAF flew a few sorties into enemy territory to drop not bombs, but propaganda leaflets. For nineteen-year-old Arthur Taylor, the air force was a step in the direction that he had originally wanted to go when he had joined the Territorials. He found himself in the specialised position of an RAF wireless operator linked up with troops. 'We were sent to a place just outside Arras,' he said. 'We were getting settled down when they decided what to do with us. In the end they posted ten wireless operators to each regiment of artillery. Mine was the 63rd Regiment Royal Artillery and my job was forward ground spotter, liaising with the army and the Lysanders.'

Those very early days of the war were, for some recruits, tinged not only with a sense of faint unreality, but also a particularly tasty tang of variety. Bob Halliday, serving his apprenticeship in a Clydeside shipping yard, instantly found that he was able to reach for more satisfying problem-solving aspects of engineering. Before this, though, he was attached to an intriguingly esoteric unit in France.

'Map making,' he says now with a rueful smile. 'Right in the beginning. There was a brand new unit which was doing 3D work, photographing from heights. You had sections going out spying on enemy territory, coming back.' Naturally, the work was absolutely vital; 3D photography made it possible to track and map the enemy in much more precise detail, while also offering up information concerning airstrips and even potential rocket-launching pads. One might imagine that such work would have been catnip to a clever, technically minded boy. Mr Halliday did not see it that way.

'All the work was done on site in a big stable in Revannes . . . and I couldn't get out of that job quick enough,' he says. The reason? 'I wanted to do my bit. I was just . . . I wasn't happy about it.' In the time he was there, he says, 'one or two [German] planes came over, everyone dived for cover but other than that . . .' The excitement – plus the life-threatening jeopardy – was to follow.

The question of preparation for battle still makes Gareth Wright pause for thought today. Barely more than a lad in 1939, his brief couple of weeks of military experience as a teenager with the Territorials in Devon in the days before Chamberlain made his broadcast were a little less intense than he might have wished: 'There was no training. Absolutely none really. We were Saturday night soldiers. And we only had a couple of guns. We used to go up on the golf course up on top of Tavistock. There were a lot of gorse bushes. And our training used to consist of one of the gunners running in and out of bushes and popping up and waving his hat in the air and the number one on the gun, looking around, to see if he could see it.

'They used to tow a sleeve behind an old biplane and you'd fire at these puffballs. They wouldn't trust us with proper ammo, just a plastic shell which burst into a puff of smoke. Just as well. We would have brought down more planes than sleeves.

'We were due to go on a training exercise in Somerset for a fortnight on 3 September 1939.' But then, instead, the orders came through: destination St Nazaire. 'I was told to start as a dispatch rider,' says Mr Wright. 'But when I got across the other side, I started driving trucks.' By the time he and his comrades were facing the ineluctable progress of the Wehrmacht, Mr Wright had managed to spend his time educating himself with the mechanical proficiency that he knew he was going to need.

It is instructive to look back at how the French military was perceived in contrast to their British counterparts. In short, the French were understood to be much better trained, sleeker and more professional. The early verdict of one French general upon his British comrades was that they were 'barely trained divisions of questionable value'. Almost as soon as British troops began landing on French soil, Brigadier George Davy, who for his own part had been one of the few to spot weaknesses in the Maginot Line, commented that the French attitude was very superior towards the British, and 'BEF officers were treated as learners in the military arts.'

This might in part have been due to the familiar British tendency among some of those officers towards self-deprecation. John Shaw QC – who would later win the Military Cross for the part he played at Dunkirk – cheerily recalled in his memoir how he had come to be an officer in the army at all:

> I joined the army in September 1939. Before the month was out, I found myself at Officer Cadet Training Unit (OCTU) at Sandhurst, where I remained for four months. We were taught all about square bashing and trench warfare but not about modern instruments of war. I duly passed out, mainly I am told because I played rugger for the 1st team and not for my knowledge of anything military.[6]

In contrast, it was at that time that the novelist Evelyn Waugh – thirty-six years old, distinctly rotund, a wearer of spectacles and not immediately obvious soldier material – was 'banging on' to his friend Brendan Bracken for a commission. He got one. Waugh's friend Mary Pakenham said of him: 'He was one of the few people who was not made more distinguished-looking by military uniform.' Yet Waugh was lethally serious, both about the conflict and indeed the role he should play in it. His friend, the writer Christopher Sykes, later said: 'He had no use for cloud cuckoo war aims. The only war aim was to win by killing great numbers of the enemy's population.'

But in common with so many others, Waugh – or as he became, Captain Waugh – found the opening stages of his military career an exercise in matters other than the waging of war. First was the training, both for him and for the men under him, in the gustier, wilder corners of the kingdom. Waugh seemingly had very little patience for other ranks, and he was frequently rude and brusque to them. The class divide had very obviously and disadvantageously opened up. Waugh would berate his men in language so ornate and baroque that sometimes the soldiers literally had no idea what he was talking about. They came to know him as 'Captain Wuff', mispronouncing his name from the spelling, and were heard remarking to one another, 'What is Captain Wuff on about now?' And the training exercises involved chores such as the clearing out of an old camp in west Wales, and then being sent off to patrol rural Cornwall. 'Our task was to defend Liskeard,' wrote Waugh. 'None of us could quite make out why anyone would want to attack it.'

Yet perhaps in this story we can detect one underlying positive note: furiously eager as Waugh – like so many other commissioned officers from his educated background – was for battle, he was forced instead into a period of acquainting himself with the fighting men who served under him; and all ranks were forced to adjust themselves to a repetitive, hard-slogging life that had been all too easy to romanticise. For every captain like Waugh, there were men drawn in through conscription who wearily resented the martinet NCOs and the monotone nature of drills. Married men who had been pulled away from wives and babies; men who had enjoyed their pre-war work, and the lives and the community that went with that work. They were afforded this period at least to acclimatise to the new restrictions thrown up around their lives, and even to acquire a taste for this alien way of doing things.

Whatever the actual level of training, the Germans were quick to probe any potential fissures in the partnership between the British and French armies. A sour joke was very soon to be heard in German propaganda broadcasts: 'Britain will fight to the last Frenchman.' As celebrated historian A.J.P. Taylor later said: 'The war machine resembled an expensive motor car, beautifully polished, complete in every detail, except that there was no petrol in the tank.'

Yet there was an immediate impact, if confined to French soldiers and citizens alike: 'The presence of British troops in France was a useful boost to the French morale.'[7]

Artilleryman James Bradley had been fired with enthusiasm from a very early stage, joining up before being conscripted. 'I thought it was necessary for all young people to consider that their freedom was at risk,' he recalled. 'I couldn't sit back and just let the invasion of other people's countries go on. I felt I ought to be one of the people – and there must have been millions of them – who wanted peace and an honourable world to live in.

'I was a Bren machine gunner, first class,' he continued. 'I was very enthusiastic . . . We went to France and landed at Cherbourg, drove all the way along the coast and went to the Belgian frontier. At that time I thought it would be like the First World War because we were putting up barbed wire . . . When we first arrived in France, it was like peacetime. We got on very well with the French people and we used to go for day trips.'[8] The baffling absence of conflict was to make both army life, and life for the anxious sweethearts and families back home, highly unsettling. Minimal training, trench digging, heel kicking: yet many soldiers were to find their time in France – before the storm broke upon them – rich and formative.

They brought some distinctively English musical entertainments with them. The trilling Rochdale vibrato of Gracie Fields now instantly evokes the war, although in fact her signature song 'Wish Me Luck' had been written for quite another purpose – it formed part of the 1939 musical film comedy *Shipyard Sally*. None the less, the tune was quickly appropriated for patriotic use: 'Wish me luck when you wave me goodbye/ Cheerio, here I go, on my way.' Miss Fields swiftly understood that entertaining the troops was a very important job; especially at a point, with a freezing winter looming, where it seemed that there was little else to occupy them. Her concerts in France during those months of Phoney War were hugely popular: standing room only. The older tunes were calibrated to bring sentimental tears to the eyes of the old sweats: 'Too Old to Dream', 'Little Old Lady', 'Little Sir Echo', 'The Sweetest Song in the World'. When Fields's fellow entertainer Noel Coward once sharply noted the extraordinary potency of cheap music, his remark was not entirely pejorative; such compositions last while other, more highbrow stuff disappears into oblivion. Besides which, Fields's act was not all mawkishness; she also adapted a previous number to include barn-storming lyrics about 'stringing Hitler up' on 'the biggest aspidistra in the world'. Musical accompaniment was provided by bands from Lancashire regiments. Fields would not have been nearly so popular had she not meant it.

On the parade grounds, other songs were calculated to appeal directly to the more boisterous of the recently conscripted soldiers. Most famous is Captain Jimmy Kennedy's composition 'We're Going to Hang Out Our Washing on the Siegfried Line', a song which received a hilariously huffy response from a German radio station, which was broadcasting propaganda. The English-speaking presenter declared primly that the German people 'had a serious mental and moral attitude' and that 'no German had written doggerel about hanging out washing on the Siegfried Line'. Yet this was not true: German troops had done that very thing – taking the same tune, but adding lyrics about British soldiers 'filling their trousers'. So much for the serious moral attitude.

This was, however, emphatically not the music that young men were listening to before they were called up. Throughout the 1930s, the proliferation of dance halls and gramophone players had led the young to import a rather more exciting musical style: swing. In the north, traditional brass bands in the industrial cities had either been struggling to recruit new young players or were rather startlingly swinging it up. For men and women alike, it was the faster-paced, more thrilling American music that they wanted to hear. The BBC had reluctantly begun to acknowledge this, with programmes dedicated to dance bands. But many young people, even then, were tuning their radios to Radio Luxembourg. The dance band sound spoke of a certain urban sophistication as well as an undercurrent of illicit sexual excitement. It was not just the later

American GIs who wanted to hear from the Boogie Woogie Bugle Boy of Company B.

Meanwhile, back in Britain, as the country waited for this strange war to get going, for young single women there were still young men – yet to be called up – available as potential dance partners. One exceedingly popular refuge from the blackouts, after all, was the dance hall. In those early weeks and months of the war, the Mecca chain, which boasted clubs from Tottenham to Brighton, had noticed ticket sales rising, and clearly, their young clientele were in no mood for the fancy ballroom styles enjoyed by the 'nobs'. But it was more than that: the halls, as Mecca manager Carl Heiman observed, offered 'bright lighting' and 'fascinating illumination'. In these gaudy halls was to be found precisely the sort of escapism that an evening at home in dimmed lighting with the radio playing could not match.

For all the youthful idealists and adventure-seekers who reported to barracks and were kitted out with comically ill-fitting uniforms, there were men – like Charles Searle's brother William – left behind in what were termed reserved occupations; those jobs of such skill and experience that they could not be spared. Unemployment was still high; even though in the broadest terms the country had left the depression years behind, in big swathes of the northern industrial belt, conditions were still every bit as grim as those recorded by George Orwell. Yet for the skilled machinists and other experienced factory operatives not called up, this was curiously a time in which the unions were able to display some strength. Conditions and pay in many places were the sources of dispute; and the Trades Union Congress also wanted to be able to sit in on Whitehall discussions to do with war work, and the use of large manufactories for making vital equipment.

During this nervy period, the wireless was ever more central to the heart of the nation – and to soldiers home and abroad. The BBC's radio output had been reconfigured under the 'Home Service' and the fare on offer for army and civilians was an amusingly patrician mix of the culturally wholesome and the unashamedly populist. In one evening's programming in that autumn, a teatime 'Contralto and Piano Recital' is followed at 6.30 by a broadcast from 'Northern Music Hall' (the Alexandra Theatre, Hull). To make up for that, there then follows an episode of the serialisation *The Four Feathers*, then a 'Cello and Piano Recital'. But at 8.15 p.m. – primetime – everyone, whatever their tastes, settled down for ITMA – *It's That Man Again*. These days, the title is as familiar as the songs of Vera Lynn, but what is now beguiling is the degree to which this hugely loved radio comedy show began to gently poke fun at the authorities. In the very first episode, the insanely popular comedian Tommy Handley played a character called 'The Minister of Aggravation' who presided over 'The Office of Twerps' (as opposed to 'Works').

Gentle ribbing, but also indicative of a wider, ruder scepticism about the edicts flowing from Whitehall and the wisdom of those who issued them. In the real-life Ministry of Information, it was certainly being found that rather than narrowing the social chasm, the war seemed to be widening it. There was a sense that those in the government and the civil service were in a class far too high and rarefied to understand the concerns and fears of the ordinary man and woman. The findings of Mass Observation were that working-class audiences tended not to wholly trust or believe pronouncements from those who sounded 'upper class'.

The Ministry of Information was quite robust enough to withstand Tommy Handley's satire. In fact, such jokes might have helped allay deeper suspicions of such a department. The Ministry was somehow the very embodiment of the establishment while being staffed by many who were not quite of that establishment; from the BBC's pioneering female executive Mary Adams to the young novelist Graham Greene and the aesthetically sensitive Harold Nicolson. 'For the purpose of war activities,' said one unnamed Ministry official, 'the BBC is to be regarded as a government department, although I wouldn't put it quite like that in any public statement.'

The Ministry was for a time headed by Lord Reith, the famously austere Director General of the BBC; yet his appointment of Mary Adams was a step away from the gentleman's club approach of other departments.

Adams, by training a scientist, had joined the BBC in 1930 and by 1936 was the first woman television producer, working out of Alexandra Palace in north London. Now here she was, Director of Home Intelligence. She was acutely aware of the sensitivity of her job; to this end, she cannily formed an alliance with the men and women behind the ambitious Mass Observation project. MO had already proved a popular means for the public to look at itself – paperback collections of pre-war diaries sold in the hundreds of thousands. So, crucially, the project was not initially seen as an intrusive or oppressive elitist Whitehall operation, designed to catch ordinary people out. Mary Adams thrived at the Ministry and incidentally, after the war, resumed her hugely successful BBC career: she inspired a young David Attenborough and even oversaw the inception of children's favourites Muffin the Mule and Andy Pandy.

In that first autumn of war, questions of freedom of speech versus the wider public good were debated hotly in Parliament. What constituted a public mischief? As the Ministry of Information would have cause to ask itself, how exactly was anyone to measure morale, and the amount that it might have been damaged by, say, someone talking with drunken authority in a pub? Earlier that year, Winston Churchill had picked up on the subject in a speech, regretfully declaring that in a time of conflict, individual freedoms of expression had to be curbed, as newspapers and radio broadcasts and films had to be submitted for censorship. For these were ultimately the very freedoms that were being fought for; a temporary suspension would only benefit Britain in the long run. Initially, many were impatient with the idea of broad censorship. That was to change after Dunkirk.

Curiously, in this time of crisis, domestic crime remained a constant. The blacked-out cities were altogether too tempting for veterans of organised crime; they made certain targets easier. 'Thieves have stolen five tons of tea from a Government storage warehouse in the Paddington district,' went the report of one London robbery. 'The warehouse stands by a canal and the police are examining the theory that the thieves may have loaded the tea on to a barge.' Without the absolute darkness of blackout, such a raid might not have been possible. In the East End of London, the blackout provided a bonanza for smash and grab raiders; jewellers from Old Street to East Ham had their windows targeted by criminals whose unlit cars were difficult to pursue down unlit roads.

For the fighting men, some rather incongruous and comical properties had been widely requisitioned by the War Office; these were Britain's holiday camps, dotted around the coastline near pleasure resorts. Billy Butlin and his competitors were recent additions to British popular culture; the first Butlins camp had opened in Skegness in 1936. Now young soldiers found themselves billeted in the empty camps for the purposes of training. The Skegness establishment was remembered by veterans for its murderous coldness; they slept in double beds, with a wooden board partition down the middle 'to stop them getting at each other in the night', as one put it. But given the impossibility of sleeping in those freezing draughts, many removed the boards and slept close for warmth in defiance of instructions.

What we might now call an 'embedded' journalist sent an enthusiastic dispatch from an unnamed holiday camp in the west of the country in November 1939. 'It was hard to believe that these men were engaged in the deadly serious business of preparing to take part in a war that was actually in progress,' he wrote. 'As one officer remarked, the sense of strain, or at least of preoccupation which pervades the wartime atmosphere of any large town seems entirely absent here.' The correspondent went on to describe the 'neat lawns, gay flowerbeds and clean concrete paths' which separated the buildings. 'The sleeping quarters are little chalets, each accommodating three men or one officer.' Even in Butlins, that sense of a separate officer class of privileged background somehow managed to peep through. Here too the other notable matter was a complete lack of heating; the camp was only ever opened for business in the summer months, and so there had been no previous call for it. A great deal of wooden bed partitions would have been removed.

The reporter was keen to talk to 'old sweats' – the men who already had experience of military service, as opposed to the raw and untested teenagers who had just been conscripted. From the start, whether in France or in domestic barracks, these experienced men had fast acquired the reputation for fearless straight-talking. One old sweat in the holiday camp proclaimed that 'some officers did not know their jobs'. That quote may now be read as a hilarious bowdlerisation of his actual words. There were also complaints that in the haste to assemble an army, men 'had been removed willy-nilly from useful jobs'. Also, given that the men were supposed to be on parade at 5.30 a.m. in the frost, how was it that they had not been issued with overcoats?

For others, there were comically practical problems to do with mutual understanding. East End lad Charles Searle, now attached to the Medical Corps, found himself at a training barracks in Fleet, Hampshire. In among a great mob, he recalls, there were just four or five fellow cockneys. The rest hailed from Lancashire. 'We couldn't understand what they were talking about! Their dialect,' laughs Mr Searle. 'But we mingled in.'

Mr Searle found the training so hurried, it was almost disorientating. It has been suggested that in a wider sense – lacking the luxury of time – raw recruits to the army did not receive the immersive training that they should have done, and that this in turn was to have a profound impact on events in May 1940. 'We were there at that camp for six weeks,' says Mr Searle, 'and we had to absorb the knowledge, the language, which would ordinarily take nine months. We were a bit short-handed.'

*

It was only to grow more abstract, this war that was not a war. Apart from the occasional scuffle involving German reconnaissance planes, the BEF, primed and prepared for the sort of conflict that a previous generation had fought, had to find ways, in the silence, of adjusting to the small communities to which they were attached. Yet if their time was quiet, for those who patrolled the waves, those weeks swiftly gathered in intensity. On England's east coast, and especially around the Thames Estuary and the Straits of Dover, the air was alive with speculation about Hitler's diabolical new secret weapons. And it was in these waters that, even prior to their pivotal role at Dunkirk, some rather unexpected, colourful vessels found themselves being pressed into the dangerous work of sweeping the grey waters for mines. It was during this period that Britain's maritime strength – private, as well as naval – was proudly enriched with a new generation of eager sea-going recruits, and some vessels with gloriously eccentric histories. These were the boats and the crews who would later become emblems of the nation itself.

3

'They Threw Us In'

December 1939–May 1940

While the inhabitants of London and the larger cities waited – and waited – for Germany's bombers to fill the sky, the conflict had actually begun out in the ocean, prefiguring the most desperate hours of the battles to come. For a maritime nation, it was fitting that so much importance would come to be attached to its shipping, both large and very small.

The first outrage against the British had been committed by U-boat U-30, captained by Fritz-Julius Lemp, that September. His vessel was lurking in the waters 250 miles north-west of Ireland. Sailing ever closer to it was a passenger liner that had departed from Glasgow and was heading for Montreal: the SS *Athenia.* The crew of the ship felt confident that they would be free from attack: a treaty called the London Protocol had been signed concerning passenger liners. During the Great War, Germany had found that targeting such vessels had resulted in neutral countries turning against them.

It was anxious not to hand its enemies such easy propaganda again. Academic Jeffrey Legro wrote: 'When Germany started World War II by attacking Poland, strict orders had been issued to the U-boats that the war was to be conducted with meticulous restraint towards merchant and passenger ships in accordance with international agreements.'[1] But when the *Athenia* sailed into Captain Lemp's sights, he couldn't hold back: the U-30 fired two torpedoes that shattered the hull. One hundred and twelve passengers drowned, 1,088 took to lifeboats. This was the incident that opened the vicious warfare of the Battle of the Atlantic. In her diaries, Virginia Woolf captured the horror of the sinking, its profound emptiness. 'It seems entirely meaningless,' she wrote, 'a perfunctory slaughter, like taking a jar in one hand and a hammer in the other. Why must this be smashed? Nobody knows.'[2]

Almost instantly the war at sea began to intensify. The Germans launched a U-boat attack on the Scapa Flow base in the Orkney Islands, during which the naval vessel *Royal Oak* was sunk in harbour. The day afterwards, a stunned First Lord of the Admiralty Winston Churchill told the House of Commons that it had been assumed that naval security was so tight that any attack would come from the air. 'The Admiralty,' Churchill said, 'upon whom the broad responsibility rests, are resolved to learn this bitter lesson.'

Further south, the cockle pickers and fishermen who operated from the mouth of the Thames Estuary – and who were later to play such an emotive role in the Dunkirk evacuation – were finding the wider waters filled with fresh hazards. The Germans were seeding estuary and Channel waters with advanced mines. These devices started blowing up British and neutral ships alike.

And so minesweeping was intensified, a focus on the English Channel that would later prove useful. 'Now [the Navy] has hundreds of ships engaged in this work and the number increases daily,' reported *The Times*. 'The craft range from units of the minesweeping service proper, which was a pre-war branch of the Navy, to trawlers, drifts, yachts and paddle-boats brought in since war began.' Already, before their appointed time, the little ships were proving their worth. 'The crews of mine-sweeping craft are largely drawn from men of our fishing fleets who were trained to the work by serving instructional periods . . . consequently, these fine seamen – and there is none better for this particular job – have a specialized knowledge of the task.'

Some familiar civilian boats that were later to play their part off the Dunkirk beaches were called up early. Several years previously, in 1936, Red Funnel ferries, which ran services to the Isle of Wight, launched a pretty steamboat which they called the *Gracie Fields* in honour of the madly popular entertainer. In the months before the conflict, the vessel had ploughed her holiday-making passengers back and forth across the Solent. Diarist Elizabeth Ackerman recalled: '[She] had proper engines, and I loved to go below and watch the engines turning . . . One could stand beside the paddle and watch the revolutions and the sea dripping down.'[3]

Gracie Fields was now requisitioned by the government and put to work as a minesweeper. The Germans were using new kinds of magnetic mine: not, as the term would suggest, mines that would be attracted to iron hulls, but bombs engineered to go off as a certain mass of iron passed over them. Unlike mines constructed to the principles of the Geneva Convention, which would become defused if separated from their moorings, these bombs would remain entirely active, no matter where they floated. In storms, many washed up on Britain's coastline. Countering the threat would require a serious effort – and here again we hear a forward echo of the efforts made at Dunkirk: for the Royal Navy was swiftly able to find ways of employing civilian vessels for this vital work.

Fishing trawlers were rounded up and pressed into service. As one naval officer remarked: 'They threw the fish out – and threw us in.' It was fantastically important – the estuary, and the east coast, were vital supply lines for Britain. On the bleak flats of Shoeburyness in Essex, looking out over the grey waters, one such mine, spotted and gingerly recovered from the sea during the hours of darkness, was defused –

with quite incredible courage, and over some hours – by Lieutenant Commander Ouvry, to enable scientists to examine its workings. In the meantime, the little ships that had been commandeered ploughed up and down the tidal waters; trawlers were sunk and lost their crews. But there was no shortage of eager and enthusiastic volunteers for the work, among whom were amateur yachtsmen of the Royal Naval Volunteer Supplementary Reserve 'who had learnt the elements of minesweeping during their holidays with the First Minesweeping Flotilla at Portland'. The RNVSR had been set up some years before and was particularly popular with those who had land-locked civilian jobs but craved the sea. Elsewhere, in Lowestoft, Suffolk, a naval base called *Pembroke X* (later HMS *Europa*) attracted thousands of sailors for work with the Royal Naval Patrol Service, the fleet of small boats that carried out the bulk of minesweeping in the Channel. Originally nicknamed 'Churchill's Pirates', they also went by the affectionate epithet 'Harry Tate's Navy'. (Harry Tate was a popular music hall comedian noted for his scrapes with all things mechanical. Though its precise origin is unknown, the nickname was thought to refer to the clunky old boats the sailors worked on.) Among those helping to keep the route of the convoys clear, all the way up to Lindisfarne, was John Gregson, later to become a film actor and the star of *Genevieve.*

Lieutenant Commander Berkeley Moir had had early experience of the little ships, having joined the London club of the same name. 'Here they ran various courses in seamanship, leading up to the Board of Trade's Yachts Masters Ticket, which I took,' he wrote. 'The Port of London Authority called for volunteers and small craft to patrol the Thames basically as mine-watchers . . . I found myself as a deckhand on a converted RNLI boat called "Wandered".'[4] In the months to follow, many other sea-salty civilians would follow suit; some of the men who sailed out to Dunkirk were to be lectured in the arts of anchors and astrolabes in a quirky but smart navigation school round the corner from Piccadilly.

Among the vessels to see distinguished service in the early months of the war was steamer the *Medway Queen.* Built in 1924, and popular with holidaymakers up and down the Kent coast – when engaged in her proper business as a pleasure boat, she was festooned with a variety of flags – she sailed in 1939 to the Deptford Creek shipyard where her black, white and cream livery was painted over with battleship grey. The rear of the boat was modified to make way for minesweeping apparatus; machine guns were fitted; and the bridge was sturdily enclosed. If there was something a little incongruous about an old pleasure steamer being converted for such use, the dedicated crew – themselves largely men of a certain age who had seen action in the last war – ignored it.

The *Medway Queen* began her serious duties in the Thames Estuary and through the exceptionally cold winter of 1939–40, her structure was put under immense stress in unusually icy waters. Come the New Year, she was out in the Straits of Dover, either minesweeping or acting as a lookout. Similarly striking was the minesweeping career of the *Crested Eagle*, built in 1925.

This pleasure steamer, another paddle ship, was quite large; it had a capacity for about 1500 excursionary passengers. Throughout the late 1930s, it – alongside the *Golden Eagle* and the *Royal Eagle* – would start at the pier by Tower Bridge, and then make its way down the Thames. The *Crested Eagle* – known as 'the greyhound of the river' – would stop off at Greenwich, before sailing on to Southend and thence to the seaside resort of Clacton. There were sun-decks, on-board games and bars, 'Excellent breakfasts, luncheons and teas' served in a dining saloon that could seat 310, and 'a varied musical programme'. In fact, such vessels were sadly on the brink of obsolescence; the new diesel pleasure boats, faster and more reliable, were edging in. But to look at the old photographs now – the vast paddles, the angled telescopic funnel (allowing the vessel to pass beneath London Bridge), the decks packed with excited families – there is more than a simple twinge of nostalgia; there is also a stab of melancholy. For the ship, so valiantly sailing for Dunkirk in May 1940, was doomed.

*

Before the war had even begun, the Royal Navy had been looking seriously at the port of Dover; just twenty-two miles from the continental mainland, it was clearly going to be of terrific strategic importance in the coming conflict. But in the 1930s, Dover Command had been seriously neglected. Located at the site of the medieval castle, the base had beneath it a labyrinth of tunnels, burrowed through the chalk in 1803 in expectation of a Napoleonic invasion. There was sufficient room down there to house 2000 men in dormitories. Of course that invasion never came – though Napoleon was actively preparing for it in 1805 – and the tunnels were eventually forgotten. By 1938, it was time to look at them again. The man asked to do so was a semi-retired rear admiral called Sir Bertram Ramsay; he was pulled out of reluctant retirement in the Scottish Borders in the autumn of 1938 specifically to see how the base could be made suitable for modern warfare.

Some might have thought that employing a retired admiral was the human equivalent of pressing into service an old paddle steamer. But in fact, one of the reasons that Ramsay had departed from the naval hierarchy in the mid-1930s was that his methods and his thinking were paradoxically considered altogether too modern. He was moreover a man of sharp edges, querulous and combative; in a few crucial respects, in the 1930s, he mirrored another great political outsider – his friend Winston Churchill. This admirable rear admiral has never fully received his dues; it is no exaggeration to say that his efforts had a profound effect on the course of the war.

Bertram Ramsay was born in 1883 and early on, his path crossed with that of a very young Winston Churchill when the latter was a pink-cheeked subaltern. Ramsay was a junior naval officer in the Somaliland expedition of 1903–4, and also saw service on the revolutionary battleship HMS *Dreadnought*. Later he found himself drawn towards the realm of signals. 'Signals training brought him into contact with those parts of the navy dealing directly with new technology,' wrote Brian P. Farrell. Ramsay was passionate about the possibilities of such technology. Intriguingly, he was also sceptical about certain hierarchical traditions prevalent in the navy – especially any that rested on the idea that the higher social classes had an innate and infallible instinct for war. A technocrat, not an aristocrat, he was much more interested in the capacity for formal training to bring out the finest in the officer class. Ramsay respected tradition deeply – but where it was proved to work, and not for its own sake.

He saw action in the Great War and received the MVO afterwards. The interwar years saw him command vessels in the Mediterranean and the Far East; these were the last rosy sunsets of Britain's imperial glory, with a world of dominions to be patrolled and guarded. In the 1920s and 1930s, Ramsay was regarded as a moderniser, bringing new, sharper methods to naval practice. 'Professionally,' wrote Brian P. Farrell, 'he was seen to be a stickler, always commanding the respect but not always winning the affection of his subordinates.' Ramsay was 'an authoritarian', 'brash' and 'impatient with anything that seemed outmoded or inefficient'.[5] And as he steadily climbed the rungs of the naval hierarchy, this unyielding trait eventually brought him into direct conflict with Commander-in-Chief Home Fleet Sir Roger Backhouse. Ramsay started work with Backhouse in the summer of 1935. Both men were ferociously dedicated but there was very soon friction; and it was Ramsay, after a period of intolerable conflict, who had to leave the field. Just months after joining, Ramsay requested that he should be allowed to stand down; permission was granted, and this left him with nothing to do, and on half pay.

Thankfully, even though in official terms he remained retired, it was not long before Ramsay was summoned down from family life in Berwickshire. The man who was responsible for summoning him: Backhouse. For despite the sulphurous nature of their working relationship, these two strong-willed men had contrived to remain friends, and there was a genuine mutual respect. The first inkling came in a 1938 letter to Ramsay from Admiral William (Bill) Whitworth, soon to be appointed Second Sea Lord. 'My dear Bertie,' it read. 'For your secret and personal information, I write to tell you that in the event of war in the near future, you will probably be appointed Rear-Admiral, Dover.' In rather chummier handwriting, as opposed to the typescript of the official communication, Whitworth added: 'Your official letter about further employment has arrived but it is unlikely you will get a definite answer until things in Europe are more peaceful. I expect you will be glad to get settled in Brightrig; we will certainly come and look you up when next we find ourselves in Berwickshire.'[6]

There was little time to settle into Borders life: when the official summons came in late 1938, Admiral Ramsay, by then a mellow fifty-five, was on his way to the south coast. He understood just how much work needed to be done; in the event of invasion, this would be one of the most crucial points.

Here, then, was the naval base at Dover Castle; and here was a man with a keen sense that war could only be fought using the most modern methods. Ramsay set about his new work with grim enthusiasm. He identified a number of problems, writing to his wife Helen Margaret: 'We have no stationery, books, typists or machines, no chairs and few tables, maddening communications. I pray that war, if it has to come, will be averted for yet a few days.'[7] Yet he was equally swift to set forward a range of solutions.

As early as October 1938, he was putting the old port on quite a new footing. He wrote to his superiors:

> The Western entrance should be closed. This would entail a few months work and would cost about £750,000 but it would render the harbour safe in all weathers . . . it would also render a large part of the harbour safe from torpedo attack . . . a protected oil fuel depot [should] be constructed in the chalk cliffs of East Cliff . . . A mine depot [should] be established, making use of the shelter afforded by the chalk cliffs and utilising the present tunnels in East Cliff.

Ramsay's office, rooted deep in the white cliffs of Dover, had the feeling of a whitewashed cave; in letters to his wife, he referred to it as his 'igloo'. There was a window, outside which were some railings, and a view out over the roiling waters of the English Channel. It was not long before these tunnels, recently little used, were teeming with life around the clock.

Also within the caves and tunnels was established the impressive operations room; here, on a vast three-dimensional map rendered on a near-circular wooden table, ships were tracked and traced, while elsewhere were the tangled mazes of radio equipment. There were many sub-corridors and subsidiary operations rooms; when the war really got going, great quantities of young Wrens (recruits to the Women's Royal Naval Service), were to work there, operating the radios, tuning in not only to ships but also to enemy pilots. Dover Castle was transformed into a great naval establishment. And, unusually in this war, the transformation was achieved in very good time. Admiral Ramsay prepared the way expertly for the days that were to come.

Yet in that time of the twilight war, and despite all his brilliant work, we now see in Ramsay a sense of the curious uncertainty that was felt up and down the land. He was a terrific letter writer; and in his surviving letters we see that even such a senior figure, privy to the most secret information, had no more idea about what was coming than anyone else. Nothing in war is ever pre-ordained or inevitable. There are just too many thousands of factors for one single mind simultaneously to absorb or anticipate them. And so Ramsay, at times, could not even be sure whether there would be full-scale conflict, or whether the summer of 1940 would be his to enjoy with his 'darling Mag'. It emphatically wasn't.

But whatever his regrets about being torn away from home, they must have been more than counterbalanced by a terrific sense of pride that he had been called to serve in such a pivotal role. Early letters from that time to 'darling Mag' show Ramsay growing in good humour and energy. 'Fellows are getting accustomed to their duties and have more confidence,' he wrote. 'Soon we will be able to compete with the demands made upon [us]. But heavens, the cost of all this . . .' The subject of money sent Ramsay spinning off on to other topics. 'I've found some very nice sherry in Dover,' he added, 'nicer and also a little cheaper than what we have at Bigwistry. So when you are getting towards the end of your own stock, let me know and I will send you a case.'

And so his 'igloo' overlooking the misty Channel became firmly established. The staff that he requested gradually started arriving; the white cliffs, so piercingly captured in that later song, were fully utilised for the less romantic purposes of storing munitions and mines. If the story of the start of the war is partly one of a lack of preparation, then this at least was one corner of the effort where quite the reverse was evident; a huge amount of foresight and work had gone in. The enthusiasm that Ramsay brought to his work – from dining and 'gossip' with the local brigadiers and the Warden of the Cinque Ports, to roaming the echoing tunnels of his base, checking on the smallest details – was immediately noted with delight by his superiors.

One of Ramsay's crucially important – yet also symbolic – lines of defence at the old port was the Dover Patrol; naval ships that zigzagged the frequently stormy waters, guarding a point of real vulnerability. The patrol had been a by-word for dependability in the First World War; with the advent of Ramsay, it was now joined by a collection of decidedly un-military vessels. Again this was a foretaste of the crisis to come.

One embedded correspondent described the scene as he sailed out on a shroud-grey morning:

> The boom defence swings open and the destroyer creeps out to sea; it is the beginning of her new turn of duty on the Dover patrol. As we move out of harbour, we pass several ships which have suffered a strange sea-change since the coming of war. Over there is a two-funnel steamer which only a few weeks

> ago was crowded on every deck with care-free holiday makers. People who have been to the Isle of Man for their holidays will remember her well, for she took them to Douglas. Now she has other and sterner uses.

The navy seemed primed; but was the army in France properly prepared? The German forces who had fought in Eastern Europe were being hardened to the very edge of psychopathy. Any natural nausea these Wehrmacht soldiers might have initially felt when blazing through towns and villages would have been violently quelled. In some men, there developed a thirst for more. In other words, there was every sense that the Allied armies did not have the fullest idea of what they would be facing.

In fact, there were some British soldiers who – transplanted from the earlier hardships of their lives back home – were finding their days in northern France a deceptive idyll. That autumn, some 158,000 British soldiers – together with 310 tanks – had sailed over anticipating an immediate prospect of bloodied mud and barbed wire; instead there was the sudden submersion into a new and unexpected way of life. They worked hard, obviously, and there was military discipline: but this was a land with which they were gradually falling in love. Some had come from towns where the pavements were greasy with rain-moistened soot, and where lingering coal smoke lodged permanently in noses and throats; by contrast, the small villages of rural northern France presented new sights, new flavours. There was food and drink never before tasted; a rich and complex language to grapple with; beautiful girls – and very few young male French locals to compete with for their attention, since they had been called up.

Bob Halliday, whose war was to take him from Glasgow to the heat of the North African desert in 1941–2 and thence to the Normandy landings, found that it was France of the Phoney War that surprisingly haunted his imagination afterwards. Even now, the subject causes him to look far into the distance. 'The people in

France that I was billeted with . . . because of my young age, they took me in. [They lived in] this café. There were two young daughters, mum, dad and granny . . . When I went back home on leave, my mother had given me coffee and Oxo cubes and stuff like that and I always managed to get those things back over – the welcome I got!'

The bucolic quietness of his billet was for Mr Halliday, just a teenager in 1939, a seductive contrast to the industrial hardships of his native Glasgow. 'My French was non-existent. There was a little chap, a farmer, and we used to go up to his place in the morning and we would have coffee and cognac with him. He had a bent pipe. And he stuffed it with tobacco that looked like straw and when he lit it, there were flames about six inches high. Lovely old man. We were sent up to get a goose for Christmas. The Major said I should go and get it. The man grabbed the goose by the neck and chopped its head off. Same with the farmers' wives when we wanted a chicken – just grabbed it, cut its beak off, put the scissors down there and cut it. That's the way they were. They had rabbits as pets, feeding them. One day doing that, and then eating them the next.'

Indeed, the place so lodged in his heart that he tried in later decades, long after the war, to seek out the kindly café owner and his family. 'I used to go on these pilgrimages,' says Mr Halliday. 'But I never, ever managed to get back to where I wanted to go.' Until one day not long ago when he found it. 'I went up to the café – it was all changed. Thought I had not a hope in hell of finding anyone. But then a voice behind me said: "Can I help you?" I told him about the café family. And this man told me that the girls – Lucianne and Ellianne – now lived together. I went round there. It was astonishing. I had been hoping to find them all those years. When we got up to their apartment, they had all the neighbours in and you couldn't get through the door. My friends and I decided to stay overnight at the hotel so that we could have a day out with the sisters. So that was wonderful. And I stayed in touch with them until they died.'

Affectionate stories of the kind that we now hear from Mr Halliday and others only serve to underline the brutal shock that was to be visited upon this French idyll. Observing the forces closely in France at that time was *The Times*'s special correspondent, a young man called Kim Philby. Prior to his immersion in intelligence and some distance from his rather more infamous role as a Cold War double agent for the Soviets, he was reporting at a time when journalists were coyly bylined as being 'Somewhere in France'. 'A new pidgin Anglo-French language is being evolved,' proclaimed Philby in one dispatch. 'Many of the soldiers are seriously trying learning French. They realize it may be an asset to them after the war.'

While Clydesider Bob Halliday was in Ravennes negotiating cognac and cigars and freshly killed chickens, others were being beguiled elsewhere. Having been posted to France to link up with the army's Royal Signals regiment, RAF signalsman Arthur Taylor found the experience enjoyably strange. 'We were stationed at Arras,' he recalls. 'Beds up in the loft of a farmhouse. One morning we woke up and we were under snow. After that, they moved us to a house. We dug in the garden – and found all the shells and the bullets from the First World War. I put them in my kitbag.

'We weren't doing anything. We were just waiting for a posting or a move. As signals, my job was to contact the aircraft. I had my own RAF radio. Transmitter receiver. Posh one it was.'

Mr Taylor describes a typical day: 'We were told there would be an exercise on, and that the aircraft would come over and contact us. And we would just do the drill and that's all I had to do. We were doing nothing except exercises. There was no war. Nothing. Just had to keep everybody occupied. We were all right, we were getting paid, there was a bar just opposite from where we were. We were quite happy. We were allowed out on weekends with a pass. I went out on a Saturday and the sergeant said, "Do you want to go again tomorrow?" I said yes, so he took my pass, crossed out the dates, and off I went. I had both days.

'In Amiens,' he adds, 'the social life was in the bar. We got on well with the local French. There was a nice bar lady.' As was quite natural, such a setting and such circumstances frequently sparked romances, though Mr Taylor was more concerned with a matter of some social awkwardness: although, as an RAF man, he says, 'I got on well with the army,' the fact was that as a skilled RAF signalsman, he was significantly better paid than his 'Tommy' counterparts. 'Of course the Royal Signals, I don't know why they had poor money but I always seemed to have more money than them,' he says, laughing, 'and I even bought them a radio so they could tune into England. Unfortunately that ended up in my kitbag.' The kitbag ended up as part of the collateral damage from those days to come in May 1940. 'I've still got the receipt for that radio,' says Mr Taylor ruefully.

As these men waited for the action to begin, still it was as if no one could quite envisage that this war would be any different from the last. That was certainly the case when the Prime Minister visited. 'Mr Chamberlain inspected several units which had just returned from patrol duty among the woods of no-man's land,' read one report – and even the use of that Great War term, still emotive and raw for so many, is indicative, given that the new landscape of conflict was scarcely the same thing at all. None the less, the need to illustrate a readiness for valour and sacrifice was important. 'The force, which is composed largely of men from the Midlands and northern England,' continued the report, 'contains a high percentage of men from rural districts who find little difficulty in moving across the country on their perilous missions after dark, though occasional snowfall increases the risk of exposure.' That was also the case elsewhere – indeed, many units found that even their ordinary parades were being cancelled for fear that snow-prints would be seen from above by German reconnaissance planes.

But where was the action? 'The period of inactivity has been an emotional anti-climax,' continued the report. 'Instead of the exciting and dangerous warfare for which they were keyed up, they have had hard monotonous work, no excitement and hardly any variety. The result is that many of them are bored and some are inclined to grumble.'

Strikingly, this was understood by pilot (and later literary historian) Samuel Hynes, who wrote: '[The soldiers] would go into war in a mood very different from that in which their elders had volunteered in 1914. They would go without dreams of glory, expecting nothing except suffering, boredom and perhaps death – not cynically, but without illusions, because they remembered a war: not the Great War itself, but the Myth that had been made of it.'[8]

There had been a German plan to strike into the Low Countries and France swiftly, in the late autumn of 1939, and in such a way as to maximise surprise. But this was continually deferred. By the spring of 1940, the highly experienced Colonel General Gerd von Rundstedt, a Prussian aristocrat who had been brought out of retirement for the war, and had been unhappy overseeing operations in Poland and the east, would be on the Western Front. It was on Rundstedt's advice that Hitler would eagerly seize on the Manstein plan, to strike fast through the Ardennes region and charge to the Channel coast. A later decision from Rundstedt would be the hinge on which events were to turn.

Elsewhere, throughout that dark winter, a top secret meeting in London between the most senior British and French naval personnel anticipated the need for a wider variety of boats than the purely military. For the British side, crucially, there was 'a request made by a Flag Officer-in-Charge, Cardiff' about 'little ships conversion' and whether 'it would be possible to ensure that small craft being converted are taken in hand at or near their home'.

From all around could be heard the approaching drums. The British public, and services, read of the Winter War between Finland and Russia, imagined easily the horrors of ice and blood. The entire continent was swirling in a maelstrom. France and Britain could not expect to escape its gravity for much longer.

And it was a particularly bitter winter across Europe. While Allied troops sought to keep circulation and mental faculties moving with drills and exercises across the iron-hard frosted soil of France, back in Britain there was a sympathetic awareness of battles taking place further north in regions where the cold could kill as surely as a bullet. For those in Poland, or Latvia, or Estonia, there had been no phoney war. Even among the civilian British population, there was an understanding. Bloomsbury member Frances Partridge, living deep in rural Wiltshire, wrote in her diary of January 1940 about an almost instinctive need to huddle inwards, to keep the coldness of this world at bay. 'The frightful accounts in the papers of arctic warfare in Finland – war, cold, fire and blood – all combine to turn one in on one's nipped and frozen self, and fasten powers of satisfaction on to small sensual things, pots of cyclamen, the shine on holly berries and cats fur, the texture of materials.'[9]

Air Minister Oliver Stanley, addressing soldiers in France, took care to remind them of the salient facts. 'No one who saw the last war could under-estimate the Germans,' he told them. 'Whereas we have been preparing for war at full speed for one year only, they have been preparing for four years and they have been pouring their sweat into their war machine. The German regime can only break down after the collapse of that war machine.'

Yet despite these words, one man was anxious that there was real, dangerous complacency among senior commanders: Hore-Belisha, Secretary for War, was acutely worried about the Maginot Line and its potential gaps. He was privately critical of defence plans; and this infuriated Lord Gort, as well as many other senior military personnel. Feeling against Hore-Belisha (fuelled, some have suggested, by an element of anti-semitism) reached magma point, and in January, Chamberlain removed him. But that electric uncertainty remained.

Sitting tight in his 'igloo' office, Admiral Sir Bertram Ramsay mused in letters to his wife about the increasing awkwardness of this war. 'What are we to do with all the troops we are throwing into France I can't think,' he wrote. 'They really will be an awful embarrassment to the Commander in Chief who will have a job to keep them quiet.' Moreover, he wondered, did Hitler himself possibly lack the necessary stamina for an all-out conflict with Britain? Yet in other letters, he told 'darling Mag' quite freely of his belief in an imminent Nazi assault upon English shores. As much as the man in the pub, Ramsay's mood seemed to ebb and flow with every fresh rumour that he heard, any potential invasion advancing then receding like a tide. In one letter, he signed off with this sentiment: 'But at least we have the summer ahead of us. It's something pleasant to look forward to.'

As a base for ferrying troops and goods back and forth from France, Ramsay's Dover eyrie was continually busy; all the more so for a seemingly non-stop parade of VIP visits, ranging from the Duke of Kent to His Majesty the King himself. 'It came on a blizzard,' wrote Ramsay to his wife. 'It really was frightful and we just had to rush [the King] along to the eastern breakwater . . . He had come over all cold and chilly so we gave him hot tea with whisky in it, followed by neat whisky, which we all drank.'

As the spring sun began warming the earth, however, there was still a certain languor to be found in north-eastern France. One correspondent wrote:

> The big camouflaged lorries still bump along the cobbled roads, and the handful of soldiers still stroll . . . in villages with that touch of long-legged grace which battle dress gives to a strong and fit man . . . The men look subtly different in some way that I have not been able to define – perhaps more confident, more at ease with their world. They might well be so, for many of them have now done their spell of duty in the Maginot Line and learned something of what war conditions were like.

These very same men – having adjusted to 'war conditions' – still seemed to be preparing the way for a modern remake of the Great

War, with a great many pill-boxes and trenches. After all, General Sir Alan Brooke, the melancholic ornithologist, had been convinced that the coming fight would not involve tanks to any great degree. 'The trenches have been strengthened,' noted the embedded reporter. There was a great deal of 'material' to be seen everywhere: 'duckboards, wire, timber, gravel and sand for concrete. Everywhere, too, parties of soldiers were digging.'

There was, too, room for some swagger. Highland regiment the Seaforths and Gordons had arrived in France to an unlikely controversy: should they – or should they not – wear the kilt? 'They are striding through the towns and villages of France in the new sombre battle dress capped with the khaki bonnet,' observed *The Times.* 'The traditional costume is worn only by pipers and clandestinely by such officers as were able to smuggle their kilts across the Channel . . . It is acknowledged freely that battle dress is the more efficient fighting uniform but, as a staff officer remarked today, "a Highlander in his kilt is a man and a half".'

There were very small skirmishes and minor scrapes; in March, a British reconnaissance flight miscalculated and landed in a field that the pilot assumed was just over the French border. In fact, the crew had landed in Germany. They found themselves being approached by what they described as 'peasants', and as they took off, shots were fired.

An equally low-key encounter took place on the Rhine, when a small party of Germans in a boat launched anti-British propaganda via 'streamers', aimed at the French. The result was that they were fired upon by an equally small party of French troops.

One other aspect of British soldiers' lives in France had been investigated by a society calling itself the Association for Moral and Social Hygiene. This organisation's aim was to ban soldiers from using brothels, or what they primly termed 'licensed premises'. Instead, they wanted to divert the soldiers away from sex and towards what they called 'social centres to promote the cheerfulness and good conduct of our men'. It is not too difficult to imagine what the

Tommies' reaction to that would have been. In fact, the association seemed unaware that the army hierarchy was recommending French brothels to soldiers – because with 'licensed premises', as opposed to casual encounters, the chances of sexually transmitted diseases were reduced.

There were rather more romantic stories in the weeks before May 1940. Private Bill Hersey not only fell in love with the daughter of a local café owner in the small town in which he was billeted. He married her in the weeks before the German invasion.

The Allies seemingly had no way of seeing what was coming. On 4 April, Chamberlain remarked in a disastrous speech to Parliament that 'whatever may be the reason – whether it was that Hitler thought he might get away with what he had without fighting for it or whether it was that after all the preparations were not sufficiently complete – one thing is certain: he missed the bus'. Days later, on 9 April, the German army smashed through Denmark and invaded Norway. The tactical importance of this region was the catalyst for a sort of action among the Allies – but the action was chaotic and misdirected. The War Cabinet became fixated upon Hitler's access to iron ore, and particularly to the supplies of ore to be found in Sweden; these shipments were then transported back via Norwegian waters and the port of Narvik to German blast furnaces. Therefore, despite Norway's neutrality, the British could find a way to use that territory to disrupt the movement of ore. The plan eventually settled into an idea to lay mines along that stretch of Norwegian coast, in neutral waters. This gave at least the impression of being some kind of war objective; some became convinced that the iron ore question would decide the course of the entire conflict. It didn't, but it would have deeply repercussive and unexpected effects in Britain and France a few weeks later. The British navy scored some success at Narvik but there were losses too; and on land, the situation was hopeless for the Allied troops, who were both outnumbered and outgunned by the Germans. In another forward echo of what was to come, it shortly became obvious that thousands of troops would have to be evacuated.

The incoherency of the Norwegian action fanned an already incandescent mood in Parliament; for weeks, months, the so-called 'glamour boys', a group of Conservative MPs (including Leo Amery, Harold Macmillan and Harold Nicolson) who had the deepest misgivings about Chamberlain's leadership, had been gathering and talking. As they saw it, tribal party loyalty simply had to be set aside in the interests of putting together a government that looked as though it had the necessary ferocity to fight; a government that did not have the continual suspicion of future appeasement lingering around it like a cloud. Indeed, there were two of these dissident groups within the party; one set aligned itself with Anthony Eden, the other with Winston Churchill. But it wasn't just a cabal of Conservatives who were anxious; there were profound concerns on the Opposition benches too. Said senior Labour figure Herbert Morrison: 'I have the genuine apprehension that if these men remain in office, we run the grave risk of losing this war.'

On 7 May, the painful confusion and failure of the Norway campaign resulted in what is now termed the Norway Debate, which was spread over two days. The Prime Minister naturally had a core of strongly loyal MPs, who believed that he was the right leader for these times. But many of the Conservatives, in consultation with the Labour opposition, were making their move. Their fear was that in the face of this aggressive and seemingly technically superior German army, Britain's chances would be slim.

For the Opposition, Labour leader Clement Attlee said: 'It is not Norway alone. Norway comes as the culmination of many other discontents. People are saying that those mainly responsible for the conduct of affairs are men who have had an almost uninterrupted career of failure. Norway follows Czechoslovakia and Poland. Everywhere, the story is "too late".' This was a debate of confidence in the wartime leader; and Chamberlain could not command the confidence he needed. Some wondered whether he had confidence in himself. And yet the simplistic picture of Chamberlain as an 'appeaser' is not sufficient, as his First Lord of the Admiralty understood.

There is an instructive story from a few months earlier, in 1939: Chamberlain, Winston Churchill and their respective wives had gathered to have dinner one evening. And Chamberlain – greatly to Churchill's surprise – held the party spellbound with an account of his younger life. He had been sent out to the remote Bahamas by his family in an effort to replenish their fading fortunes. He was on an island with a 'difficult' workforce trying to grow sisal. The experience was long, exhausting and unsuccessful. 'I was fascinated,' wrote Churchill, 'by the way Mr Chamberlain warmed as he talked, and by the tale itself, which was one of gallant endeavour. I thought to myself, "what a pity Hitler did not know when he met this sober English politician with his umbrella at Berchtesgaden, Godesberg and Munich, that he was actually talking to a hard-bitten pioneer from the outer marches of the British Empire."'[10]

Yet this 'hard-bitten' man was felt by many to have no enthusiasm for conflict. Leo Amery, one of the 'glamour boys' who precipitated the Prime Minister's fall, said of him: 'He was a civilian to the very marrow, hating war, obsessed by the sufferings it would cause and determined to avoid them if humanly possible. Prepared to do his patriotic duty and to urge others to do it . . . he had no conception of the daemoniac drive behind the enemy or of the heights of sacrifice . . . to which our own people are ready to rise if rightly led.'[11]

To Henry Buckley, a *Telegraph* journalist who had been in Spain throughout the Civil War, and witnessed the appalling new technological miracles that could inflict mass slaughter, Britain in the late 1930s looked extraordinarily old-fashioned; in London, he watched a ceremonial occasion involving the King, and other dignitaries, and noted uneasily that Britain seemed quaint and sclerotic next to the sleek, electric modernity of Europe's totalitarian powers. In a curious way, Neville Chamberlain, that son of the old Empire, exemplified a sort of strangulated patrician paralysis. It is ironic that the man chosen to guide Britain through the shock of its own modern age was of a family older and grander even than the King himself. And it is truly extraordinary that he assumed power on the very day that the old world was swatted aside by Hitler's forces.

PART TWO

4

Blitzkrieg

10–19 May 1940

No veteran will speak directly of fear. Rightly so; not because it would be unmanly to do so, but because it would be a tangential form of boasting, a means of suggesting grit and endurance. Yet it is very hard to imagine how the young men waiting for war early in 1940 could not have experienced moments of profound anxiety. Even if they had been given years of training – rather than, in many cases, a few weeks – nothing could have prepared them for the days that were to come, when they would cross that shadow-line. The German soldiers, along with the single-mindedly sadistic SS divisions, the Gestapo squads, that were shortly to swerve unstoppably and with sickening speed past the Allied defences, were a force that had never quite been seen before.

Imagine also then the turn of the screw: for so many of the very young soldiers in northern France as that invasion spread, confusion would be followed by isolation. Men were to find themselves separated from officers, from units, from comrades. There were individuals who would be left to fend for themselves as best they could; inexperienced soldiers, wandering a strange land with no solid command or orders. Some would not have the time to become disorientated; they would find themselves constantly on the move, on the search for shelter in open, exposed country, foraging for food – and constantly aware that they were targets. These young men, either singly or in small raggle-taggle groups, would find themselves not only in a lethal game of hunter and hunted with Panzers and hidden snipers; they would also shortly witness the real meaning of total war. They would watch helplessly the long lines of civilian refugees, very young and very old, being casually machine-gunned by German bombers roaring out of the sky: death for death's sake.

For the vast majority of the men, these were to be the first obscenely exposed corpses that they would see; the first experience of true visceral horror, of dismemberment, of the startling purples, mauves and blues of interior organs displayed. No soldier, having witnessed this onrushing fury, would expect civilised treatment from such a savage enemy. For the young British soldiers who were to find themselves in bewildered retreat, there was to be one certainty: the absolute need at every cost to avoid capture.

What would make those days the more piercing was the stomach-dropping lurch of shock. It now seems as though, back in Britain, there was something akin to a national exhalation of breath as the news came through on 10 May: 'Hitler strikes at the Low Countries! Belgian, Dutch and French towns bombed!' Those were the headlines; the papers sounded almost giddily exhilarated. Yet the fact was that Allied senior commanders were ready for the wrong war.

The Germans penetrated Belgium, Holland and Luxembourg – from the air, by rail, by road – in the small hours of 10 May. The incursions, so long anticipated and so often delayed, had the speed of a nightmare. Railway stations around Rotterdam – which only twenty-four hours before had awaited the day's commuters – now echoed to rapid gunfire and the city itself was bombed so savagely as to be rendered almost unrecognisable. In Luxembourg, which had no army, German commanders seized the ducal palace almost instantly, for some reason expecting a cordial welcome. To the west, before the first streaks of light appeared on the horizon, clouds of parachutists landed in Belgium and communications faltered in the pandemonium. Bombers swooped over aerodromes, which blossomed into flowers of flame. The pilots dived on Brussels; terrified families, their houses shaking in the pre-dawn dark, had no idea that war had been declared. British soldiers and their officers, billeted in northern France, heard the news via the wireless early that morning. Over their breakfasts, men eagerly discussed their anticipated mobilisation. There was the quicksilver injection of adrenaline: the high confidence of youth eager to face the future. Yet they were also piercingly aware that they were facing an utterly implacable enemy. One soldier recalled that just a few weeks earlier, he had been working in a furniture factory; now he was being called upon to face the most formidable army the world had yet seen. Who among these men would not also have quietly experienced stomach flutters of apprehension?

That morning of 10 May, great numbers of the BEF were moved up towards the new front in Belgium. 'Guns were decorated with flowers,' wrote languorous *Times* correspondent Kim Philby. 'The mood of the BEF changed perceptibly today and in place of dogged resolution, tinged perhaps with boredom, there are smiles and singing as the troops move off to the Front.' Even as civilians cheered them, though, the men were marching into the German trap.

Philby's inadvertent echo of the Great War was captured a little more saltily by the *Manchester Guardian*'s correspondent. 'Beside the roads,' he wrote, 'the Belgian population have stood cheering, pressing glasses of beer on the troops . . . and garlanding their guns with lilac. In spite of all the prospects of blood and horror which have been before us since three o'clock this morning, the move of today has been a happy one. One British unit crossed the Belgian border singing the Marseillaise.' But there were others who had their own fears: French civilians. 'In the towns and villages,' continued the correspondent, 'women were standing together at every door talking seriously . . . and the shop assistants were out in the streets waiting apparently for whatever might come.'

'Now it could be seen why we had been building defence lines and pill-boxes on the Belgian frontier,' wrote Colonel J. Lee of the 2nd Battalion, Hampshire Regiment, not long afterwards. 'I returned to the office after breakfast to find the Adjutant busily engaged on an Operation Order. This could mean only one thing – advance.' Just hours later, he wrote, 'we crossed the Belgian border at about 3am and we were greeted by the Belgians in the same way that we greeted them – thumbs up . . . We made towards Brussels and our convoy must have stretched for miles.' The initial mood, according to this account, was jocular, upbeat. They watched as a Hurricane chased and then downed a Heinkel; watched as the surviving German pilot was taken prisoner, and his pistol – a much-admired piece of workmanship – was taken from him. If there was foreboding among this vast number of men, it was not articulated; instead, the cheers were more in keeping with a football match. The first inkling Colonel Lee and his men gained of the gruelling time to come was on the road before them:

> Just outside Brussels, we saw the ever-increasing columns of refugees. They were all over the place and it was exceedingly difficult to get through them without causing any harm. It was a pitiful sight, people old and young, all intent on doing the same thing, and all making their way to supposed safety. Little did they know what was going to happen.[1]

Indeed, little did Colonel Lee himself know at that stage.

As the troops – the experienced old hands and the inexperienced youngsters – marched on, all those back in Britain were absorbing the other pivotal moment of 10 May 1940.

'The Right Hon Neville Chamberlain has resigned the office of Prime Minister and First Lord of the Treasury this evening,' ran the announcement, 'and the Right Honourable Winston Churchill accepted His Majesty's invitation to fill the position. The PM desires that all Ministers should remain at their posts and discharge their functions with full freedom and responsibility while the necessary arrangements for the formation of a new administration are made.'

According to the (sometimes excessively) colourful account of his bodyguard, when Churchill returned from the Palace and his audience with the King, the new Prime Minister slumped with tears in his eyes and said: 'I hope it is not too late. I am very much afraid it is.' Was Churchill – in the moment when he assumed control of the nation's destiny – convinced that Hitler would snatch it away? Certainly there would be other occasions in the days that followed – even in his most famous speeches – where Churchill seemed to be hinting that the British fightback would be a desperate one, guerrilla warriors with improvised weapons. Yet he was also particularly noted for his vertiginous temperament, and it is possible to square these moments of ink-black gloom with the figure who minutes later could energise everyone around him with bellicose humour.

Meanwhile, Neville Chamberlain took to the airwaves for a valedictory address; he felt the need to explain and contextualise his own actions in those last several years. 'Now as this is my last message to you as Prime Minister from Number 10 Downing Street,' Chamberlain said in that tired, quavering Received Pronunciation, 'there are one or two things I should like to say to you . . . I have borne a heavy load of anxiety and responsibility. As long as I believed there was a chance of preserving peace honourably, I strove to take it. When that last hope vanished and war could no longer be avoided, I strove equally hard to wage it with all my might. Perhaps you remember,' he added, in the curious folksy way that the BBC encouraged at the time, 'that in my broadcast of September 3 last year, I told you that we should be fighting against evil things. My words have proved to be insufficient to describe the vileness of those who have now staked everything on the great battle just beginning.

'Perhaps it may be at least some relief to know that this battle . . . has ended the period of waiting and uncertainty. For the hour has come when we are to be put to the test.'

This address did nothing to quell the rising fury of a small group of young politicians and writers who would make themselves heard a few weeks after.

Nor was the BEF alone on a new, urgent war footing; in Britain, on 10 May, there was a sudden flurry of action and preparation. New official guidelines to do with the use of gas masks, and the location of bomb shelters, were distributed; it was not if, but when. There were now special gas masks for toddlers, fashioned to look like Walt Disney's Mickey Mouse – painted red and blue, with the addition of large ears. Some school teachers cleverly extemporised practice drills by means of piano tunes; whenever the children heard the music, they would stop whatever they were doing and run to put their masks on. In general terms, it had been so long since the previous autumn that it was felt that everyone needed reminding of old drills. There was also a sharp tightening of defence regulations; these ranged from the correct way for civilians to approach armed sentries (to avoid accidental shootings) to the need for civilians to keep watch for the first signs of enemy incursion, while there were fresh restrictions on what could be written and indeed what could be said out loud in public. The latter was an area that did not trouble Mr Churchill too greatly. He was in favour, in the short term at least, of censorship. Others were less blithe. A fairly new organisation called the National Council of Civil Liberties protested about what it saw as the draconian dangers of the restrictions; these rules harked back, it claimed, to the tyranny of Charles I.

Others were exercised by more quotidian concerns. 'Two girls at the office, due to be married tomorrow, are in a flutter,' reported one diarist from Sheffield. 'Guests coming from afar, all preparations made . . . and to crown it all, Chamberlain resigns.' Even more quotidian was a widespread peevishness about the government's cancellation of the Bank Holiday. 'People who had intended to go on holiday are urged to remain at home,' went the announcement. 'Special trains are cancelled.' In fact a great many people were on their holidays already. Magazines, from which it had been too late to withdraw advertising, still carried colourful enticements such as 'ample rations of sunshine at Bournemouth!' But the scramble to reset the national consciousness was on. More than just a simple readjustment, the entire world now had to be viewed on wholly different terms.

This was a country now in full expectation of an immediate Nazi invasion. Another official pronouncement from the Home Office exhorted ordinary citizens to 'keep watch for enemy troops landing by parachute and to report any such attempt at once to the nearest police station, giving the most accurate information possible as to the place and number of persons landing'. There were small outbreaks of black comedy. At a mill in Huddersfield, one loom girl caused outrage by suddenly goose-stepping up and down the factory floor. She explained that she was getting in practice for when Hitler came. Her actions were ascribed to 'light-headedness'; one woman commented: 'It's making a lot of people like that, this war.'

While BBC radio news was carefully sombre and unexcitable, to the point of somnolence, the newspapers were in quite a different mood, which in turn might have helped stoke up the passions of their readers. Even the highbrow *Observer*, on Sunday 12 May, abandoned its customary measured tone. 'The Trumpets of the Apocalypse are sounded and its seals are broken,' the editorial boomed. 'Illusions are shrivelled as by the breath of fire. Our awakening is final. Our resolve is steel . . . These are hours of destiny.'

Vague reports began to filter back from Belgium; of brave gunners embedded in trenches, of German fighter planes being shot down. Understandably, the reporting now became much more nebulous. And clearly the truth was rather more complex. Colonel

Lee of the Hampshire Regiment recalled days of marching, and of slightly jumbled directions; of finding new HQs – old farmhouses, an empty chateau – which would then almost immediately have to be abandoned after bombing raids. There was an awareness of advancing tanks; but where? In that quiet, flat countryside, shelling found its first British military victims. 'The wounded soldiers looked very young and taking that into consideration, they did very well when their wounds were being attended,' Colonel Lee wrote later. He and his men seemed constantly to be withdrawing, yet without ever quite getting a chance to 'have a crack' at the enemy. At 10 p.m. one night, he and his men were almost deafened by an almighty exchange across a canal that the Germans were trying to cross. 'Mortars, rifles, and bombs all at it,' he wrote. The noise was unholy. In this scenario of almost ceaseless movement – the precise reverse of the last war, and of what had been expected of this conflict – half the battle, it seemed, was for any man to get into a position where he could grab at least a couple of hours of decent sleep.

The public back home was not yet to know any of this; nor were their elected representatives in Parliament. Events were simply moving too fast. Yet people could obviously not help speculating. And if the public was not to take its cue from the news from over the sea, then the tone of government pronouncements certainly would have triggered strong responses. 'Action Stations!' bellowed one domestic government poster, bearing an illustration of a destroyer. 'This is WAR . . . and everyone must help. Everyone!' This was no poster for conscription or for local defence volunteers: rather, it was a plea for money. The government was exhorting the public to plunge its savings into savings certificates and defence bonds. The cash was badly needed.

How much spiritual comfort was on offer for those at home? Though church attendance was clearly a very great deal higher than it is today (and indeed in the early days of the war, crept a little higher yet, before falling back somewhere around 1942), that does not mean that services always offered much to congregations in the way of succour. One diarist in the north was taken by the spectacle of his wife and the woman next door heading to church for the first time in years, in search of some solace. It didn't work. They came back and declared that 'they had been disappointed and a little bored'. Nor were the preachers always satisfied with the reactions of those sitting in the pews. One vicar in Manchester complained of 'the cold listless stare, the drowsy indifference of the faces before him'. Yet he might have misinterpreted those stares; they might have been of silent apprehension.

On 13 May, Winston Churchill made his first speech as Prime Minister to the House of Commons, famously declaring that 'I have nothing to offer but blood, toil, tears and sweat.' His larger message was equally stark:

> We have before us an ordeal of the most grievous kind. We have before us many many long months of struggle and of suffering. You ask: what is our policy? I can say: it is to wage war, by sea, land and air, with all our might, and with all the strength that God can give us. To wage war against a monstrous tyranny, never surpassed in the dark lamentable catalogue of human crime . . . without victory, there is no survival.

The response in the House was, curiously, mixed; on the Opposition benches, there was a great roar of enthusiasm, the air fluttering with the white of waved order papers. From the Conservative benches was a more muted, muttered approval; indeed, the appearance in the chamber of former PM Neville Chamberlain evoked a rather greater shout from those benches. Sir Irving Albery, Conservative member for Gravesend, followed Churchill's speech by saying that 'a great many people in the House and in the country resented the action in last week's debate of certain Privy Counsellors and others in turning what should have been a debate on affairs in Norway into a political manoeuvre. When history comes to be written,' added Albery, '[Chamberlain] might rest assured that he will get his due.' Indeed so. But Bethnal Green MP Sir Percy Harris declared that 'the Prime Minister has two qualities essential to win the war – vigour and imagination'.

And the response from the wider British public? At the time, parliamentary business was not broadcast either live or edited. Only a little later would Churchill consent to repeat his speeches in a BBC studio for broadcast to the nation. Before that, it was left to the parliamentary correspondents of the newspapers to provide transcripts and convey to their readership the mood and atmosphere of each day's proceedings. Strikingly, *The Times*'s leader column compared Churchill's speech to that made by Garibaldi when he promised 'hunger, thirst, marches, battles and death', concluding that 'with that spirit, no one can doubt that the government and nation will achieve victory'.

Writing many decades later, Lord Jenkins of Hillhead (Labour Home Secretary from 1967 to 1970), who was nineteen years old in 1940, recalled that to him,

> the national mood . . . was not so much defiant as impregnable. The prospects were awful but people pushed the consequences of defeat out of their collective mind. It was not a question of bravery. It was more that they chose to believe that the worst would not happen. To what extent this was a product of the mesmerising quality of Churchill's rhetoric is a difficult question to answer . . . What he did, almost more in the recollection of my 19 year old state of mind, was to produce a euphoria of irrational belief in ultimate victory. This at least stilled any paralysis of apprehension and made it possible to pursue normal activity, some parts of which were more useful to the war effort than others, and to live surprisingly happily on the edge of a precipice.[2]

This activity included Jenkins's own war effort; he rose to the rank of captain and, later on in the war, was pulled into the pressurised hothouse of codebreaking at Bletchley Park.

Certainly Churchill's public projections of growling confidence were at odds with the private communications he was receiving from the French. On 15 May, French Prime Minister Paul Reynaud had telephoned Churchill in the small hours and declared: 'We have been defeated . . . we are beaten.' Elsewhere, the French military chief of staff, surveying the German attack, observed: 'From what I see around us, the campaign in France is over.' Such pessimism was communicated to and shared by many senior British personnel. 'At this moment,' reflected the new Chief of the Imperial General Staff, Sir Edmund Ironside, 'this looks like the greatest military disaster in all history.'

Very little in the way of detail about the German campaign was given by the BBC or the newspapers. It was as much a matter of intelligence as morale. Yet we now might wonder if full knowledge of the situation would have changed the national mood, or whether Churchill's rhetoric – like the spell of a powerful sorcerer – would banish fretful rationality and instead summon faith. One evacuated civil servant was listening a few days later to Churchill's first radio broadcast: 'Upon all . . . the long night of barbarism will descend . . . unless we conquer, as conquer we must, as conquer we shall.' He and some colleagues were in a basement kitchen in Harrogate, Yorkshire. 'The effect of that broadcast,' said the civil servant, 'was magical. A confused and frightened lot of people became courageous, hopeful, determined to see it through and no one that I came across ever slipped back into the defeatism that disgraced the country from Munich to that May.'[3]

For Colonel Lee of the Hampshire Regiment, any sense of 'magic' was absent from the weirdly defamiliarised country he and his men were moving through:

> The road was full of bomb craters. Nearby was a house that had been demolished, and near it was a Frenchman who was frantically searching the ruins . . . we saw the Frenchman walking

slowly away from the building with a body in his arms. About 100 yards from the building, he stopped and laid the body gently down. We asked a Gunner what had happened and he told us that the body was that of [the Frenchman's] daughter. She was terribly mangled, and we watched the Frenchman digging a grave for her. When this was done, he took the body up, covered the face with a handkerchief and laid her in the grave. When the burial was completed, he picked up two pieces of wood, and made them form a cross, which he stuck in the ground. He looked up and said something in French which we did not understand, and walked away.[4]

The chief and immediate concern in the letters columns of newspapers as the Germans made their sweep through the Low Countries was to do with the likelihood that the British skies would soon be darkening with enemy parachutists; Sir Anthony Eden, Minister for War, had addressed the subject briefly in the Commons, promising some form of a special body to deal with this contingency. One letter writer, a doughty old warrior, declared: 'I have spent this Sunday in my village in Sussex. An air-troop carrier landing on the Downs – indeed, a handful of German parachutists – could take possession of the village and of the look-out posts on the cliffs . . . some dozens of able-bodied men and myself, armed with rifles, could handle the situation with at least some measure of success.'

Elsewhere in Sussex, Virginia Woolf wrote in her diaries:

Apple blossom snowing the garden . . . Churchill exhorting all men to stand together . . . These vast formless shapes further circulate. They aren't substances; but they make everything else minute. Duncan saw an air battle over Charleston – a silver pencil and a puff of smoke. Percy has seen the wounded arriving in their boots. So my little moment of peace comes in a yawning hollow.

And she and husband Leonard had their own macabre plans for the worst. 'But though L says he has petrol in the garage for suicide should Hitler win, we go on. It's the vastness and the smallness that make this possible.'[5]

Preparation was solace in itself. Sir Anthony Eden called for Home Defence volunteers to be on the lookout for Nazi parachutists. He also unveiled the name of the new force that would help to foil them: the Local Defence Volunteers. On hearing this broadcast, Leonard Woolf was immediately keen on the idea of joining such a force (not least, perhaps, because their village would have been a prime target for such an invasion). He was not alone in his enthusiasm; in the first week after the formation of the Local Defence Volunteers, some 250,000 men had rushed to join. There were, according to historian David K. Yelton, immediate tensions, some of which were class based. 'Many initial officer appointees were roundly criticised,' he wrote, 'particularly among working class volunteers, as incompetent, inexperienced, unenthusiastic or simply unpopular.' There were other problems too: almost nothing in the way of equipment or arms was available for issue to the volunteers. Given that the BEF itself was not luxuriously supplied, this might not have been a surprise; yet for a country facing the prospect of ruthless invaders, it was not an immediate comfort to think that the last line of defence was down to using shotguns, old pieces confiscated from museums, including in one or two cases muskets and an antique Chinese bronze cannon.

The lack of uniform – to begin with, the men had to make do with armbands – was another source of discontent, not least because the Germans in their broadcasts had made it plain that anyone bearing arms in civilian clothes would be treated as resistance forces, and subject to execution. A sharp cartoon depicted a butler in a stately bedroom placing an LDV armband on his master's bed and saying: 'I've laid out your uniform, my lord.' As Yelton remarks, in the first couple of weeks that LDV units assembled themselves up and down the country, 'many British citizens saw [them] as more indicative of their country's military weakness.'[6]

The government also signalled the rounding up of 'aliens'. There were some 3000 German-born people in Britain. In the initial round-up, quite a few of these Germans were taken and held at the offices of the Tote racing organisation. A conversation was later reported between a German boy waiting in a queue for lunch in the Tote building, and an army officer holding a gun. The army officer said to the boy: 'Are you Jewish?' 'Yes,' the boy replied. 'Are there many Jews here?' 'About 80%,' replied the boy. The army officer exhaled sharply. 'Damn!' he said. 'I knew we'd got the wrong lot!'[7]

On the south coast, young signals cadets based in the port town of Ramsgate had their own German paratrooper emergency, which was recalled by former cadet John Shelmerdine: after a rare night off, when a party of the young men had been refreshing themselves in a local pub, the alarm was sounded at 4.30 a.m. – intelligence had been received that German parachutists had landed at the local airfield. This was it! The invasion was on! With a sense of trepidation in those pre-dawn hours, men piled into an old civilian truck. They got to the airfield as a warm May sun was rising, and found no sign of Germans. But what about the intelligence they had received? Perhaps the invasion would be the next day. And so the men set about making Ramsgate airfield impossible to land upon. They gathered up old ironwork, discarded pipes, barbed wire – and covered the landing strip with it. The next day, recalled Mr Shelmerdine, the soldiers once more hurried to the airfield. Somehow, despite all their careful precautions, a plane – completely undamaged in any way – was now sitting there on the runway. Happily for them, it was a naval Swordfish. After those false alerts, the port of Ramsgate would, just a few days later, be involved in a rather more nail-biting emergency.

The frothier side of life somehow went on. In city cinemas, huge audiences sought escape in the fizzing comic backchat of the Bob Hope/Bing Crosby/Dorothy Lamour vehicle *The Road to*

Singapore. There was also Marlene Dietrich and James Stewart in *Destry Rides Again,* which had opened that week to affectionately scoffing reviews.

But as those audiences settled back, the German army was making its lethally fast and decisive push across the French border, through the heavily forested Ardennes region, and then bridging the Meuse river; territory broadly overlooked by French generals and politicians on the grounds that it would be impossible to move large numbers of troops at sufficient speed through such rough, hilly, densely wooded terrain.

There have been many suggestions over the years that the same authorities were repeatedly tipped off long in advance by those with knowledge and foresight that such an assault was in fact perfectly possible; and there are sound theories about why the French might have psychologically tried to will the possibility away. In particular, there was General Gamelin's strategy, described by one historian as 'a cut price war on the peripheries [i.e. the Low Countries] to avoid battles on French soil'. Historian Joel Blatt went further:

> Profound memories haunted inter-war France. First, World War One, with its horrendous 1.3–1.4 million French dead and many more wounded, left war cemeteries, memorials and widows. Understandably, most of the French regarded entry into a second charnel house with serious qualms. Generals . . . accordingly devised a defensive strategy and sought a war outside France that might somehow spare French lives.[8]

What, then, of British military strategy at this point? Anglo-French understanding had never been smooth; from the early French desire to launch action in the Balkans, to disputes over the German assault on Norway, there were differences. Yet, as some have suggested, the British were also acutely aware of the size of their contribution to the effort; although substantial, it did not match that of the French. Therefore it was a matter of diplomacy to accept French thinking in strategy. 'My responsibilities were confined to ensuring that the orders issued by the French for the employment of the BEF were capable of being carried out,' wrote Lord Gort later. 'And indeed events proved that the orders issued for this operation were well within the capacity of the force.'

There was another mistake too, as summarised by military historian Martin Alexander: 'The near universal British complacency about the impregnable shelter provided by the Maginot Line and the French Army . . . even Churchill harboured limitless faith in French military prowess.'[9] This was also about the use of advanced equipment; while in terms of numbers and indeed materiel the Germans and the Allies were well matched, the Germans had found new ways to deploy their armaments. As Great War veteran Brigadier General John Charteris explained in an essay at the time: 'With mechanised forces, all . . . is changed. The advance is led by hordes of tanks moving at a pace which may reach twelve miles per hour, against which ordinary obstacles offer no protection. The heavy artillery is replaced by swarms of fast moving bombers raining down upon the defenders heavier and probably better-directed shells than before.'

One might also ascribe the lightning German swoop through the Ardennes – and the failure of the Allies to keep a sufficient defensive force in the region – to a colossal failure of intelligence. Back in Britain, although the codebreakers of Bletchley Park had already succeeded in cracking the principles of the German Enigma code, this triumph was still brand new; Alan Turing's cypher-sifting bombe machines had only started clicking into action. It would be some little time yet before it became the vast, highly efficient operation that could read messages from every theatre of war.

Moreover, intelligence is only ever of use if soldiers are prepared to act on it. It was noted, for instance, that some time beforehand, an inspection of the French troops in the Ardennes region was made by Edward, Duke of Windsor, of all people, who was at that time surprisingly attached to a liaison mission. He voiced scepticism about how much the troops would be able to do if a lightning strike was made. But, as one historian put it, 'the discredited ex-King was not taken seriously.' The raffish abdicator was not the only one to have detected vulnerability; General Sir Alan Brooke also had doubts, and had voiced these to his superiors. At the time, he was viewed as a 'carping defeatist'.

Another element was that communications between the British and the French were at best unreliable. They completely lacked the fluid and fast organisation required. And so, as the sheer numbers of German forces pushing through the rough tracks of the Ardennes actually at one point slowed to a crawl because of gridlock – tanks backing up on tanks – British news reports continued to tell of brave RAF raids, of lines in Belgium and France being held, of British troops standing steady. Eagle-eyed readers might have frowned briefly as they alighted upon a statement from the American embassy: 'The State department has advised all Americans in Great Britain to go to Ireland,' it read starkly. This was upon the recommendation of the new US ambassador in London, Joseph Kennedy (the father of Jack). He insisted at the time that his reasoning was all to do with 'the increasing difficulties in passenger services from England to America'. There was clearly some concern that this should not be seen as a panicky evacuation of US citizens from a country that might shortly be invaded.

Winston Churchill travelled to Paris – there were several such visits before the fall of France – to meet with French Prime Minister Paul Reynaud. Their meeting was held against a backdrop that featured angry denials by the French government that it was about to abandon Paris, and that the Germans were materialising in ever greater numbers within France's borders. 'Stupid alarming rumours!' exclaimed Reynaud, even as it was announced that France's 'Army Zone' would now be extended to include Paris, and that the city's administration had been passed over from the civilian to the military authorities. 'Paris is becoming rather empty,' wrote one correspondent with careful understatement. 'Though there has been an influx of refugees. Many Belgian cars are seen in the streets with mattresses over their hoods to protect them against the full force of machine gun bullets. The seven thousand Paris buses have disappeared,' the correspondent added. 'They are busy transporting refugees.' And it was here that Churchill is said to have received the gravest fright of his entire war. Not only did he arrive to find officials setting fire to government paperwork, but when he asked General Gamelin of the 'strategic reserve' forces that might be deployed against the German invaders, Gamelin replied: 'There is none.'

Against this palpable sense of catastrophe, there were continued outbreaks of pleasing and occasionally absurd optimism back in Britain; manifestations of a determination simply to get on with it. 'Hampers for the Forces', cried one mouth-watering advertisement from the upmarket Piccadilly grocery shop Fortnum and Mason. What better way to send comfort to soldiers in France than 'The Piccadilly Box', which contained – among other slightly random-seeming delicacies – Dundee cake, game pâté, strawberries in syrup, whitebait, grilled mushrooms, lime tablets and veal and ham pie. All for twenty-one shillings. There was a slightly posher version – 'The Grand Fleet Box' – for thirty shillings, which as well as the tinned veal pie contained Nescafé, a whole roast partridge, lemonade tablets and anchovy paste. It is difficult to know how many were sent, and whether the recipients had any chance to enjoy the contents.

On Sunday 19 May, Winston Churchill made his first radio broadcast as Prime Minister. His talk was aimed not only at his British audience, but a wider American listenership too. Introducing the situation as 'a solemn hour in the life of our country', he continued plainly:

> A tremendous battle is raging in France and Flanders. The Germans by a remarkable combination of air bombing and heavily armoured tanks have broken through the French defences . . . and strong columns of their armoured vehicles are ravaging the country.
>
> After this battle in France abates its force, there will come the battle for our island, for all that Britain is and all that Britain means. That will be the struggle. In that supreme emergency we shall not hesitate to take every step, even the most drastic, to call forth from our people the last ounce and the last inch of effort of which they are capable. The interest of property and the hours of labour are nothing compared to the struggle for life and honour, for life and the freedom to which we have vowed ourselves.

There were stirring words concerning the French leadership, how Churchill had been given 'the most sacred pledges' that they would fight on until the end. But the mere fact that he felt the need to say so would have indicated perfectly clearly to everyone – from the beleaguered and sometimes bewildered soldiers in the north of France, to families sitting in the yellow light of their parlours – that crisis was imminent.

Before that, very quietly on 15 May, in a small down-page item in *The Times*, there appeared an announcement that would have been ignored by the general reader, but seized on keenly by anyone with an interest in boats. This small item, no more than a paragraph in length, ran as follows:

> The Admiralty has made an order requiring all owners or occupiers of self-propelled craft (including motor boats) in Britain between 30ft and 100ft in length used for their own pleasure of for fare-paying passengers for pleasure which have not already been offered or requisitioned to send particulars to the Admiralty within 14 days of yesterday.

The notice was in fact aimed at rounding up as many vessels as possible for minesweeping work. Yet its timing could not have been more serendipitous.

5

'They Just Kept Marching Us'

19–24 May 1940

Arthur Taylor sits with his file of photographs and documents before him, in his house on the south coast, as he recalls the fraught experience of having been a young RAF signals operator attached to an army unit in the spring of 1940 – a position spiked with unexpected hazards. It was not merely the shattering engagements with German forces along the banks of the River Dyle; the shelling and the bombs that would make the very ground vibrate like jelly; or indeed the sickening moment when his company learned that the enemy had managed to bypass the French and were now *behind* them. It was also the fact that Mr Taylor belonged to a different service – and one that, quite quickly, and wrongly, was perceived as funking the war. In other words, as a young man in the wrong uniform, he faced almost as much physical danger from his own side as he did from the enemy.

'I was on my own with the other wireless operator,' Mr Taylor says. 'Just the two of us attached to the Royal Signals. No air force. No one to fall back on for help. Nobody. My boss was a Lieutenant Thomas.'

It was Thomas who knew that Mr Taylor was not only proficient with Morse, but also with the driving of heavy military vehicles. 'I had [a truck] allocated to me personally – but we were stopped by the military police and told "You've got to drive it into the canal with everything you've got and you can go away with your rifle and your clothes."' Such wanton destruction of army property, otherwise regarded as sacrosanct, gave Mr Taylor, along with many other men during those days, an inkling that something terrible was going on.

And so his truck went into the water. But this still left him in the anomalous position of not quite knowing who to answer to. 'When I got to the other side of the bridge,' continues Mr Taylor, 'the lieutenant said "You can be my map bag-holder." So thank you very much. "But the other thing," he said, "is that you've got to get rid of your uniform and we'll get you a pair of gumboots and get rid of your Air Force shoes."'

This was not a question of military etiquette but a means of protecting young Mr Taylor. His lieutenant knew all about the rivalry between services, and in particular the ill-will that soldiers felt for the air force – an antipathy that was to sharpen greatly over the next few days. Never mind the Germans; there was every chance that Mr Taylor would be attacked by his own side. 'So I had to get rid of the shoes,' he says, 'and put gumboots on. And my uniform went. Lieutenant Thomas gave me a black mackintosh. And I had a tin hat. All because they heard that air force personnel had been beaten up by the army. Because there was no support.' In fact, he says, they were wrong about the question of air support for the BEF. 'There were twenty-six RAF squadrons in France. Plus there was help from across the Channel. So the idea that the RAF weren't there wasn't true. But there was ill-feeling. Hence not displaying my air force uniform.

'So I had the coat, the helmet and the officer's briefcase with all his maps in,' continues Mr Taylor. 'And a rifle. And away we went, ten miles. Well, we got, shall we say, three miles, when we came across some three tonners.' These were vehicles that had already been abandoned. 'The lance corporal got one of them going. So then we jumped in. The police came out and demanded that we take some wounded with us.'

Retreat is a curiously emotive word, and yet for Mr Taylor the experience was more one of intense practicality. In the growing tumult, and amid the chaos of terrified refugees and increasingly haphazard communications, the order to pull back seemed to come to different units at different times. But even in the confusion, it seemed clear to all that they were being pressed back to the coast under the weight of the German onslaught. Arthur Taylor was one of many thousands borne along by a rapid tide of events, so those days felt neither like a withdrawal nor a defensive manoeuvre; it was simply about keeping moving and staying watchful. There was certainly no time for dreams of glory; yet nor was there any sense of defeat. Before the men actually saw the German forces that confronted them, there was some underlying optimism that the British could overcome the enemy, that this strange, powerful tide would turn in the right direction again. Even after those German forces materialised, a certain dogged spirit persisted. The alternatives could not really be considered.

Mr Taylor and his comrades were trying to save as much in terms of equipment, as well as in terms of the wounded, as they possibly could. There was not a great deal of time for him to speculate on what exactly would happen. 'All we had to do was pack everything up, go and take the lorries down to the rear party and make sure they were all filled up and the guns had all the ammunition they wanted and were all stocked up for two days and then off we went. Adrenaline? No. We just kept busy, packing up, one thing and another. We were going to war. Let's go!' But, he adds crucially, he and his young comrades also had a blanket of ignorance draped around them. 'We didn't know about the German war machine.' Before they had broken through, he says, 'we thought we could walk over them with what we had. The British and the French. We outnumbered them in tanks and what-not.' And even during the days and the nights when they were scrambling backwards towards the coast, that curious confidence somehow persisted.

'We knew we had to get to Dunkirk.' Given the relentless speed of the German advance on the ports of Boulogne and Calais – plus the necessity to use a port that large ships could get into – it seemed from an early stage that there was no alternative. And on the way there, 'the message came through that the German tanks had been seen. Action stations! And Lieutenant Thomas said to me, "I'll have to give you a two hour anti-tank rifle course."' Mr Taylor now gives every impression of having appreciated the speed of that anti-tank course. 'Now you've done it, the lieutenant said, get under that Land Rover and point your gun!'

Mr Taylor is now admirably blithe about the idea of squaring up to fast-approaching German tanks. But before he had the chance to put this newly acquired skill to the test, he found that his older skills as a radio signalsman were required more urgently. He was hauled away to sit hunched over a radio set attempting to glean some sort of order from a hissing, fuzzy world of anarchy and confusion.

'The lieutenant was getting all the information. When the Lysander [planes] went back to England' – the few that survived the German onslaught, that is: eighty-eight were downed in battle and thirty destroyed on the ground, with a grievous loss of crew – 'we had no job to do then, we packed up, so the lieutenant commandeered me and this other chap. We were superior in Morse. We passed out at eighteen words a minute.' Mr Taylor was now effectively the ears of the retreating party. 'And this was my work for the rest of the retreat. I had a standard van with the army radio in and we did shifts in that.'

Obviously the work was intense, although again there was little sense of fatigue; rather, there was an awareness that it was essential not to let up until the company concerned was beyond the reach of the Germans. The airwaves were filled with noise; Mr Taylor was there in his van, painstakingly picking out the frequencies he needed to keep them updated on just how close that enemy was.

'They were long shifts,' he says. But there was, for Mr Taylor and his colleague in the van, at least a fleeting, illusory sense that they had some mooring in this mad tidal rush; that by intercepting signals, they could gain a sense not merely of the enemy's positions and intentions but also – even through the medium of Morse – of what the enemy was actually like: how they spoke to each other, even the state of German morale. Proficient signalsmen could learn much from what was called 'the fist' – the personal Morse-tapping style of each wireless operator. The blank dots and dashes of Morse might sound identical to the untrained ear, but each operator had a style and rhythm unique as a fingerprint.

In this much, Mr Taylor had the small privilege of a little knowledge, which it was his job to pass on. But he had no control over a more pressing need: nutrition. As he and his company drew further back, supplies were growing scarcer. This was the point at which more serious chimes of unease would have been felt among the men.

'We were short of food because no one could get rations to you. But there was a certain village where the houses were all empty.' As the Germans advanced, a great many of the civilian population had instantly fled; the memories, not even yet a generation old, of mud and blood and bone were too much. Much-cherished houses and possessions, land that was loved, were abandoned without any further thought. For those English soldiers left behind in empty countryside and empty villages, the taking of food from such abandoned properties was not so much a matter of theft as simple practicality. The defending forces had to eat. Mr Taylor recalls: 'Lieutenant Thomas said to us "Right, take your hats, fill up what you can – eggs and whatnot." And he said to one of the cooks, "Get your rifle, go in there, kill one of those baby cows and we'll have that." And that's how we got on. They just left their animals, the French. They just scrammed. One chap – we got talking to him – he says, "I'm going now. Here's my key." He said he might be back.' And he might have been at some point; but Mr Taylor was never to see him again.

The exodus that he saw as the days rolled on was haunting. 'There were mothers, kids in prams. We came across one small village and there was a bloke dead in the road. German. How he got there . . . no idea. He was just dead and there was nothing we could do. Might have been a fifth columnist. Plenty of them. Nuns coming down on parachutes. But wherever we went,' adds Mr Taylor, 'there were military police, so you couldn't get lost along the whole route.'

That incongruous dead German was somehow just as startling as the sight of an approaching German tank would have been. Another veteran recalled how he and his comrades were marching along a country road when, suddenly, a motorbike went past at leisurely speed. They did double-takes – the rider was in German uniform. This is what invasion looked like: not just lines of tanks, or planes screaming from the skies, but an altogether quieter, horribly assured presence; the unsettling suggestion that the invaders were already quite at home.

Glaswegian Bob Halliday found himself making a more circuitous retreat as the emergency came upon the Allies. 'It was a bit rough when all the Germans turned up,' he says with magnificent insouciance. 'The speed of them. We had to get on a troop train and find our unit. And when we got to our transit depot four days later, they were evacuating. We got on that train.'

It was not an easy place to be; as well as all the fruitless speculation, not to mention the frustration, there were practical difficulties. 'The train was put into sidings,' says Mr Halliday. 'We couldn't get fresh water. There was nothing to eat. All I had was what my mother had put into a little pack: half a dozen little tins of rice. And I used to open them, offer them to the lads around, and that's what we had to eat for a few days. Water – well, we got it from the engine. The driver,' he adds with a smile, 'made tea for us.'

But then, after that sojourn on the train, came a period of disorientation and chaos. 'The unit was split. There were about fifty of us. The others, we didn't get together at all. Just wherever we were at the time. We were just making our way to Dunkirk.'

Mr Halliday was luckier than most; his unit managed by and large to stick together, giving their journey a deeper sense of cohesion. Many others elsewhere recalled that they suddenly found themselves either in very much smaller groups from disparate companies, or indeed completely alone. In Mr Halliday's company, the men found themselves first a camp, then another base, all the time making that desperate effort to stay ahead of the fast-advancing Germans. 'They just kept marching us. I was fortunate: we took a break, by a farm. We helped the refugees, milking cows. The road was absolutely packed – women, children – and we were keeping off the roads as much as possible, we were dealing with them, feeding them.'

While Mr Halliday was taking his break, he saw a dispatch rider amongst the crowd and unable to get through. Recognising the rider's call sign and managing to get across to him, he said, 'I'm here with the unit.' The rider replied, 'Yes, I'm HQ section, I'm going back there now.' Mr Halliday said, 'Can you take me?' and the rider answered, 'Yes – sit on the side.'

'He took me back to headquarters,' says Mr Halliday, 'and I joined up with them and then continued the trek.'

For the teenage Devonian soldier Gareth Wright, that initial sight of the enemy was a shock – but it also happened to come when he was facing something of a crisis within his own unit. 'The Germans hit us with every damn thing they could,' he says. 'They were real professional soldiers. And the shock: it also shook the civilian population. The roads were choc-a-bloc. There was no communication whatsoever. Refugees going back. Us trying to get up and meet Jerry. Absolutely impossible. No movement at all on the roads. And Jerry was strafing and bombing all the time. Every day. Causing absolute chaos.' The chaos was an extra complication for the soldiers; there was what would now be termed gridlock on the roads leading to the sea. In front of them, the obstacle of fleeing humanity; behind them, an enemy approaching murderously fast.

Yet Mr Wright was also facing an extraordinary individual crisis, one that was itself quite pressing. 'I was going to be shot for looting,' he says lightly.

The accusation, naturally, was quite unjust, but it is also an intriguing insight into how frayed the sensibilities of the commanding officers became in the aftershock of the German assault. 'As the RAF pulled out and sent the planes back to Blighty,' says Mr Wright, 'all the NAAFI (i.e. the stores, food and liquor) was going to – well, whoever wanted it. By 4 a.m., I took a thirty hundredweight' – an army truck – 'and I went into the NAAFI block and sure enough it was like Aladdin's cave. There was whisky, chocolate, fags – you name it. So I made a beeline for the whisky, which was in wooden cases. These cases had a golden wrapping. I got four of them on board the truck. I had a load of fags and chocolate.

'So when I felt I had enough,' he continues, 'I came out – but as I was driving round the perimeter of the aerodrome, this major was coming in to the NAAFI stores to see what *he* could get.' Mr Wright already knew of the major and felt a flicker of anxiety, for the officer had quite an aptitude for alcohol. 'For a second, I looked at him and he looked at me and I thought: this is it. I'm for the high jump.'

After a moment the major walked into the stores. Mr Wright drove off in his loaded truck. There was a short period of jangling suspense as Mr Wright made his way back to his quarters, before the major caught up with his truck and the contents therein. The major said to him, 'I suppose you know what the penalty for looting is?' Mr Wright replied: 'It's not looting, sir, it's salvage. I've liberated some stuff.' The major said, 'In my book that is loot. And you are going to pay the penalty for looting in wartime.'

Mr Wright knew that this was serious, not least because the major's drink problem had already seemed to threaten his mental stability. And in the midst of the pandemonium of retreat, it was all too easy to envisage a general slide towards lawlessness.

'The major put me in a Nissen hut and locked the door,' says Mr Wright. 'He was going to put me in front of a firing squad. First I thought, it's just the beer talking. But then I thought, even if it was the beer talking, this was the bloke who – just the day before – had been running up and down this French village street with a revolver firing at planes a mile high. Sozzled to the eyebrows. So there was nothing at all to stop him with the idea of the firing squad.'

There was something blackly comical about Mr Wright being made to feel more anxiety about his commanding officer than about the approaching Wehrmacht. 'Anyway, there were footsteps outside the hut,' says Mr Wright. 'And it happened to be Harry Rogers, who was captain of the battery.' And with whom, happily, Mr Wright happened to be on first name terms; both men hailed from the fringes of Dartmoor. 'He said, what's all this I hear about you looting?' A hugely grateful Mr Wright didn't have time to give Captain Rogers a coherent answer. 'He said, "The Germans are coming, let's wipe them all out." And, the captain added, "You get out of the major's way until he's sobered up – and by the time he has done so, he will have forgotten all about it."'

The incident now makes Mr Wright laugh. There was a little poetic justice in the gash that he sustained when manhandling a case of liquor. 'My only war wound was from those cases of whisky,' he says. 'So I got out and stayed out of the way until the heat died down.'

But there was fresh heat to come as – together with so many thousands of others – Mr Wright made the trek to the French coast. 'I remember one hot afternoon I was sat in a little French village and I went in the café and got a beer and I went and sat on the kerb. Now,' Mr Wright adds, 'before, as soon as a squaddie sat down or stopped moving in France, he was instantly surrounded by kids and dogs. This little fella came over and sat beside me and we were yapping away, me with my beer, and I gave him a chocolate from my loot. And we were talking.

'Suddenly the boy sprang up and he said *Allemagne, Allemagne!* I looked up – and not far away, this blooming SS truck was going along across a T-junction. Oh blimey, I thought.' Mr Wright waited until it had disappeared, and then made good his own exit from the village.

Back in Britain, on 19 May, Admiral Ramsay was summoned from Dover to an urgent meeting at the War Office to consider the increasingly precarious position of the British Expeditionary Force. Ramsay himself noted afterwards that this meeting 'discussed 1) temporary maintenance of the BEF through Dunkirk, Calais and Boulogne and 2) evacuation of personnel through Dunkirk, Calais and Boulogne. Under this last was included, amongst other items, the problem of the hazardous evacuation of very large forces.' This was the first serious official discussion of evacuation. According to David Woodward, the main purpose of the meeting was to let Admiral Ramsay know that any such efforts would be masterminded by himself, and that all available shipping would be placed at his disposal – naval or otherwise.

None the less, a public front had to be maintained; especially once reports from around the country about the state of public morale from 'Cooper's Snoopers' (a rather unpopular web of 'regional information officers' and local volunteers at Duff Cooper's Ministry of Information) had been collated and the first batch of responses analysed. The Ministry officials sought to find ways to lead opinion, as a secret memo stated:

> Fear needs to be expressive, not repressive. Thus while private individual fears are bad, socialised fears can be made positive and turned to account . . . people should be made to share

> their fears; to fraternise, to be neighbourly . . . It is important to stimulate a feeling of being a united nation (at the level of the street as well as the level of the cabinet).[1]

Yet perhaps the public didn't need telling. 'There is a half-hearted rumour that Nazi parachute troops have landed at Dover,' wrote one London-dwelling female MO diarist. 'Nobody believes this. Arranged to play tennis.'

What if the rumours grew wilder? The Ministry of Information felt that real honesty and a reasonable level of disclosure were better than official obfuscation. 'Facts, even bad facts, are some protection against bewilderment and suspicion,' another memo stated. 'Even at the eleventh hour, people are seeking and needing a positive purpose, something aggressive, dynamic, beyond themselves, worth dying for; not just survival or "blood sweat and tears."'[2]

But what was that positive purpose? There were those in the department who then dared to ask: yes – what exactly is this all for? They were doing so rhetorically on behalf of what they perceived to be the more radical sections of the younger generation. Echoes of such questions were being heard, from around the country, by the 'snoopers'. 'The opinion has been expressed in various quarters that some fundamental statement on a postwar social policy coming from the new government would have an effect in rallying the extreme left-wing sections of youth organisations,' read yet another Ministry of Information memo, this one from 20 May 1940. 'Youth is "waiting for a sign" . . . that the future is being thought about in a constructive way.' The writer also cited mulish behaviour from young left-wingers, but there was little evidence of it from the unions or the shop floors, where huge changes in working practices were being contemplated to speed production. 'Reports show,' the memo concluded, 'young people are not content with "we are fighting for our lives, nothing else matters."' We might say that the first pulse of the welfare state was being felt.

*

Incredibly, back in France, there were a few who still seemed oblivious to the threat. The expatriate novelist P.G. Wodehouse – living with his wife Ethel in Le Touquet, and almost childishly heedless of the shadow fast moving over the land – had just published *Eggs Beans and Crumpets,* to enthusiastic reviews. Indeed, his essentially optimistic view captures a wider dichotomy: the idea that people at once acknowledged the coming threat, yet at the same time contrived to dismiss it. The Wodehouses were not the only British expatriates in Le Touquet. Some had left some weeks before and returned to Britain, uneasy about the war. But others, like the Wodehouses, held out. He and his wife provided a billet for two French military doctors, and were in constant contact with the British consul. They were reluctant to return to Britain – aver their supporters – first because this would mean consigning their beloved Pekinese to many months of quarantine; and second because they had an abiding confidence that the British would hold back the advancing Nazi forces. To evacuate would give the impression of defeatism. Even as late as 20 May, Ethel was being assured by British commanders that the German advance was being slowed, and that there was still time for them to consider their options. That very night, the Germans took Le Touquet, and Wodehouse was consigned to an internment camp.

A day later, as the newspapers were beginning to report seriously on the German 'spearhead' and the Nazi plans to rush for the Channel ports the better to secure them for the coming invasion of Britain, Duff Cooper felt it important that the public was both calmed yet readied for what lay ahead. His declaration, made in a BBC radio broadcast, was a smooth admixture of soothing sentiment and stirring rhetoric:

> The Army of Great Britain and the far greater army of France are still there. They are neither in retreat nor have they suffered heavy losses. It is hard enough to understand what has

taken place in a battle once it is over; it is quite impossible to understand while it is taking place . . .

It is for each of us to play his part. The battle is being fought so close to our shores that every one of us is taking part in it. Therefore we are all soldiers and as such, we must acquit ourselves . . .

These grave events will act – indeed, they have already acted – as a tonic to the nation.

It is always easy – and almost always wrong – to laugh at a previous age's idea of propaganda. For what else was the Minister of Information to say? Though the army was very much in retreat, there was little to be gained in broadcasting this to the enemy. Cooper was also quite right to lay a new emphasis on the Home Front; in those turbulent days, there was every expectation of an imminent German invasion. Yet one MO diarist captured the dualistic nature of the public response. 'The truth is that human desires and behaviour are not . . . changed by history,' wrote this young Londoner, 'and so even when history is being made, men cling to their normality.'[3]

Even with bowdlerised newspaper and radio reports, it was obvious now to all back in Britain that the BEF was not merely in retreat but in desperate danger. 'It seems they [the Germans] raid with tanks and parachutists,' wrote Virginia Woolf. 'The feeling is we're outwitted . . . The Gs [Germans] seem youthful, fresh, inventive. We plod behind.'[4]

In fact this was not entirely the case. News had not quite come through of a gallant Allied fightback in the north of France that had the effect of stunning the Germans. The Battle of Arras – involving the Durham Light Infantry and the Royal Tank Regiment (about 2000 men and 74 tanks) and French armour from the Light Mechanised Division – may have had more profound consequences than anyone at the time could have known. At this stage, Rommel's forces were very close to cutting the British off from the French. But the Allies not only stood their ground; outside the town of

Arras, on 21 May, the British pushed aggressively back, with Matilda tanks that were more than able to withstand German firepower. For a few hours, the element of surprise, if not perhaps of shock, was all theirs, as Rommel's 7th Panzer division found itself, to its confusion, on the defensive. According to some historians, had the 1st Armoured Division been present, there might have been a slim chance of severing the Panzer 'corridor'. Instead, the Germans soon rallied, the tank formations were rearranged and, swiftly, the fightback began. The British were once more forced back, although a brave intervention from the French tanks bought invaluable time.

The importance of the battle, however, is not only the terrific spirit on display – along with a vital glimpse of momentary German vulnerability – but also the short-term effect that the Allied resistance had upon German tactics. There have been suggestions that Rommel and his commanders imagined that the Allies had many more tanks than they actually did. There have also been suggestions that the British show of force gave the mighty German war machine pause. Its spearheads were deep into France – but that resulted in a certain amount of exposure too, until reinforcements and supplies could get through. In other words, the Germans knew that an effective Allied fightback could snap the spear in two. There was nothing inevitable about their victory. As a result, the interregnum that followed – Rundstedt famously mirroring Hitler's anxieties by calling a temporary halt to the advance on 24 May – was pivotal. Over the years, there has been speculation that Hitler deliberately ordered the halt himself, for he did not want to wipe out the BEF when there was still the faintest possibility of making terms with Britain. But it was Rundstedt's strategic concerns that caused the Germans to stop and take stock and refuel – giving Allied soldiers precious extra hours to pull back to the coast.

This pause however was fleeting. Subsequent events in Britain could leave no doubt of what was coming. However spirited the domestic newspaper coverage of the efforts of the RAF against the ineluctable

Nazi forces bulldozering towards the Channel coast, few could have been unaware of the subtext. The Prime Minister made another flying visit to Paris, and so it was left to his coalition deputy, Clement Attlee, to guide the swiftly drawn up new Emergency Powers Act through Parliament. Again, there could be little doubt what it all meant. 'It is necessary that the Government should be in complete control over persons and property,' said Attlee, though adding, as any scrupulous socialist should, that such action would be painstakingly fair and equal: such control would be exercised 'not merely over some persons or some particular class of the community but over all persons, rich or poor'. Indeed, control was exerted over the wealthiest estates; among the stately homes and smart boarding schools requisitioned for military purposes were Castle Howard in Yorkshire, Woburn Abbey in Bedfordshire and Marlborough public school. Attlee added: 'The Government's demand does not arise from panic and there is no need for panic.' But the fact that the term was used at all was significant.

These emergency powers enabled, among other things, the Minister of Labour to 'direct any person to perform any service required', and to set pay, hours and working conditions. Once again, the official emphasis was on fairness; if anyone found that they were losing out financially as a result of these war directives, then they would have the chance to get compensation. The emergency powers also extended to banks, though in a radio broadcast, Sir Robert Kindersley declared: 'I am empowered by Mr Attlee to assure you that your savings are not affected in any way by the Emergency Powers Act. You will have just the same freedom in regard to those savings as you have today. You have no need for anxiety.' Again: don't panic! Yet obviously the chief apprehension was not so much about Attlee interfering with savings accounts, or even plundering them; it was to do with the prospect of German invasion. If the Nazis were to gain a foothold, what would happen to the banks then?

Further emergency legislation was enacted with the passing of a new Treachery Bill, the intention of which very baldly was to set the death penalty for 'grave cases of espionage and sabotage when the intention is to help the enemy'. A great deal of excitable, though muted, talk about fifth columnists – the sinister, silent German sympathisers believed to have infiltrated every nook and cranny of society – was now doing the rounds; there were rumours of nuns with hairy hands. The British ambassador to Holland had stated quite clearly that he attributed the fall of that country chiefly to the activities of hidden agents, working from within to erode the foundations of security, while to this day, some BEF veterans are convinced that such figures were very active in France.

Oddly enough, though some of these theories had traction in Britain, they had far greater impact in America; President Roosevelt's assistant secretary of state, Adolf Berle, recalled how a Hearst newsreel executive had told him in May 1940 not only that fifth column agents had engineered the fall of France, the Low Countries and Scandinavia, but that they were very close to doing the same to Great Britain. And once the UK had fallen, America would be next. 'His story of how the Fifth Column was already in control of New York was so graphic that it frightened me completely,' recalled Mr Berle. 'Only after I got the FBI . . . to check, did I begin to pull myself together.'

The British government was taking no chances either. It also had greater justification for nervousness; there were some who – unlike fifth columnists – wore their totalitarian beliefs openly. That week, a squad of plain-clothes policemen entered a smart London address in Smith Street, near the Palace of Westminster. They were there to arrest everyone within. It was the headquarters of the British Union of Fascists. Among those arrested and placed in Brixton prison that day were John Beckett, secretary of the British People's Party and – in a move that caused some shock within the House of Commons – Captain A.H.M. Ramsay, the Unionist MP for Peebles, up in the Borders. He was described in reports as being 'President of the Right Club'. The man that the detectives were most anxious to seize, however, was not there. They caught up with him at home a mile along the river. Sir Oswald Mosley was arrested at his flat in the exclusive Dolphin Square development, and he too was taken to Brixton prison. The aim of such actions, said a government spokesman in the House, was 'to order the detention of members of organisations which have had association with the enemy or are subject to foreign influences or control and which may be used for purposes prejudicial to national security'.

The Prime Minister was understandably concerned by the entire question of maintaining domestic security. In War Cabinet, it was Churchill who volubly supported the idea of arming the police force. The nation's police constables, he thought, should be fully prepared for eventualities such as parachute landings. And, Churchill added, other countries were happy to see their police bearing arms. Perhaps he was thinking of the US. His colleagues, however, were thinking of those European countries for which they already had a deep distrust, and objected strongly to the idea. It simply wasn't quite British, the idea of a police constable carrying a gun. The Minister for Home Security cited the feelings of Scotland Yard on the subject: 'The police should be kept for civil police work, of which there was plenty.'

Across the Channel, the reality of the German forces was far worse than shadowy speculation about invisible saboteurs. Despite the temporary splendour of the Arras fightback, the Panzers, along with the Luftwaffe bombers and the expert parachutists, had reduced the French and British forces to a state of stuttering confusion and had driven a wedge between the two armies. The invaders were ineluctable. And so, in War Cabinet at Downing Street, Churchill raised an uncomfortable notion with his colleagues. 'The Prime Minister,' stated the minutes, 'thought that as a precautionary measure, the Admiralty should assemble a large number of small vessels in readiness to proceed to ports and inlets on the French coast.'

It was a measure that the Prime Minister had already raised with

Admiral Ramsay in Dover; that same morning, the Admiral held a meeting with his own colleagues to give consideration to the unthinkable idea of a huge evacuation. Ramsay let it be known that day that such an eventuality still seemed to him unlikely. Either he said this for the sake of his colleagues' sensibilities, or he then succeeded in accepting the 'unlikely' with terrific speed. Just forty-eight hours later, with members of a shocked and exhausted British Expeditionary Force making their stumbling way to Calais, the pursuing German tanks were just ten miles outside the town.

After that previous War Office meeting on the 19th, Admiral Ramsay had been aware that simply to keep all the soldiers of the BEF in rations – or 'temporary maintenance' – would mean having to set sail with some 2000 tons of stores a day; and obviously to land them safely, and to keep his naval vessels from harm, he would need at the very least for the Allies to keep control of the ports of Calais and Boulogne. The Germans were making their way there fast. According to David Woodward, on 22 May, 'V and W class destroyers set out for the threatened harbours with demolition parties in case the worst should come to the worst.'[5] But the worst was already happening. The day before, at a meeting in Dover, Admiral Ramsay tried to convince colleagues, including French commanders, that it was time to seriously consider 'the emergency evacuation across the Channel of very large forces'.

There were some in French high command who still scoffed at the idea that their troops should be forced not merely to retreat, but actually to be carried out of their own borders; they felt that a counter-attack on the German assault would be feasible given time. The position is understandable on an emotional level: what sort of defending force is it that abandons a country and crosses a sea, leaving its civilian population at the mercy of a savage and vengeful enemy? But by this time, even a full evacuation was starting to look optimistic.

However, even as Admiral Ramsay sent naval officers across the south coast in search of suitable boats to requisition, other senior figures thought the very idea of such a vast evacuation was madness. 'Personally, I think we cannot extricate the British Expeditionary Force,' confided General Edmund Ironside to his diary. 'Only hope a march south west. Have they time? Have they the food? God help the BEF. Brought to this state,' he added, 'by the incompetence of the French command.'[6] Equally, those who thought such a retreat viable were struck by another consideration: the idea that allies would thereby be abandoned to their fate. 'My outstanding impression of the French attitude of mind,' wrote Major General Howard Vyse some time later, '[was] that of fear that we were about to leave them, and of suspicion that we were not playing straight with them . . . the amazing reluctance of the French to face up to unpleasant possibilities and to make preparations accordingly resulted in many preliminaries on our part being immediately suspect.'[7]

One of those French senior commanders looking on at the British with a suspicious eye was Admiral Abrial, who later bitterly observed: 'The British never took part in the struggle as faithful and loyal fighting comrades – but only, and on occasion not without bravery, for their own personal ends . . . the evacuation of British personnel.' Even as the heat of the mortar rounds could be felt against the skin, there were those who still believed that it might be possible for the Allies not merely to halt the Germans, but to start pushing them back. Those who believed so were diminishing in number.

In the outskirts of the port town of Boulogne, the German forces were gathering; within the town, numbers of British soldiers were roaming around in a state of disorganisation and confusion, having lost track of their officers and platoons. A great many wounded men were lying on the quay, intensely vulnerable; and a sense of anarchy was augmented by the panic of the many civilian refugees who, seeing British ships, attempted to board them. Admiral Ramsay's destroyers had got into the port but now they were in serious jeopardy; mortar fire from the enemy, followed, as they got closer, by intensive machine gun fire from the hills around.

According to some accounts, it was actually possible – from the window of his office in the white cliffs – for Admiral Ramsay to see the shell-bursts of the attack of the 2nd Panzer division on Boulogne. Two battalions of Guards – Irish and Welsh – had been sent out there with the boats to co-ordinate the operation and they brought a measure of order. Admiral Ramsay had also sent the ship *Vimy* with around 200 seamen to control the dock area itself. Invaluable food and water for the BEF were disembarked and a great many wounded were conveyed aboard SS *Biarritz*. In the meantime, the destroyers launched countering fire at the town's outskirts, trying to pick off the roads to make further German advance impossible.

While the troops of the town were assembled, and then scrambled aboard the *Venetia*, the cacophony of destruction had reached a height; the destroyers firing upon the enemy at full blast, to the extent of bringing houses down, and the Germans launching in return all they could, from mortars to field guns to bullets. For the soldiers being evacuated, it was profoundly disorientating; for the men crewing the ships, to keep a steady head and eye as the flames shot up around them was the most profound test.

As a result, however, over 4000 soldiers were retrieved safely from a town that was on the brink of collapse. For Brigadier General John Charteris, giving his analysis in the *Manchester Guardian*, the relief was mixed with a sense of dawning horror about the many hundreds of thousands of troops left in an increasingly desperate situation:

> The news that the bulk of the British forces defending Boulogne managed to withdraw does little to allay the anxiety that the fall of the port must necessarily cause. The lines of supply to the northern group of armies upon whose resistance so much depends are seriously compromised . . . the fate of the Allied armies north of the gap now hangs in the balance . . . Time is

> the essence of the problem. Given time, there can be no doubt that the great mass of the mobile French army operating close to its own bases would prevail against the exposed flank of the invader dependent on long and precarious communications. 'Ask me for anything but time,' said Napoleon, and the words ring with strange intensity in the minds of all at the present moment.

Meanwhile, Kim Philby, *The Times*'s correspondent – who, having previously covered the Spanish Civil War, was among those to have seen the atrocity of blitzkrieg – paid reluctant tribute to the guile and nimbleness of the enemy:

> The Germans, in fighting their way from the Belgian border to the Channel coast in a fortnight have achieved their first objective. They have separated the bulk of the BEF and the Allied forces associated with it from the main French armies . . . momentarily, their faith in lightning movement as providing the key to the riddle of the offensive in modern warfare, has been justified. As the French Prime Minister has declared, the enemy is exploiting a new technique.

This technique made 'scant use of field artillery . . . The bombing aeroplane has superseded the gun . . . The role of the tank is to over-run the fortifications and field defences and press forward as far as it can.' Then, an unsigned Philby added, there was the lethal menace of the 'parachutists', gliding down in darkness way behind enemy lines and combining the roles of 'spy, wrecker and guerilla', courting 'unbelievable hazards in the execution of their tasks. They are formidable opponents.' His steely conclusion was that in order to face such an enemy squarely, the British had to match it every way in terms of ruthlessness.

It has to be said that – in a demonstration of the insouciance that would subsequently allow him to maintain a career as a treacherous

Soviet double agent – Philby's own behaviour during this moment of national crisis edged towards the admirably cool. Holed up in a besieged Boulogne, as the bombs came screaming down at dawn, a friend and colleague was amused by Philby's comment as he dressed at top speed that trousers were – psychologically at least – the best defence both against women of a certain type and against the German army. Even later that day, on the brink of evacuation, Philby and his friend allowed themselves a moment of fantastical rumination about a road trip they might take: beetling down to the south of France, taking in the Côte d'Azur.

Others found the façade of cool a little difficult to maintain as each hour passed. In Britain, the tiredness was telling. 'No bed for any of us last night,' wrote Admiral Ramsay to his 'darling Mag':

> I'm so sleepy I can hardly keep my eyes open and we are all the same . . . We've been on the telephone to everyone from the Prime Minister downwards and the situation only becomes more and more difficult from hour to hour . . . it's hateful having to order ships to do things and go places where one knows they are going to get bombed to blazes and to send troops into what I know will be an inferno. But one must obey orders, though one wonders if those in London can have any idea of local conditions . . . It's nice to know that you and the children are safe and sound, miles away from the scene of conflict . . . My room is full of people, I write a sentence or two, and then break off and put this away in a drawer while we discuss frightful problems.

The problems were poised to become more frightful yet. Just a few miles along the coast, the fires that had been unleashed on Boulogne were now at the walls of Calais. In the former, the idea had been to retreat; for the latter, the plan had first of all been the same. Now it was being reversed. The BEF was to hold it at all costs. The result was a lethal carnival of confusion. 'Communications were difficult,' observed one writer, 'messages often had to be delivered by hand and orders became obsolete after they were issued.' Rather more pertinently: it was a bloodbath.

6

'A Ring of Steel and Fire'

25–26 May 1940

The unearthly howl of the German Junkers Ju87 'Stuka' planes – thanks to a slew of 1950s and 1960s war films – is as familiar today as the air-raid sirens. The result is that a great deal of the meaning and impact of this noise has been blurred over the years. That steadily rising note as the plane nosed downwards and dived in towards its prey on the ground was specifically invented to generate terror and unreasoning panic. The noise was created by a special addition to the aircraft: the Trumpets of Jericho – the name of the sirens attached to the legs of the planes, a reference to the trumpets that destroyed the walls of that city in the Old Testament.

The use of the Stukas – which could dive almost vertically on their targets – was calculated to destroy the nerves of infantry battalions. For the soldier on the ground, it was quite unlike the more straightforward business of facing the enemy across a battlefield, or a river, a canal or a bridge. This was lethal malice shrieking from the sky, with little chance of hitting back against it. In psychological terms, the incessant persecution of the soldiers on the beaches – the dismemberment and disembowelling in the sand of friends and comrades by German pilots who seemed utterly sadistic, bordering on gleeful – was to be one of the most damaging elements of the evacuation. And if it felt like that for the soldiers, imagine how it must have felt to be a civilian refugee; a member of a family, moving slowly along a pitted, clogged road in pony and trap, with no protection from the red-hot bullets fired down upon them.

A great many veterans of Dunkirk would, a few years later in 1944, find themselves on the beaches at Normandy, once again facing terrifying enemy firepower. But by that time, they were at least better prepared. In France in 1940, there were young soldiers who seemed to have been trained for quite a different war. Moreover, there were terrible things that no one could ever be adequately conditioned for: the impact of a mortar shell, for instance, either filleting the flesh with shrapnel or displacing the internal organs with the power of its shock wave. The same with bombs dropped from planes: a blast that could lift you bodily, throw you through the air, shred your clothes, leave blood pouring from your ears. It seems quite easy to understand now – though apparently it was less so then – how exposure to this sort of attack could leave a man leaping with fright at any suggestion of noise resembling the whoosh of a fired mortar. Nor was that sensation of demonic persecution to end at the beaches; consider the intense feeling of vulnerability on board a tiny pleasure boat, designed for cruising along lazy rivers on sunny afternoons, while being fired upon from the sky and knowing that at any moment, the hull might touch a mine and the entire vessel be blown into razor splinters. For thousands upon thousands of men, this was the ordeal to come: days and nights where every nerve was alive to the possibility of agonising injury, permanent disability or capture, or death. It is perhaps little wonder that some veterans now recall that time as a kind of fugue state: hours and days that seemed to melt into one another, passing in the manner of a dream.

Yet for those soldiers still in training over in England, events across the Channel – the gun battles, the roaring tanks, the fire, the pandemonium, the death – were both largely unreported and unimaginably distant, even to those who had finer imaginations than most. On Saturday 25 May 1940, in Hampshire, Evelyn Waugh wrote wryly of the progress of the training of his company:

> This morning, just as the battalion had decided its training was so deficient that we must break up into cadres, the Brigadier, having boasted that we would have held Boulogne, reported us as trained and ready for service. Cadre training will continue. The major put in charge has eluded all responsibility and left me in charge of the NCO's cadre.

But, Waugh continued, describing a curious period which he would later fictionalise in the marvellously sour novel *Put Out More Flags*, there was sweet respite from the tedium of the parade ground:

> At midday Saturday, Laura and I set off for an idyllic weekend at Alton in the Sun Hotel. A charming town, not only devoid of military but full of personable young civilians of military age. A hotel full of foliage plants and massive elaborate furniture. We went to church, read P.G. Wodehouse . . . watched old men in panama hats play bowls and forgot the war.[1]

That sort of forgetting by 'old men in panamas' was also being encouraged in advertisements inside that weekend's edition of *The Times*. 'For sunshine, come to Worthing,' read one such. 'South for sunshine and safety – it's Worthing for preference. Excellent music and entertainments . . . Boating, fishing and safe bathing.' Though regulars might have noticed, in that extraordinarily fine May weather, the odd absence of paddle steamers.

*

All the while, just a few short miles away across a placid sea, country roads were blocked with horses and carts filled with fleeing families, desperate and desperately hungry; other refugees, on foot, were vainly trying to use roadside trees as cover when the German bombers flew overhead. The corpses of those slaughtered from above lay all around, the discoloured bodies left in the roadside ditches. For these people, hell had somehow erupted from nowhere.

Just a few miles south-west of Dunkirk, the Germans, determined to cut off all the escape routes they could, had been moving ineluctably on the ports of Calais and Boulogne. In the centre of Calais – now under sustained fire, shops and bars and offices and homes in flames or simply flattened, the stones and bricks cracking with the heat, the shattered glass molten to the touch – a young captain called Airey Neave staggered through the streets. Years later, he was to be instrumental in Margaret Thatcher's rise to the office of Prime Minister. Now he was in a situation of mortal jeopardy, having been shot in the side. Painfully – excruciatingly so – he managed to make his way to a local hospital; but as the building was shelled by the Germans, and as windows shattered, he left his bed, despite the intense physical discomfort, and made his way back out into the streets where he thought he might be safer. He wasn't: Neave was eventually captured, and had to eke out the following years as a prisoner of war. Elsewhere in the town, according to some accounts, a dangerous air of anarchy was prevalent among the French and the British troops, with suggestions that the French were failing to obey orders. Other accounts described a plague of drunkenness involving military and civilians alike; an apocalyptic scene in a burning port as the people sought oblivion in brandy and champagne.

The side effect was rising paranoia. As houses and shops were shelled, some soldiers turned upon others; there were reported instances of British soldiers suddenly suspecting that their French counterparts were spies, and shooting them. The meme of the fifth columnist found its apotheosis here, with suspicion spiralling into irrationality. If there had been as many double-dealing agents as some believe, the Germans would have conquered and captured the Allied forces with the greatest ease.

Elsewhere, others maintained an almost surreal and comical air of calm. A Major Ronnie Cartland took himself off for a picnic in a park; it involved duck, wine and Cointreau. In another part of the town, at a defensive position, one soldier was standing ready with a bow and arrow; according to author Walter Lord, the very last time any such instrument was used in battle.

Soldier Samuel Albert, who had been with the 2nd Battery at Liques, had in the last few deceptively quiet weeks been billeted in an old church; the priest there had given him a rosary and had blessed it, thereby protecting him and whatever family Albert might have in the future. As the Germans invaded, he and his comrades were sent to defend Arras; but how could men with rifles defend a town against such ferocious aerial bombardment? The noise, he recalled, 'was so intense and deafening that it seemed impossible to survive'. He and the other men were pulled back further and soon found themselves, as the shades of evening drew on, within view of the distant port of Calais, which by that time was 'an orange glow'. The plummeting drop of dismay that he had experienced was merely a foretaste of the ordeal to come. There were refugees everywhere; all he had to offer was chocolate. Some were waving money at him, 'but all the money in the world could not have helped them'.

And then into Calais itself, in the hope that somehow they might find a way to get evacuated from there. The immediate prospect was a nightmare; he described the sparks leaping from slates under machine gun fire, and the sight of cellars filled with French troops who, according to his account, refused to come out. The aerial bombardment was intense, the noise infernal; shells were bursting all around. Albert received a bone-exposing wound in his thigh, which someone close by with a Red Cross satchel managed to patch up and put into a splint. He was then loaded into a military ambulance, which itself seemed to be a target for the planes above. Eventually they made it to a subterranean regimental aid post: a cobbled tunnel in which, recalled Samuel, the dead and the dying were packed tight together. The orderly who removed the dressing on his thigh was forced to look away; and that is when he knew how serious his own wound was. But what would be the chances of ever getting out, still less getting home?

News came through that they were going to try to evacuate the wounded; but as the ambulance left the tunnel, the bombardment started again and Samuel was told they would have to wait until dusk. He was left lying helpless in the grass on the white cliff-top overlooking the sea, with England just twenty-two miles away. He put his tin helmet over his face and, in an effort to drown out the noise and concentrate on managing the pain, started singing 'all the songs that we used to sing around the piano'.[2] Come evening, it was time to try and reach the harbour. Deliverance materialised in the form of a stretcher party. All Samuel could remember of this – perhaps mercifully, given the pressure and the pain of his wound as he was carried to the jetty – was that the boat waiting for them 'was a merchant type vessel'; rather more piercing were the memories of civilians on the stone steps at the harbour's edge screaming for help as he and other wounded men were loaded aboard, under fire from Stuka bombers shrieking down from the skies. Samuel Albert made it back to Dover, but then had to spend many months in various hospitals around the country.

Admiral Ramsay meanwhile somehow still found the time to write to 'darling Mag':

> We've been through and are going through an indescribable time. Days and nights are all one and we are dealing with a situation as complex as it is unsavoury . . . it's been my lot to operate the naval part of this and anything more difficult and unpleasing I've never been faced with. At this very moment, we are racked with anxiety about the situation in Calais. I can't tell you of it, or of the anxieties with which I am confronted; I can only say that the latter increase with each hour and we

> are helpless to retrieve the position. We are also working in several dimensions, and at the same time, and the offices are a veritable bee-hive of naval and military officers . . . What we are experiencing is nothing of course to what the poor devils are going through in Calais . . . I get new destroyers daily and throw them into the fray where they remain until they are so damaged they have to be sent away . . . I am optimistic that we shall pull through and win the war in the end. But admittedly, I have no cause to say so.

Ramsay also wrote of the loss of captains and other naval personnel. The destroyers offered large targets for German Stukas. One of his captains was killed by a machine gun bullet. But there was also the shelling, and the bombing. For all the horror in the town of Calais itself – the bewildered, frightened Belgian and French refugees, the townsfolk themselves watching their homes go up in bright orange flame and choking black smoke – the crews of the destroyers sent to Boulogne and Calais also gained a sharp taste of that terrible inferno, as they sat patiently outside the harbours waiting to do their bit.

There was a clutch of British civilians in Calais at that time; some who worked at a local rayon factory, others who were involved with a bicycle manufacturer. Some days beforehand, as the air of panic in the town began to build, and news of the fast-approaching enemy spread, these families were shipped out. The surrounding countryside and villages were already swarming with confused Allied soldiers, some of whom had lost their groups and companies, and were unclear as to their orders or where they were going.

Even at this stage, such things were known only to a few back home. German propaganda, broadcast over the radio, was blandly menacing and teasingly noncommittal. 'It cannot be expected that the great battle of the west will be decided within the next few days,' drawled the English-speaking announcer. 'The area in which the

French, British and Belgian troops are surrounded by a ring of steel and fire covers 1400 square miles. The enemy armies consist of chosen troops and it must be emphasised that their fighting power is unbroken.'

But the British public well understood by now that one had to be careful in speculative conversation not to be seen to be lowering morale. Where could reasonable anxieties – about one's relatives in the forces, about the threat of invasion – find expression? Curiously, there is an echo of such concerns in some lively correspondence to *The Times* – letters sent as Boulogne, then Calais, were torched, and when it was quite clear that the British forces were increasingly beleaguered, yet which focused almost eccentrically upon domestic matters. 'Are We At War?' asked the headline of one letter. 'Is it really necessary,' wrote the correspondent, 'to employ able-bodied men to stand outside hotels with the sole duty apparently of opening car doors for guests? Is it right that so many young men should still be employed as shop assistants and bus conductors?' The paper's newsdesk agreed, and explored the theme further, the unspoken subtext being that all these spare men would very shortly be needed to help the nation fight for its very life. 'Another "army" of young men staffs the scores of "amusement" halls dotted about the West End,' wrote the *Times* reporter. Worse than the arcade machines was the capital's naked materialism at this time of national crisis; there was something not quite patriotic about it: 'The wide range of expensive clothes, hats, furs, jewels and knick-knacks still on view throughout the West End make something of a mockery of the call to sacrifice and a need for thrift.'

Some – including George Orwell, who observed with disbelief the staff and customers of a pub purposely not listening for the latest news on the radio – found the continuation of ordinary life an affront; others, equally, saw no harm in it. In London, it was not just the luxurious shops of the West End that attracted opprobrium. There was also the matter of the dog tracks; as German bombers rained down death on the French coast, greyhound racing was still being carried on from Catford to Wimbledon. The stadiums drew big crowds for the races; those who attended clearly felt gambling to be a legitimate form of wartime escapism.

Racing was also very big business; was Herr Hitler to have the pleasure of shutting it down? The question was raised in those days of late May as members of the grand Jockey Club met with officials from the Home Office to discuss the short-term future of the main horse-racing fixtures. For the moment, it seemed, the horses should continue to run: there was confirmation of the following week's meetings at Bath, Salisbury and Redcar.

But while for some, the horses were a necessity, others found the reporting of such meetings intensely distasteful. R.A. Hayes of Cambridge wrote to *The Times* on 25 May:

> I cannot believe that I am alone in feeling a sense of shame that, at a time when the whole world must be listening in on British broadcasts, when the life of France, when the life of our own Army in France, and of all nations who love liberty seems to hang by the slenderest thread, our news bulletins should be associated with racing results . . . if indeed an appreciable number of Englishmen still exist who require racing results to satisfy their craving for excitement at the present time, then at least let us keep the deplorable fact out of the limelight instead of following broadcast news from France with news of the turf.

There might well have been a class element here; in the late 1930s, a few racecourses became synonymous with the murkier side of life: conmen, fraud and terrifying gangland razor violence. By way of contrast, *The Times* – and presumably its readers – was quite happy on Saturday 25 May to devote a good portion of the page to that day's cricketing fixtures. Some of the teams at least had a suitable wartime flavour. Members of the Marylebone Cricket Club would be able to see a match at Lord's between the 'BBC' and 'London Balloon Barrage'; unlike racing, cricket had a sort of unimpeachable purity to it. None of the soldiers facing the German onslaught in France could have begrudged anyone else playing a match.

And across the nation, that weekend, a reported 326,000 more men were registered for service. The notions of duty and of escapism could coexist, it seemed, quite easily. In Birmingham, one diarist recorded that in her husband's manufacturing firm, '25% of their lads – mostly the learners – had been strutting about the place all day' having registered.

Admiral Ramsay had been making intensive preparations for a large-scale evacuation for the last week. There had been something of a small-scale dress rehearsal just a few days before in Holland. Intelligence had indicated that a German assault on Rotterdam was coming, and it was Ramsay's responsibility to mastermind the evacuation of some 200 Royal Marines, along with a battalion of Irish and Welsh Guards. As the bombs fell and the sky turned red with sunset and flames, the evacuation ships stayed steadfastly moored until all the men had been safely embarked. Ramsay, from his chalk eyrie, had found the operation churningly tense yet also a little awe-inspiring. 'My losses have been heavy,' he wrote to his wife, 'partly from enemy air action, partly from accident and partly from stupidity.' But, he added, 'the behaviour and the success of the destroyers has been phenomenal in achieving the almost impossible.' He also noted 'the plight' of fleeing Dutch officers, sailing over in any craft they could lay hands upon, with 'not a stitch of clothing but what they stand up in, their families left behind, no money and dog tired. And they behave magnificently!'

The evacuation of men from the Low Countries on that scale was one thing; to achieve the same with hundreds of thousands more men was quite a different prospect.

As Calais teetered on the brink, one German Panzer group was rather closer to Dunkirk than any of the retreating British Expeditionary Force. And the bombers had seen the potential of the town. On the morning of 23 May, a squadron of them had flown over and attacked the harbour, the bombs starting vast fires. Meanwhile, not far away, the Belgian forces were faltering fast. Lord Gort established a defensive line on the Ypres–Comines canal, to the west of Dunkirk. Like a heavy bulkhead door slowly closing up, the gap for Allied soldiers to escape through was narrowing inexorably. And across the Channel, even if details were not known to the public, the general sense of it was pervasive. Novelist H.G. Wells, in a letter to *The Times*, wrote: 'Never mind what happens to us in England. If we at home can help by diverting a few bombs, then so much the better. Let us hit them hard in France now with our utmost strength, and win.' But in that igloo office in the white cliffs, Admiral Ramsay was perhaps alone in grasping the full appalling magnitude of the evacuation of nearly half a million men. Only he could fully understand the ordeal and the nightmare to come.

7
Dynamo

26 May 1940

When, just two weeks before Calais collapsed in molten ruins, the government had quietly placed those announcements in the press and on the BBC about the general need for smaller boats and vessels, it was not initially known how successful the appeal would be. Hundreds of responses came in, and naval officers were dispatched around Britain to check on the suitability of the craft being offered. A great many of the boats were not up to scratch, or at least, they would not be able to survive the rigorous transition from boatyard, river and reedy fen to the demands of cross-Channel sailing with vast loads of passengers.

To evacuate that colossal number of men from Dunkirk, the burden would obviously fall upon the largest of ships – the navy's destroyers. But these vast vessels would have difficulty berthing in a harbour that had already been seriously damaged by bombing. The men would have to form vast, vulnerable lines on the long jetties (or 'moles') that jutted out into the sea as the ships moved alongside. More men would have to be embarked from the six or seven miles of wide shelterless beaches that lay outside the town. But the destroyers would not be able to get close in those sandy shallows; this is where so many little ships would be required, moving back and forth from shore to ship.

And those boats that did make the grade were proud to come forward; even though the owners and the captains still had no idea – for security reasons – what exactly it was that they were being called up to do. In Teddington, Middlesex, there was a boatyard on the Thames owned by the splendidly named Tough Brothers. Somehow maintaining the intense security, Admiral Lionel Preston made contact with Douglas Tough and – while smoothly eliding the specifics – outlined what it was that the Admiralty needed and what sort of feats any little boats involved would be required to carry out. River vessels: how suitable would they be for sea crossings? Boats that in peacetime would ordinarily only be licensed to carry seven or eight people at a time – how many might they hold in case of the gravest emergency?

Douglas Tough knew almost at once what sort of boats would be required, and how many. He also had contacts with the Little Ships Club in London; again, once contact was made, members were told nothing save that their little pleasure boats – those elegant confections of walnut and white paint – would be required to travel rather further than usual.

A typically striking story – though not an average one – is that of Dr Basil Smith, whose motor yacht, called *Constant Nymph*, was berthed at Isleworth on the Thames, just a dozen or so miles upstream from Westminster. He received a vague naval summons; namely that he was to sail his boat down the Thames to Sheerness, on the north Kent coast. Yet in one of those wartime twists, he had to negotiate a labyrinth of bureaucracy to do so: he needed a permit to sail the boat so far. And without being able to give a clear explanation as to what the boat was required for, this was initially awkward. The Port of London authorities finally saw sense and Dr Smith sailed out of the city and down to the Thames Estuary, still not quite guessing exactly what it was that he and his boat would be required to do. But, as he recalled, even at that stage, with no information at all, 'the opportunity of playing boats for a month seemed too good to miss . . . and I had been able to warn my partners that I would be away for a bit'.[1]

The Royal Navy would have preferred to exclude civilians from the operation simply because, through a lack of training and experience, they might have hindered as much as they helped. But they couldn't really stop the eager volunteers, who simply exaggerated their skills or – in the case of a Thames tug boy – lied like a trooper about his age, having first cycled home to ask permission from his parents to join the other crewmen.

A similar story was recalled by Henry John Osborne, who as a young man had an inbuilt fascination for the various boats and ships that ploughed up and down the khaki Thames. As the war broke out, he was working in a large toiletry and soap manufacturing outfit in Silvertown, a peninsula of east London with vast docks, and a view of the river beyond stretching down for miles. Mr Osborne even contrived for his commute – from the south London suburb of Sidcup – to involve a brief taste of sailing: this by means of the venerable Woolwich Free Ferry, which took him across the river and enabled him to gaze alike upon the vast steamers and the smaller skiffs, all the teeming traffic that plied the Thames; the sort of boats that would, just a few months later, be called upon. His holidays, too, were spent with friends sailing; so, as he recalled, when the war broke out he had a good sense of seamanship.

Days after war had been declared, Mr Osborne had tried to get himself signed up:

> A friend and I drove to Chatham on his motorbike, a 350cc Rudge, to offer our services as volunteers in the Royal Navy. We were surprised, and a little disappointed, to find that the

> only volunteers who were being accepted immediately would be enlisted as cooks. That was not our idea of fighting a war although we were both to discover, in very different active service circumstances, to what extent cooks and stewards could improve or mar life afloat. So we returned home to await our 'call-up' papers.

The wait was a little more prolonged than he would have thought, but in the meantime, Mr Osborne had applied himself to his passion. 'I was . . . told that those in possession of a Yacht Master's (Coastal) Certificate would be considered for direct entry into the Royal Navy as RNVR Officers – Sub-Lieutenants or Midshipmen, according to age . . . therefore I commenced studying for this Board of Trade Certificate at Captain O.M. Watts' Navigation School in Albemarle Street, London W1.'[2]

Captain O.M. Watts and his establishment in well-heeled Mayfair had been doing very brisk business in the weeks before the catastrophe in western Europe. As well as eager lads like Mr Osborne, other students included actors and writers. In some senses, it was quite the place to be seen. The navigation school was a proper chandlery, but near fashionable Piccadilly. Captain Watts himself was a master mariner who had come onshore in 1927 and started running courses, enjoyed by many well-to-do young adventurers, in sailsmanship and particularly in astronomical navigation, tutoring young students in the positioning of the stars, the sun and the moon. Captain Watts wrote a book called *The Sextant Simplified.* One of his many appreciative disciples was journalist, editor and graphic designer Robert Harling. Just before the outbreak of war, Harling had met up with a young journalist called Ian Fleming; burrowed deep in the heart of naval intelligence, Fleming had ideas for Harling, but at that stage, Harling was most keen simply to sign up for the navy. He received the expert tutelage of Captain Watts. The Albemarle Street premises – a grotto of wood and brass and astrolabes and sextants and rulers of brass – had quietly if unknowingly prepared a great many prospective and enthusiastic amateurs for an operation that would require the greatest skill and deft judgement, as well as cold courage.

Those amateurs were a pleasingly random selection: for instance, a young American theatrical director called John Fernald, who faithfully attended the captain's classes every Thursday evening, carefully following the diagrams chalked up on the blackboard. He went with his scenery designer friend David Homan, until one particular spring evening when Captain Watts took the young men aside and told them that, today, instead of a theoretical lesson, they would have a chance to see the more practical side of yachtsmanship.

In terms of available vessels, thanks to an exodus of shipping from Dutch ports, there were a number of scyutes, or skoots, berthed both in Poole Harbour in Dorset and also up the Thames, not far from the Royal Docks in the East End. These were shallow-bottomed craft with quite sizeable capacities. They were requisitioned with some excitement by naval officials, and a memo from the Admiralty stated that 'the operation for which these ships are being prepared will be known as "Dynamo"'.

Together with the skoots came the gathering in of other vessels: the pleasure steamers; the tugs; the ferries; the lifeboats; the hospital ships. And of course, the immaculate motor launches, with their polished wooden and brass fittings and their small elegant saloons. Craft such as the *Constant Nymph* were an inherently cheering sight, carrying with them that perpetual atmosphere of summer dawdling on the turbid Thames, the sheer pleasure of drinking cocktails while sitting back on elegant leather, gazing up at green hills and grand houses. These boats came from a world that very few of the soldiers of the BEF would have had any idea about, let alone contact with. We are once more reminded of Clement Attlee's parliamentary exhortation that people of all classes would be required to make their sacrifices.

And with this gathering of craft came the responsibility for organising – at extraordinary speed – the entire operation. Commodore Gandell, who had managed to escape the fires of Calais, went to visit Admiral Ramsay in his igloo: 'I remember going to his office in the small hours, and found him immaculately dressed, cheerful and fully alive, though I understand he had been up all night; although pallid and slight of frame, he seemed to be quite tireless.'[3]

How could Ramsay have slept? From that window overlooking the dark waves under black skies, he must have been able to see the eerie glow from Calais, the orange embers of that pulverised harbour. It would have taken no imagination at all for him to picture what the Allied soldiers were now facing. Not merely a crisis of rations – the crisis that only a week before the Admiral had sent destroyers to try and alleviate. But also a crisis of shelter, of access to fresh water. Admiral Ramsay would have been one of the few people in Britain at that time to understand how hideously precarious the situation was, and exactly how fast the catastrophe had come sweeping in.

After some time on the road, and in a state of disorientation, soldier Gareth Wright eventually found his bearings as the Germans overran the French countryside around him. He was very close to the coast. The closer he came, the less it could be mistaken: 'I made my way up into Dunkirk. That night you could see the glow of it.' The road, he says, 'was choc-a-bloc with refugees. Jerry was taking advantage of the chaos. Going along the roads, machine gunning, bombing. Absolute chaos, havoc, no communication. Everything just collapsed.'

Some had simply lost all sight of their comrades. 'We were given the order to go to Dunkirk,' says medic Charles Searle. 'It really was every man for himself. I lost the others in my company. I had been in Arras and there really was nothing for it but to walk.' This was a horrible prospect: a distance of some eighty miles through exposed country. 'I was on the road with all sorts of other people, refugees too. Taking cover in the ditches when the bombers came over. It was just pandemonium.'

In the midst of this free-for-all, some soldiers found practical

– and bizarre – means of reaching that coastline. A few managed to obtain rickety bicycles; one apparently contrived to get there by means of roller skates. That can't have been a fast journey; old-fashioned skates were prone to jamming. There was also a report of a soldier hurrying along the road and refusing to relinquish a parrot in a cage that he was carrying.

Others had more romantic concerns. Private Bill Hersey, of the 1st East Surrey Regiment, 11 Anti-tank Company, had also received the order to make his way to Dunkirk. He did so, determinedly, with his new bride in tow. During his time in France, he had met and fallen in love with Augusta, the daughter of a café owner in Tourcoing. When the Germans turned west, Private Hersey had been among the brave men sent into Belgium to shore up the line. Impetuously and bravely, Augusta refused to stay behind in France; she took herself off to Belgium to find her young husband and did indeed track him down at Roncq. But now the retreat was under way. Augusta was adamant: she wanted to go to England with her husband. By his side. Obviously the very idea went against every military regulation and in normal circumstances, would have been rigorously forbidden. But these days were different. Hersey's immediate superiors relented. They arranged for Mrs Augusta Hersey to be stashed at the back of the HQ truck, attired in some old battle-dress so that she did not draw attention to herself. When they got to the beaches, however, the true level of danger that Mrs Hersey faced was soon to become terribly apparent.

Another unconventional married couple – Staff Sergeant Gordon Stanley and his French bride Jeanne (they had wed back in February 1940, and indeed she was the first British Expeditionary Force bride) – were equally determined not to be parted. According to an account from one of their grandchildren, when the Germans invaded, Jeanne 'went to her mother's house in Servins . . . Suddenly,' the account continued, 'Gordon appeared with a staff car. The Germans were coming, he told her. Jeanne flung a few things into a suitcase. In an hour she was ready. Typically French, she was dressed in a blue dress, blue coat and matching blue broad-brimmed hat. Off they went in the car accompanied by a corporal.' Again, this seems to have been one of those occasions when strict army rules were bent without qualm. The account goes on:

> The first night was spent in the car, others in ditches. Once they slept in the barn of a Belgian farmer, he wouldn't give them permission so Gordon shot off the barn door lock. They got dirtier and dirtier. On one occasion, Jeanne bought a bucket of water for ten francs, but mostly there was no time to wash.
>
> At the small French town of Bailleul, they received hospitality from an elderly spinster Mlle Jonkerick who, unlike many others they met, welcomed them to her house. The journey was starting to take its toll on Jeanne, exhausted and with her once smart clothes in shreds. She told Gordon that she could not go on. The decision to leave my grandmother was tough, but Jeanne convinced Gordon to go. And he promised to return.[4]

The story – romantic as it is – also conveys a sense of the growing anarchy as tight military units started to dissolve and disintegrate. A Vorticist world in which no individual man or woman could get a firm grasp. Jeanne Stanley had, in part, been disorientated by the seemingly endless howls of the Stuka aircraft, swooping in to drop their bombs.

This free-falling dislocation must have found an echo to some extent even among the invading German forces, who surely marvelled that they had got so far, claimed so much, with such extraordinary speed. The senior ranks after the Battle of Arras continued to feel some disquiet about the security of the German supply lines; certainly they had pierced deep and far into enemy territory but there was always the possibility of a counter-attack that could leave tank divisions cut off. There were arguments about the amount of time divisions would need to secure their hold on the territory they had invaded.

There are also conflicting accounts about the efficacy of British weapons against German tanks. Some aver that it was a case of pea-shooters versus elephants; others that the anti-tank fire was actually perfectly adequate. But still the Germans rolled ineluctably on. What seems reasonably clear is the extent of the chaos; at one point, when the Allied GHQ was shifted from Arras, before the Germans could get there, no one thought to inform the French commanders when or indeed where they were going. There was also some – perhaps understandable – ambiguity around the idea of evacuation. Even as the idea rapidly solidified over the Channel, things were by no means as certain on French soil. There, many persisted in imagining that a successful counter-attack would stop the Germans and cut off whatever gains they thought they had made.

But while the arguments see-sawed and resolution swayed, it fell to an unusual degree to the soldiers on the ground not merely to obey the retreat order, but also to use their instincts about how best to do it. Medic Reg Gill, a radiographer at Etaples, had with his colleagues been tensed for the medical emergency that would accompany the invading onslaught; the anticipated procession of jagged shrapnel and jagged wounds. At first, they were hazy about the commands being fed down the line. 'We were warned to be prepared to leave everything as it was,' he recalled, 'to pick up our kit bags and equipment, water bottles and everything, and march north . . . but we couldn't leave yet because the order to move had not been given.' At Le Touquet, he said,

> one or two of us looked rather longingly at the rowing boats across the estuary . . . it wouldn't have been easy, and we would have been shot as deserters, but we considered taking them. We thought that if we were indeed to be cut off . . . a forty or fifty mile journey by rowing boat would be a lot better than being in a prison camp for the rest of the war. But as we didn't know what the exact situation was, we didn't feel despondent.[5]

That factor – the crucial element of simply not knowing what was happening elsewhere – was, at least briefly, a psychological help. But for Mr Gill, moving with colleagues from his medical unit – Gill's commanding officer was a radiologist called Major Lees, and there was a colonel with them too – any comfort started to give way to a creeping apprehension as they marched, and passed ever-increasing numbers of terrified refugees heading in the opposite direction. 'As we started to march up the coast, German bombers were coming over in vastly increasing numbers, dive bombing the whole time,' he recalled. 'The roads were impossible. We were told we couldn't retreat via the roads because they were being bombed and completely choked with refugees . . . it was complete chaos. We were told to march across country roads, across fields . . . It seemed interminable. We were dog tired. We were hungry.' By day, they tried as best they could to dodge what seemed like an unending procession of Junkers firing upon them; if in open fields, they would run like 'bats out of hell'. One evening, as they rested, one man produced a bottle of whisky; Gill had no idea quite where it had come from, but, he said, they all had rather too much of it. 'I think the colonel was very disapproving but I felt a lot better after that.' Not too long afterwards, they were on the outskirts of Dunkirk, and Gill was shortly to face a profusion of unexpected medical tasks.

Dunkirk (or Dunkerque) before the war had been a town with two lives: the grey unaesthetic port, with its nearby gas-holders and canal system, deep-water harbour and all the cranes and metalwork and other surrounding paraphernalia of heavy industry; then, just a little to the north, the spectacular beaches, fringed with vast, ever-shifting sand dunes, and inland, acres of scrub punctuated by poplars. These beaches had had their period of fashion, when they had attracted artists and minor European royalty. In the summer months, they had presented a tableau of eager bathers and picnickers. Until now, many in the south of England had been under a misapprehension about the location of Dunkirk itself. 'One of the minor consequences of the great events,' went one report, 'should be to remove from minds the idea that – like Dunbar and Kircudbright – [Dunkirk] is in Scotland. If it were more often spelled "Dunkerque", the delusion would be rarer.'

Also on the fringes of Dunkirk was a monumental medical establishment, the Zuydcoote maritime hospital, stark and vast against the sands. It was here that a great many wounded Allied soldiers were to be treated in often extemporised circumstances. This was also one of the few places that would continue to have a water supply, and a stand pipe, that soldiers could use. A little way off was the seaside pleasure town of Malo les Bains, with all its genteel amusements and attractions, brightly painted cafés and little cinemas. Balanced against such seaside jollity was the climate; in the winter, freezing Channel fogs would drift far into the Bray Dunes, up to the village and the sands of La Panne across the Belgian border. Wind and storms were impossible to escape. In certain conditions, the grey of the sea, and the sky, and the silver sands would become difficult to distinguish.

And so it was this prospect – a small town in the process of being shattered by shelling, an industrial harbour burning with thick chemical smoke, a brightly painted seafront promenade with its small hotels and cafés, the cellars of which were now refuges for terrified civilians and pets, the vast, wide, empty beaches and sand dunes beyond, stretching off to the horizon – that greeted the disorientated troops as they came to await deliverance. Any soldier crossing the bridges across the canals into the town would have been aware of the townsfolk going in and out of their basements, of the broken windows, the gaping roofs, the smouldering brick and slate.

For the first arrivals, the natural inclination would have been to head for the harbour. This was not a small enclave of antique stone but a large expanse, catering for mighty ships of industry, embraced by two greatly elongated jetties of wood and concrete – the moles. The East Mole, as seen from the shore, stretched right off into the sea. It was about half a mile long. The West Mole was shorter but none the less, when it started to fill with men, the sight was extraordinary; lines of soldiers, largely still, looking out to the horizon, watching approaching boats and trying to see their native land beyond. Given the reach of this thin arm of wood and concrete into the sea, it is also distressingly easy to see how easy and tempting and fragile a target it would become for German bombers.

As more and more men arrived, the overspill went to the beaches beyond. For miles beyond; six and a half miles, over the border to Belgium, to La Panne. Imagine a photograph of a continental pleasure resort, its beaches crammed with sunseekers, then instead picture the holidaymakers as soldiers. 'We couldn't see a patch of sand anywhere,' recalled one Yorkshire soldier. The first men there, under the hot May sun, were insouciant, according to some accounts. A few removed their tunics and lay back with books they had in their packs. Others, heading off into the scrub beyond, went in search of kindling to make small fires, the better to get some tea going. Food broadly consisted of sparse rations: tins of bully (or corned) beef and biscuits. There were men who took up position with their Lee Enfield rifles pointing at the sky; not much use against a Stuka, but psychologically important. At least one would have the sense that one was trying to do something.

Then picture the hours passing, and the numbers increasing: the photos, taken from a distance, show lines and columns, almost like ants. Close up, and the reality was permanently on the edge of anarchy. A great many of the soldiers who had made it here across that open, depressing landscape, past all those terrified refugees, who had evaded the bullets of the planes above, had lost their companies. They sought to find new commanders, new units to join. And as the numbers grew, so too did the lead weight of trepidation. On the beaches, as men looked out to sea, it would have begun to occur to many just how difficult and unlikely this evacuation was going to be. The naval destroyers could not get close; the sand yawned out lethally far. And as the multitude grew, so too did the logistical dread.

If the first days on those beaches were disorientating enough for the men who continued to arrive, the nights were surpassingly strange. As long sunsets gave way to amethyst twilights, and then to warm darkness, the vast sandy dunes fell quiet; men lying awake, sometimes scanning the horizon for any blink of a signal from darkened boats, their forebodings magnified by the night. Before the Stukas became more relentless in their attacks, some soldiers even managed to sleep. The fires were put out; they would have been instant targets for any passing bombers. But the southern night sky was none the less a sullen orange as, a few miles off, the port of Dunkirk burned.

Any sense of time was, for many, concertinaed. Even eras occasionally seemed to conflate. In the countryside, stumbling towards the harbour, the indelibly nightmarish images seemed, for some, to have come from a different age. Douglas Gough was a qualified Morse operator and was nineteen in the spring of 1940. His time in France up to that point had been a curious mixture of medieval hardship – a round of very basic latrines and sleeping facilities – and quiet enjoyment. He recalled particularly going with mates to the local bar for egg and chips, washed down with the local vin rouge, which had great novelty for all the men (indeed, in other accounts, we hear of a growing fondness for local brandies – on one occasion, a paralytic soldier was tied to a post by his commanding officer and made to stay there until he sobered up after the onslaught of the unfamiliar liquor). Like everyone else, Gough was shocked by the speed at which his war really started. 'Our battery commander, Captain Terry, called us all together, and all he said was for us all to make our way back to the coast to a place called Dunkirk,' recalled Mr Gough. 'He was the only one with a map so we were to keep with him.

'We started on foot in groups of about twenty. We quickly arrived at a road where we saw other troops making their way in the same direction. It wasn't long before we came upon abandoned vehicles in the ditches. By then, some of my party had already fallen by the wayside with blistered feet. Some looked like raw steak and I thanked God for my good feet. I had no trouble with them.'

But even without the physical discomfort, there were still moments of psychological disorientation on that strange journey:

> By about midday, I found myself walking alone and approaching a river. I walked down a bank and looked for the narrowest part to cross. Suddenly a voice behind me said, 'Help me get across, I can't swim.' I have always been a good swimmer, so I said to him, 'Here, catch hold of my belt and keep your head up.' We got across but I never saw the lad again. I've often wondered if he made it home.[6]

After this came the distressing, yet almost hallucinatory spectacle of a small group of French cavalry approaching; then, out of nowhere, being blown into the sky. The Germans had attacked from a nearby tower. Mr Gough was aware just a moment later of the terrible mingled noise of maimed men and horses, each bellowing and screaming in distress. It is also quite strange now to imagine the idea of horses being used on the front line as late as 1940.

Having walked for miles under benign warm skies, Gough and his fellows found themselves on the outskirts of a town where clearly, carnage had already been wreaked, and where there was more carnage to come. Little shops had been bombed. Gough gazed with dazed interest at what remained of a music shop. 'I saw pianos, violins, piano accordions,' he said. 'All smashed up. These things stand out in my memory and my recollections of that horrible journey. I was just nineteen.' The town that he and his fellows had reached was Dunkirk. It did not seem to hold the immediate promise of deliverance.

For Charles Searle of the Medical Corps, the anarchy that prevailed outside Arras seemed dizzyingly fast to develop. 'When the Belgians collapsed, we had the order to disperse,' he says. 'We had to disperse on our own steam. In other words: we were told to piss off.' To all intents and purposes, 'we weren't in the army any more. The unit got smashed up, twelve blokes went the wrong way and got captured and imprisoned and we had to make our own way.'

Searle was barely trained, a young soldier in a foreign land who no longer had even the comfort of knowing that he was part of a unit. The enemy were close; the time, for him, now passed with liquid speed, his only aim to avoid capture. But another factor would have increased his pulse rate still further: as a member of the Medical Corps, he was unarmed. Any German soldier could take a shot at him; he would have no means of returning fire.

'I walked all the way from Arras to Dunkirk,' says Mr Searle. 'The time I spent in a ditch because the Germans were machine gunning along the road . . . They were machine gunning the civilians as well as us.

'Now in the Medical Corps you're not allowed to carry a rifle. I was a good shot, we had the training – but of course they said, "It's only for self-preservation and defence that you take up arms – that's it." If you are wearing a Red Cross, you are not supposed to.' And so his journey went on, broken by the need to take cover. Around him were the 'walking wounded. Those that were really bad were lying on the ground or being transferred to a hospital somewhere.' The idea of regiments or units had completely gone. 'When they say every man for himself in a dispersal order, you're not in any organisation.

'Along the way, we could see lorries being dismantled by British soldiers. They just put a bayonet through the water tank. They should have set light to them! Because when we went back in 1944, for the Normandy landings, the Germans were using them. And motorbikes – they were chucking them in the river. The Germans just took them out and cleaned them and dried them out. When we went back after D-Day, we saw the English motors that the Germans were using!' Indeed, the sheer quantity of materiel left, only partially damaged, was quite staggering: vans, motorbikes, cars, not to mention the various weapons. Obviously there was no choice:

either you got the men on board the ships or their equipment. There was no room for both. But in a curious way, this loss would provide emotional updraught back in Britain a few days later. For the men in the factories – and the women who were shortly to join them – there was to be a frenzy of production, an outbreak of mass Stakhanovism to replace the losses. And this great pulsation of labour energy, a generalised sense of effort and satisfaction, was to prove a very strong element in unifying the country and its spirits.

All that was to come; and it would not have been of much interest to the anxious men scattered across that corner of northern France, pointing themselves in what they hoped would be the direction of rescue. Private Benjamin Geoffrey Nickholds and his friend Harry Stretch endured a harrowing walk to the coast – the German bombers dropping vertiginously out of the skies with no warning, the lack of sleep, and the pity aroused by the refugees, many of whom, as Mr Nickholds observed, had fled their homes leaving the doors wide open.

Even in the midst of his own epic trudge, Nickholds recalled that he and Stretch somehow contrived to find a lighter moment:

> The road we took to Dunkirk went through land flooded to hinder the advance of Jerry. It was also being shelled. We decided that it might be safer to cross the fields even though they were waterlogged. Our feet became clogged with mud, making movement difficult. We came to a drainage channel full of water. The only way across was to jump. Because neither of us made it, we got wet.

It was at this point that a solution to this discomfort was spotted. 'Across the channel were several horses with harnesses on. I think they would have been abandoned by the French army as they made their way to Dunkirk. Harry and I decided to mount them and ride.' Easier said than done:

> I tried to mount my horse with the help of Harry. I failed. Harry tried and he failed. The trouble was that our feet were stuck in the mud. Next we tried stacking some empty petrol cans. Harry stood on the cans and as he attempted to mount, the horse moved and Harry dropped into the mud. We were in fits of laughter.[7]

Indeed, it is easy to imagine such laughter being completely unstoppable; the release from so much tension. None the less, the men held it together. 'We eventually managed to get mounted,' recalled Mr Nickholds. 'Harry went ahead of me. After this, I do not recall seeing him again. I wish I knew what happened to him. I hope he made it back to England.' And the horse ride took Mr Nickholds past some terrible sights. 'I was unhappy on that horse,' he wrote. 'Shells were going over. I passed the corpse of a chap who had been blown in two halves. On each side of the ditch was one half and both were joined by his intestines. I will never forget the look on his face. Just before he died, he must have realised what had happened to him.'

But as these desperate and dizzying journeys were undertaken, on the other side of the Channel there was assembling a disparate sailing force that pulsated with adrenaline as its crews prepared to sail out into the deep, dark night.

8

'Just Follow the Ferries'

26–27 May 1940

Journalist and designer Robert Harling, who just weeks beforehand had been poring over charts in the chandlery of Captain O.M. Watts, now found himself in a scene of dark, surreal beauty, while also sailing slowly into a position of extreme jeopardy. 'Midnight donged on one of the riverside churches,' he later recalled. 'The river and the night were wholly merged.' But then, as they passed the Thames Estuary and sailed southwards, the sun rose, and the sight that greeted him was at once breathtaking, stirring and not a little incongruous. 'We were moving up the coast with a stranger miscellany of craft than was ever seen in the most hybrid amateur regatta,' he wrote. 'Destroyers, sloops, trawlers, motorboats, fishing boats, tugs, Dutch skoots. Under the splendid sun, they seemed like craft of peace journeying upon a gay occasion but suddenly, we knew where we were, for someone said: "There they are, the bastards."'[1]

The 'bastards' in the Junkers might well have been rubbing their eyes slightly at some of the vessels heading off across that calm Channel. Among them was a handsome wooden steam passenger launch called *New Windsor Castle*; in its previous incarnation, it had featured on ornate hand-coloured postcards of Thames pleasure cruises, the passengers up on deck, enjoying the summer sunshine as it glided past Hampton Court. But its genteel – and open – appearance belied its other uses. As soon as the war broke out, it had been requisitioned for use on the Thames in central London as a means of trying to ease pressure on commuting routes in those days of dislocation.

Meanwhile, Admiral Ramsay and the navy had been helped enormously by the efforts of Captain O.M. Watts of Albemarle Street and his school of sailsmanship. On the afternoon of 26 May, Watts had sent word around to his varied pupils that that evening's tutorial was cancelled. Instead, they were to make their way to the Port of London Authority headquarters just opposite the Tower of London. It was here that Watts's gentleman professionals and working sailors gathered. Some, if not all, must have had a strong inkling of what was to come. Among those present were crew members of Thames tugs – doughty, unglamorous vessels that worked the river towing rather grander boats. Second mate Desmond Hill found himself ricocheting all over London that day. He recorded receiving the call from Captain Watts at 2.15 p.m. but, having misunderstood, presenting himself at Albemarle Street and then having to scramble over to Tower Hill. Only now were they finally told the nature of their mission: that they were to spend the next two days evacuating the BEF.

In what now shines a rather moving – if sometimes amusing – light on the mood among the amateur seamen before the crossings began, Desmond Hill recorded in his log: 'Split into deckhands, navigators and engineers!' But the news of his job had also left him a little giddy. 'Phone mother meet me Hammersmith . . .' he wrote. 'Pater also. And take fond farewell of Margaret, quite convinced shan't see her again.' In other words, he knew instantly the gravity of what he was about to be thrown into. 'In train: mixed feelings as to whether I'm a damned fool or not. Eventually decide it's necessary to go and won't back out, feel rather heroic.' However, this swirl of thoughts meant that he got on the wrong train and ended up in the suburb of Walham Green. After some confusion, he managed to rendezvous with his parents, collect his gear and make his way back to the Port of London Authority where, having just missed the 7 p.m. bus to the Thames Estuary port of Tilbury, he took the opportunity for a quick pint with his friend Robert in the Crooked Billet.

Half an hour later, he recorded: 'Quite a crowd gathered now and we get a Nelson speech from a very charming Rear Admiral. Departed.' He and his friends made their way to the eastern dock of Tilbury, finding time at 8.45 p.m. to 'stop for beer'. By 9.20 p.m. they were on the quayside to 'find lots of volunteers. Also lightermen and bargees. More requests for engineers. Some go off in lifeboats, of which apparently unending supply.' By 11 p.m. on the landing stage, everyone had been issued with tin hats. Hill had been allocated a boat, and they set sail after midnight, stopping at Southend to pick up vital supplies. As well as a huge case of water and a quantity of bully beef, Hill procured '5 large loaves, one and a half pounds butter and marge, 20 tins of sardines, soups, veal and ham roll, jam etc, tea, sugar milk etc'. He added: 'All hands long since frozen to the marrow but quite cheerful. Nice to be afloat again and glad I came.'[2] The sights and experiences that he would witness in the next few days make the provisions list almost heartbreakingly quotidian. Yet he and his colleagues knew that they were not merely going to be pulling soldiers aboard: those soldiers, they understood, would be ravenously hungry and dangerously dehydrated.

Meanwhile, if German pilots were ever taken aback at the prospect that was starting to unfold beneath them, there was also some surprise among naval officers at the motley nature of the armada. A young sub-lieutenant called Robert Timbrell was stationed in Portsmouth at a base called Whale Island when it looked as though Operation

Dynamo was finally afoot. One of the older captains there gave him his orders: he was to report at once for duty on the *Llanthony.* The vessel did not sound familiar but Sub-Lieutenant Timbrell got on with it. He very quickly discovered that the *Llanthony* was in fact a 77ft motor yacht – elegant lines of a white hull and a wooden bridge. The boat had rather a fancy provenance too: it had apparently been constructed for Lord Astor of Hever and was fitted with Daimler engines. Timbrell's initial orders were to take command of it – and his equally random crew of London Transport engineers and (a Monty Python touch) half a dozen Newfoundland sailors who were in fact professional lumberjacks. Obviously the craft was not fitted with any guns. Once they reached Ramsgate, they were refuelled, issued with rations, and given charts. Only then was the nature of the task ahead of them made plain.

Outclassing *Llanthony* in terms of sheer elegance and style was a Victorian sailing yacht – its sails sharp and Euclidean against the neat thin gradient of its white 41ft hull – called *Cachalot.* Built in 1900 in Folkestone, the vessel was fitted with an auxiliary engine as late as 1936. So there is every possibility that this geometrically beautiful construction voyaged across to Dunkirk under the riffling silence of sail. The craft's owner was Sir Lancelot Elphinstone, a cousin to the Queen and a descendant of another distinguished Elphinstone who had been part of the doomed 1842 British attempt to establish dominance in Afghanistan. Strikingly, just as his very own boat was being prepared by the Royal Navy for its new duties, Sir Lancelot himself was among the British Expeditionary Force officers making their bedraggled way to Dunkirk.

Some vessels happened to be in the right place at the right time. Such was the case for the small but handsome 30ft cabin cruiser *Jockette II*, built as a Thames cruiser in 1938 and owned by Judge Adam Partington. Not for him the sedate backwaters of Chertsey; he wanted a taste of the salt and the vista of the estuary, down at the limits of the Thames in Leigh-on-Sea, the Essex harbour best known for its cockle picking. From there it was possible to chug across the wide expanse of mud-brown water and explore the wide opening of the River Medway – this was Charles Dickens territory, the moody and atmospheric marsh country evoked by Pip in *Great Expectations*. It was while berthed at Leigh that the cabin cruiser received its call-up; with its owner not available for sailing, placed in charge of the boat was naval midshipman Ricky Latham, accompanied by a seaman called Bruce and a petty engineer called Jimmy. Experienced as these young men were, the workings of this rather more frivolous vessel were initially a mystery to them. Happily, Judge Partington had had the foresight to have the galley filled with provisions and quantities of beer. As with other craft, it would soon become apparent that these supplies were vital.

There were those who hankered to do their bit but had been stopped by injury or other medical causes. One such man was Bob Hilton, who had been a regular soldier before the war but was discharged in 1936 after sustaining a serious injury. Maddened by the enforced inaction when war broke out, he tried subterfuge; he volunteered, slipped through, and made it all the way to officer training before he was found out. He was discharged a second time. When it became clear just how much danger the British Expeditionary Force was in, Hilton found another way to throw himself into the fray. He let the naval authorities know that he was willing to take any boat across the Channel, and this time his services were accepted. There was one setback; he had only one shipmate and each crew required a minimum of three.

Hilton gave the matter a little thought, then doubled back to Tilbury where, for the consideration of £1 plus a great many drinks, he persuaded a longshoreman to sign up, making it clear to the man that this was purely for the purposes of bureaucracy. All Hilton needed was the signature; there was no need for the man to actually hurl himself into jeopardy. Their new companion was not put off; Hilton and his associates were assigned a motor yacht called *Ryegate II*. With a handsome hull of pitch pine and oak, and a length of 40ft, the craft was all set and packed with provisions and drinks but for one detail: there were no drinking glasses. These Hilton and his friends obtained from a pub.

Although Hilton was unusual in his sheer persistence, he was far from alone among these civilian craft and their civilian crews in their lightly worn bravery. Also at Leigh-on-Sea on the Thames Estuary was the Osborne family, whose business involved catering and shellfish. They had a cockle boat, the *Renown*, which they unhesitatingly sailed out; Frank and Leslie Osborne were accompanied by their crewmates and colleagues Harry Noakes and Harry Graham Porter (the latter a naval rating from Birmingham). Other cockle boats that made the sailing were *Letitia*, *Endeavour*, *Reliance* and *Resolute*, each with its own young crew, and under the overall guidance of Royal Naval Volunteer Reserve (RNVR) officer Sub-Lieutenant Soloman. The advantage of these boats was that they were light, with powerful diesel engines. But even before they sailed out into the open sea, the men on board must also have been piercingly aware of just how vulnerable they were: none of them armed, and nowhere practical to take cover in the event of an attack. Very often now, the story of the little ships is told with a kind of fond indulgence redolent of Ealing comedy: those magnificent men, eccentrically defying the odds to do their duty. As we shall see, the reality was much icier, and the prospects very much grimmer.

Elsewhere, perhaps mindful of Clement Attlee's admonitions concerning the sacrifices to come, one of Britain's best loved show-business acts also found a way to contribute. The popular comedian Tommy Trinder – who by that stage was a film star – had bought a motor yacht in 1939. Twenty-nine feet in length, it was unostentatious but well made. Trinder's act featured a recurring joke where he would introduce himself, spell out his name – T-R-I-N-D-E-R – and then tell the audience: 'It's pronounced Chumley.' This was a reference to the sometimes inexplicable pronunciations of upper-class names, and in honour of this, his new boat was in fact named *Chalmondesleigh* (pronounced, etc., etc.). The boat's sign-writer apparently spent three days labouring over the name. Trinder's brother later told author Christian Brann, 'Tommy sent me to pick up the boat at Shanklin (on the Isle of Wight) and deliver it to him on the Thames. I didn't know how to get her there from the Isle of Wight. Tommy told me: "Just follow the ferries and one of them would lead me up the Thames!"'[3] It didn't even have to go quite so far; once it reached Shoreham, on the Sussex coast, it was taken over by the navy. It is charming to imagine sailors and soldiers alike recognising the name and wondering if by any chance it had something to do with *the* Trinder.

One steam-engined pleasure cruiser was unique in finding a form of macabre notoriety some five decades after the Dunkirk evacuation: the *Marchioness*, constructed in Oxford in 1923, had by the time the war broke out already been pressed into service as part of the Thames Hospital Emergency Transport Service. This had largely been a precautionary measure: in anticipating ferocious bombing and poison gas attacks, the government had been keen to find ways of transporting the seriously wounded to medical help without getting caught in panic-filled streets. Eighty-five feet long, the *Marchioness* cannot have seemed very practical for that role: built for summer cruises, much of the boat was in the open air, save for a canopy. It was called up and made the journey down to Ramsgate. But it is chiefly remembered now for its afterlife: in 1989 the boat – refitted with bars and a disco for large parties – collided with a dredger on the Thames in the early hours of the morning and sank with terrible speed, claiming many lives.

Other vessels had an unexpected and colourful history. One such was a 50ft admiral's barge called, rather brilliantly, *Count Dracula*. This had seen action in the First World War – on the side of the Germans, with the Imperial German Navy. Admiral von Hipper used the craft for short hops between battleships and indeed hooked her up in 1918 to the battle cruiser *Hindenburg*. When that ship was scuppered at Scapa Flow after the German surrender, one sailor could not bear to see the *Count Dracula* lost too, so he released her before the mighty ship went down. Floating free of the *Hindenburg* out in the open water, the *Count Dracula* was picked up by the Royal Navy and then, in the inter-war years, fell into private hands. Come May 1940, its new owner and his son answered the summons, and sailed the veteran craft to Ramsgate.

Sailing in from the Thames Estuary, where she had been performing sterling minesweeping duties over the last few months alongside her sister vessel the *Gracie Fields,* was the 180ft paddle steamer *Medway Queen,* lately on diligent patrol of the Channel straits. In peacetime, she could carry almost one thousand passengers during any one jaunt. This capacity was to serve handsomely.

There must have been boat owners for whom the requisition was something of a wrench, even if they clearly never voiced this feeling. For instance, in the case of the 30ft motor yacht *Nydia,* commissioned by Harold Turner, the timing seemed a shade unfortunate; the boat had only just been finished when the initial Admiralty call for sailing vessels went out. A bijou affair, with not more than five portholes each side, the vessel would barely have been glimpsed by its owner before it sailed off to the meeting point at Ramsgate. At least Mr Turner had the chance to see his boat; in the case of certain craft requisitioned from the Tough Brothers boatyard, it proved impossible to notify the owners in time. As a result, there were some who belatedly discovered that their beloved craft were not safe behind some Thames lock, but bobbing around in the waves at Ramsgate, poised to sail through a hail of bullets and bombs.

One owner discovered that his boat had been taken away – but, thanks to the secrecy, no one offered any kind of explanation. As a result, the owner called the police, convinced that his boat had simply been stolen. The resulting wild goose chase led back to the Tough Brothers yard, where owner and constabulary were informed of the vessel's (very rough) whereabouts. In fact, the Toughs had been meticulously scrupulous about the condition of the boats that they sent over, to the extent of removing and carrying out full inventories of all the fine china, cutlery and wine glasses kept within each one.

The smallest craft to be volunteered for Dynamo would not have looked out of place in the Viking age; a tiny wooden fishing boat, completely open, with a distinctively straight stem. Scarcely bigger than a rowing boat, the *Tamzine* measured just under 15ft, with a small mast. This eccentric beauty normally saw service just off the coast of north Kent at Birchington, near Margate. And the boat was rather sturdier than it looked; it had been specially designed for year-round fishing, in waters that were often by no means easy. It had only been built in 1937, the hull made of Canadian spruce; as much a work of art as a working vessel, but one that was to be much admired in the coming days.

Given the sloping beaches and extensive shallows of the sea in the vicinity of Dunkirk, the different sizes and capacities of all these vessels offered precisely the variety that was needed. Although the great bulk of the evacuations would be via destroyer, with thousands upon thousands of soldiers beginning to gather on the wide beaches of La Panne, the tiny vessels were needed to ferry them to the larger ones. But, while it was easy to traverse, the nature of the landscape would call upon terrific reserves of courage from the soldiers and sailors alike; for it also made those thousands of men a clear and open target for an enemy that had every interest in wiping them out.

The formal go-ahead for Operation Dynamo had been given at 7 p.m. on Sunday 26 May. This was the official acknowledgement that the British forces had been routed. But even before this signal, given the nod by Admiral Ramsay, civilian passenger steamers had already embarked on the voyage to Dunkirk harbour. Among them were *Mona's Isle*, *Mona's Queen* and *Maid of Orleans*. Like all the other vessels now gathered at Ramsgate and Dover, bobbing in those listless waves, their crews would have been issued with rations and also with charts. Where had Admiral Ramsay managed to procure so many maps? There was an element of extemporisation: some were requisitioned from local sources. Others, it has been reported, had been given away free with the *Daily Telegraph* a few weeks earlier as a means of helping their readers follow the war.

The first, shortest route of thirty-nine miles – known as 'Z' – had been swept for mines. Yet it would become clear over the next couple of days that – thanks to the intensity and focus of German bombers – it was all but impossible to sail in daylight hours. Two other, longer routes had to be set out. Route Y was eighty-seven miles, and sailed past Belgium and German gun emplacements. Nor had it been thoroughly swept for mines. But dealing with the numbers that they were required to rescue – and the urgency of their mission – there was little choice but for the ships to risk it. (Later, route X came into play: fifty-five miles, along with the hazards of sailing past German guns at Calais, then the natural peril of the Goodwin Sands on the return journey.)

The rationing, too, had a freewheeling quality about it. At Ramsgate and Dover, naval ratings were on hand to supply the boats with great drums of fuel. Food and drink was a little more random, and depended heavily on what was available and to hand. One crew remembered that they were provided with a bag of potatoes and an enormous lump of raw beef.

Is it harder – or, paradoxically, easier – for untrained, inexperienced men to sail off into the line of enemy fire? In the case of the very young volunteers, you can occasionally hear in their recollections a note of that spirit of pure, reckless adventure in their eagerness to join up. Even among the older men, there seemed to be a studied blitheness. But they had not seen what the soldiers in France were seeing day and night.

Whatever the case, this was the first time in centuries – barring Zeppelin raids – that war had come quite so close to England's civilian population; and when it looked like coming closer yet, this was the first time that untrained civilians leapt at the chance – either on board little ships or wielding bayonets for the Local Defence Volunteers – to join the fight.

Partly the story of Dunkirk is about what have been termed miracles; but miracles are the result of divine intervention and the intervention here was very far from divine. It was better than that. The real story is to do with the ability of the psyche to cope under mounting suspense, anxiety and finally, terror. From the spectacle of those gaudy pleasure steamers leaving Ramsgate in the warm air of a late spring evening, to the prospect of hundreds of thousands of men waiting on beaches, without food or fresh water and under constant attack from howling bombers, it also now provides a fascinating insight – in the midst of the mind-searing carnage, the pervasive sight and stench of violent death – into the limits of quiet bravery, and even what might be termed nobility of spirit when staring into a form of hell.

9

'Blood All Over Your Hands'

27 May 1940

To the Twitter generation, inured to electronic eavesdropping and hacking and daily self-exposure, the idea of keeping a secret – properly, not saying a word to anyone – is an almost outlandish proposition. For instance, the story of the codebreaking efforts at Bletchley Park still inspires awe not just for the cracking of Enigma but the way that so many thousands of people kept this gravest of all secrets. On a similar basis, the evacuation of nearly half a million men from a small French port somehow also had to be kept quiet. Obviously the ever-increasing numbers of troops gathering there were seen by countless German bombers flying overhead. The aim of all these men, too, would have been fairly clear. Yet nothing could be said out loud.

In Britain, as the destroyers and the paddle steamers and the tugs and the skoots and the bijou cabin cruisers received their orders and began to prepare for the careful voyage, the public had at that stage no real idea of what was happening. And, strikingly, life, though dislocated, none the less carried on, under a particularly fine and balmy spring sky. In cricket, 'London counties entertained some 2,000 spectators to enjoyable cricket at Cheam and defeated the home club with the loss of four batsmen.' In football, after the weekend's matches, Fulham and West Ham – having scored five and four goals respectively – were powering ahead in the Football League. The hopes of Manchester United and Manchester City were dented. Elsewhere, north London's tennis courts echoed with the thwack of serves. 'A lovely morning,' wrote one young female diarist. 'Played tennis with Frank from 7am to breakfast.'

Nor was the crisis in northern France affecting the capital's cultural life, though again, underneath all the reporting seemed to be an implicit admission of subterranean tension. 'It takes more than the mere prospect of invasion to make the theatre inactive,' gushed a London arts correspondent just on the borders of seemliness. 'Not only do theatres continue to open but they offer four first nights this week.' Remarkably, in that week of Dunkirk, it was true: among the new productions were *The Tempest* at the Old Vic, Ibsen's *Ghosts* at the Duchess and Denis Ogden's *The Peaceful Inn* at the Duke of York. On 27 May, *Me and My Girl* racked up its 1467th performance, the occasion marked by an air-raid warden called Norman Davis 'who was seeing the piece for the 100th time'. In part, our collective wartime image of London is coloured by the Blitz; yet during May 1940, the bombing was still several months off. The city may have been deep in blackout, but its citizens – even those who feared imminent invasion – would not give up their night life.

Amid these determined distractions, it was clear that people were speculating; how could they not? 'Everybody has got the dithers,' wrote one Surrey man. 'Anyone would think Hitler was coming up the Thames in a rowing boat.' It was on 26 May, as the evacuation began, that the not wholly sure-footed Ministry of Information felt obliged to step in, on the grounds of security. 'Everyone in the country is waiting – many are waiting with great personal anxiety – for news of our men in France,' announced Minister Duff Cooper. 'So is the enemy – and the giving of news at this moment might cost the lives of men . . . we must all wait patiently and confidently until the news can be given to us with safety.'

Such patrician tones were widely resented and mocked. They were as nothing to the approach taken by Harold Nicolson, also of the Ministry of Information, in a BBC radio broadcast made that evening. 'We are now suffering from a virulent form of the rumour epidemic,' he began. 'There is the naturally nervous person who just chatters because he can't keep still . . . There are the vain and silly people who gain a sense of self-importance by imparting sensational news. And there are quite sensible people, such as you and I, who in our weaker moments become chatter-bugs, without meaning to be chatter-bugs in the least.' The idea was partly to try and establish the notion of 'chatter-bugs' as a catchword. It didn't work, but the wider central idea – that idle rumour could filter back to the enemy and be used against British troops – did have some potency.

Those British troops were now being tested in ways that just months ago they would never have imagined. From Dunkirk, and stretching several miles up that wide windy coast to La Panne just across the Belgian border, a landscape that had previously been the realm of families and gentle promenades was now a swarming mass of British, French and Belgian soldiers, as well as terrorised civilians.

A few veterans have observed lightly that because of the sand, the detonation of the bombs from the Junkers was much less effective than on the open roads; the shock wave was absorbed instead by the sand. Yet that is a calculatedly stiff-upper-lipped way of looking at it. Men were hit, or otherwise they were destroyed internally by the blasts, their organs scrambled; in either case, their bodies, sometimes in pieces, lay in those dunes. Some recalled seeing corpses repeatedly thrown into the air by successive blasts. After the planes had flown over, the lucky survivors looked up cautiously, and listened as the cries went up: 'Medic! Medic!' Some recalled how men from the Royal Army Medical Corps stayed impassive as they dealt with a range of hideous wounds. There were makeshift casualty wards a little distance away, one set up in the reception area of a hotel; the medics did what they could with blood-soaked blankets and supplies of morphine.

One of the logistical horrors facing these men was how to convey the seriously wounded on to the boats; in some cases, there were improvised litters. The medics also knew that while everyone else was waiting for their place on a boat, they would have to be among the last to leave; for they could not abandon the most seriously wounded soldiers in their care. This, they knew, meant probable capture, by an army that could not be trusted to uphold any of the ethical conventions usually attached to the Red Cross.

The German bombs aimed at the beaches also raised a question of psychological impact (even the sternest of medical reports, written up by doctors monitoring the Dover Patrol, were to acknowledge, almost for the first time, that fear and neurosis were not products of cowardice or bad character, but might sometimes be the direct result of such attacks). For the men on the beaches, even firing a rifle was only really misdirection; the truth was that they were helpless, and they felt it.

Yet according to one account, some British soldiers remained remarkably insouciant about their position; a few took the opportunity to get drunk on good red wine. Indeed, as one veteran later cheerfully confessed, 'we got absolutely plastered.'

The Isle of Man steamer *Mona's Isle* (followed in swift succession by other passenger steamers including *Mona's Queen*, *Maid of Orleans* and *Canterbury*) had been the first to make the journey across. *Mona's Isle* and her crew set sail from Dover at 9 p.m., just after the last of the evening's sunset had disappeared from the sky. The crossing took around three hours, and she arrived at Dunkirk Gare Maritime just after midnight. There were troops gathered at the wood and concrete jetty known as the mole. Embarkation began under cover of the small hours. Possibly no one could have calculated just how many men this boat – or indeed any of the others – could hold in one go. On this first round of the evacuation, *Mona's Isle* accommodated 1429 men.

Just before the sun glimmered into the sky, the steamer set off again. But its voyage back was – by necessity – painfully slow. Despite the best efforts of all those minesweepers, the English Channel was still seething with lethal traps. On top of that was the topographical jeopardy posed by the Goodwin Sands. Any boat stranded here would have been torn apart in minutes by bombers. *Mona's Isle* was on route Z, the first devised; it meant that on the return journey, for the first twenty miles or so, she had to sail troublingly close to the French coast, almost hugging it, before being able to make the turn at Calais towards England. Those few miles made her – and other vessels that followed – acutely vulnerable to German fire. *Mona's Isle* first took hits from German artillery. Then, while sailing towards Dover, she was machine-gunned by German fighters. The boat's petty officer took four bullets through his arm but in spite of the shock and the pain, he still managed to fire back.

After this shocking baptismal voyage, *Mona's Isle* arrived back in Dover around midday on 27 May, the other vessels not long after. Two things would now have been crystal clear to Admiral Ramsay and those around him: the evacuation could no longer reasonably be regarded as a secret from the Germans; and that initial voyage had taken such a very long time – in total, fifteen hours to evacuate 1429 men. There were two hundred and forty times that number still awaiting deliverance. How long did they have before they were overwhelmed by the German forces?

On that day, one of Ramsay's best young lieutenants, Captain W.G. Tennant, sailed out on the naval destroyer *Wolfhound*. He was going to France to bring an element of logic and organisation to this mad operation. He took with him twelve officers and 150 men. By now, the German planes were attending to the cross-Channel routes. Nothing could evade the persistent fury of the Luftwaffe. Some time afterwards, Captain Tennant recalled that harrowing voyage – the necessity for long detours to try and avoid the worst of the plane attacks. Then there was the lead weight of apprehension when at last the burning harbour came into view, Captain Tennant made land and took stock of the ruins around him. The scale of the job was made horribly apparent to him. 'The sight of Dunkirk and nearby districts gave one a hollow feeling in the pit of the stomach,' he told David J. Knowles. 'The Boche had been going for it really hard and there was not a pane of glass left anywhere – most of it was still lying around in the streets. There were also unremoved dead laying about from the last air raid.' He added, with an inflammatory note:

> As regards the bearing and behaviour of the troops, both British and French, prior to and during the embarkation, it must be recorded that the earlier parties were embarked off the beaches in a condition of complete disorganisation. There appeared to be no military officers in charge of the troops, and this impression was undoubtedly enhanced by the difficulty in distinguishing between the uniforms of such officers as were present, and other ranks.[1]

Many years later, any suggestion that there had been 'disorganisation' on those beaches was met with rage from within the military establishment and the War Office. Senior generals recalled, instead, calm and dignity in what were admittedly extremely undignified circumstances. Yet Captain Tennant was by no means alone in having perceived a state of near anarchy. One young man present had been sent to help deal with this anticipated eventuality.

Even before the official Operation Dynamo evacuation had begun, some naval recruits found themselves signed up for a special operation that would require both nerve and authority. These carefully chosen young men were being sent over to France not merely to help bring soldiers back but also – eventually – to bring a semblance of control on the beaches. This would mean keeping the peace among thousands of men – many of whom had been told to abandon their weapons and now felt acutely vulnerable as a result – under German attack, while trying to ensure that the evacuation was carried out as smoothly as possible.

One such candidate was 23-year-old Vic Viner, whose eyes had been opened to the wider world by his few years in the Royal Navy. From the outset, he had no idea what he had been selected to do; simply that he had been recalled from the Mediterranean. 'There were these special courses at Portsmouth. I finished my course and we were sent back to Chatham [the large naval docks on the Kent coast]. I was told to dump my gear, and go and have something to eat.' Mr Viner recalled being vaguely puzzled by the order to leave the gear. 'Then, from 6 p.m. that evening, we were to assemble in the gym where we were told that we were going to do a special project. That's all they said – special project. Then we went back to the gym. There were trestle tables. We were told: you will go and pick up a revolver from the table. Sixty rounds of ammunition. And a little pouch – which had sixty bars of chocolate in it. And then we were told that when we had got that, we were to assemble over in the corner and await further instructions.'

It still seemed opaque to Mr Viner, even though, as he says, 'I was a leading seaman by that time, I had been promoted. Then we were told – I think just after midnight – to go out on to the parade ground. There was a fleet of company buses. We were told to board the buses and then they told us, you're going down to Dover, and on the way down, you will be told why you are going. That's when we were told we were going to assist with the evacuation of the BEF.

'So we arrived at Dover,' Mr Viner continues. 'And there were four destroyers, E-class. I was told to go on HMS *Esk* with twelve other fellas. We set sail. As we were going over, the captain of the ship came round to us and he said, "What you've got to do is take away my ship's whaler and go to the beaches and bring back soldiers. I've no idea what it's like, I've no idea until I get there where I'm going to drop anchor or what I'm going to do. So just stand by."

'I think we arrived just after 4 a.m. – daylight – and we left the ship just after 5 a.m. And as the destroyer was coming in, we saw all these blobs in the water. We had no idea what they were. Of course they were soldiers. Bodies.'

This was the first intimation of what lay ahead for Mr Viner and his mates. There were men on those beaches – soldiers and civilians – who had already succumbed to fear. A few imagined that – given the relative flatness of the sea – it might be possible to swim to the shore of England. Others were suffering trauma; the after-effect of continuous bombing along the road to Dunkirk, added to the shortage of food and fresh water. They had plunged into the water without any rational sense of what they were going to do next. Theirs were the bloated corpses that Vic Viner was so surprised to see on that bright, warm May dawn.

'I took away the whaler and my colleague took the motor boat,' he continues. A whaler is a small craft with oars; the idea was that it could be used as a form of ferry to get men from the difficult-to-reach jetty and beaches and take them out to the depths where the destroyers were anchored. 'The whaler also has a sail if you want to use it. All destroyers would have this 27ft whaler. There were four of us in the boat and we picked up sixteen soldiers. They were fully equipped still. But you have to remember that this was early.' When the evacuation reached full tilt, the men were ordered to discard everything that they had, the better to make room on the boats.

That early morning, Mr Viner began his back-breaking work. 'We rowed back to the *Esk*, put them there, had a quick rest, then rowed back again – we did four trips. And the surf was running. It was quite a heavy surf. You had to get the boat into and out of it again. There was a lot of pushing going on. And a lot of soldiers with all their gear, so it was very heavy.

Before conscription in 1939, there was some concern in the military hierarchy about the physical fitness of young men from deprived urban districts. Here, new army recruits are given milk at Aldershot. © IWM (ARMY TRAINING 10/4a)

Soldiers not immediately shipped out to France in 1939–40 cheerfully endured training manoeuvres throughout Britain, including this one involving a Vickers machine gun camouflaged in a turnip field. © IWM (ARMY TRAINING 17/20)

Secretary of State for War, Leslie Hore-Belisha, addresses new recruits in 1939. His enthusiasm for capturing headlines – such as when he recruited Joe Lyons to overhaul army catering – made him an object of suspicion to senior military figures. © IWM (ARMY TRAINING 28/12)

below left: Viscount Gort was in command of the British forces until after the Dunkirk evacuation; known for austere personal habits, this was balanced with his startling appetite for humorous horseplay and japes. © Associated Newspapers/REX

below right: Admiral Sir Bertram Ramsay; the architect of the evacuation that saved Britain from making terms with Germany. Ferocious and energetic, he was also a keen socialiser and frequenter of the grander London clubs. © Bettman/CORBIS

Throughout the 'Phoney War', Mecca dance halls were a magnet for the young – oases of colour and light in the midst of the blackouts. Their popularity persisted even as increasing conscription led to a shortage of male partners. © TopFoto.co.uk

HMS *Medway Queen*, a former pleasure boat, of the type eulogised by J.B Priestley, was called up in 1939 for illustrious service as a minesweeper; then evacuated thousands of men from Dunkirk, with many voyages to and from Dover; and is now being restored in Gillingham. © Popperfoto/Getty Images

As British forces in France were pulling back to the coast in May 1940, there was a big push to recruit women for work across all industries, from the ATS to previously male strongholds such as steelworks.

As the civilian population in May 1940 lived in anxious anticipation of invasion, there were official exhortations against 'chatterbugs'. The term never caught on, but the discipline of discretion was learnt quickly. © IWM (Art.IWM PST 2837)

For some soldiers and sailors the sheer numbers gathering on the beaches were vaster than 'any football crowd'; yet even in that mass, there were some who were able to read books quietly.

above left: Out on the beaches and on the 'Mole', qualities of resilience were tested beyond imagining; especially when the Luftwaffe began attacking from the sky. © IWM (HU 1135)

above right: After days with scant rations, little water, and no sleep, even the effort of climbing a rope ladder could be too much for some severely weakened soldiers. © Popperfoto/Getty Images

The melancholy wreckage of a once-cheerful resort; bodies and a British anti-tank gun abandoned on the promenade at Dunkirk. © IWM (HU 2286)

For many soldiers, the sight of distant ships, unable to get closer, was torment, especially with bombs and gunfire raining down on them; a few swam out into the cold sea hallucinating about 'getting to England' and perished. © IWM (HU 1137)

The little ships, and lifeboats, were used to ferry soldiers from the shallows to the rescuing ships. Vic Viner rowed so hard for so long against the surf, he 'sweated blood'. © Time & Life Pictures/Getty Images

Luftwaffe bombers targeted shipping indiscriminately, even attacking hospital ships. Sunken boats formed an extra, lethal hazard – here HMS *Vanquisher* negotiates around a sunken trawler. © IWM (HU 1149)

left: Despite the fierce bombardment, men frequently waited in the water for their turn to board rescuing ships. Even in May the sea was icy; numbness and cramps made any swimming much more difficult. Many drowned. © Getty Images

above: Sightings of returning troops on Southern Trains prompted a spontaneous mass outbreak of generosity from civilians around the Home Counties, who rushed to provide them with tea, fruit, even postcards to send home to assure families they were all right. © IWM (H 1632)

below: Press reports highlighted the cheerfulness of soldiers crammed shoulder to shoulder on boats; in some cases, there were also dogs that the soldiers couldn't bear to leave behind, and which would only answer to French. © Popperfoto/Getty Images

Pictures taken by the victorious Germans having entered Dunkirk. Here, under rich blue skies, Nazis examine a memorial to aviation pioneer Louis Bleriot. © IWM (COL 296)

Two French officers under interrogation, the bizarre air of informality underscored by the nearby laid table with wine bottles. © IWM (COL 290)

On the outskirts of Dunkirk, Germans march an anti-tank gun past some of the vast quantity of hardware – in this case, scout carriers – that the British were forced to leave behind. © IWM (COL 293)

Not far from Dunkirk, and watched by their German captors, French soldiers are ordered to clear the road of an immobilised British carrier. © IWM (COL 289)

One of the many wonders of the evacuation was the way small motor boats – many built for river use – coped with the normally furious English Channel. Many veterans recall how uncharacteristically flat the water was. © IWM (HU 41241)

When some of the Dunkirk little ships sailed back up the Thames one quiet Sunday in June 1940, word quickly spread; by the time they got to Westminster, cheering crowds awaited them. © IWM (HU 104607)

An RAF signalsman at the time of the evacuation, Arthur Taylor, was in danger not just from German firepower, but the prospect of 'Tommies' turning on him in frustration at a (wrongly) perceived lack of RAF support.

Young sailor Vic Viner spent a scarcely imaginable six days and six nights on those beaches under constant fire; his job, to maintain order, with a revolver, in a column of 150 men.

At the centre of the Queen's Diamond Jubilee river pageant in 2012 were the Dunkirk little ships. Many veterans sailed on them that day; the extraordinary emotional resonance was felt by old and young alike. © Nicholas Bailey/REX

'Well, on the fourth trip back, we pulled up and John Robinson next to me said, "Vic, you've got blood all over your hands." I looked down at them – and then at his hands – and said: "So have you."' Both men, in their puzzlement and anxiety, saw that the blood seemed to be pouring down their sleeves. They sloughed off their uniform jackets and shirts and looked on with astonishment. 'We had sweated blood,' says Mr Viner lightly. 'You know the expression? Well, we were literally sweating blood.' It was the effort of constantly rowing back and forth at high speed with such a heavy load in a running surf.

Viner went back aboard the destroyer and said to the captain, 'Look, sir.' The captain looked at the blood and said, 'Right.' Viner said: 'We can't do this any more,' and the captain answered: 'I realise that.' Then he said, 'I've just received a signal that a certain operation has commenced – Operation Dynamo.'

This was the point at which any naval rating might have preferred to continue rowing and sweating blood. 'The captain said to us: "What is happening is that a flotilla of small ships are coming across the Channel from Ramsgate and Dover. And what they're going to do, they're going inshore as far as they can and the soldiers will be loaded on to the little boats – they will go back to the larger boats – and the larger boats will take them back to England. I'm discharging you now from here – you're to go to the beach and take what gear you've got with you, go and report to the first officer you can see and tell him that you are part of the Royal Naval beach party which is 150 strong. A hundred and fifty of you altogether will be there."

'And I stayed on there – on the beach – for six days.' Mr Viner was soon to discover the nature of his extraordinary mission – he was to try and bring the temperature down among the soldiers while somehow avoiding being bombed or strafed to ribbons himself.

While this command was being absorbed, others were still making their way to the port. 'I had a pocket full of sugar lumps,' says Charles

Searle. 'But you get fed up with sucking those. On the way there, you just scrounged whatever you could. A lot of the cows were dead, all swelling up. Ready to burst. No milk. Any cows that were still alive, they were all milked dry or slaughtered. Butchered. The amazing thing was that all the French were going to Dunkirk as though *they* were being evacuated. It was their country being overrun and they didn't even know where to go.'

Indeed, among French military high command, there was a persistent sense of what might now be termed denial. On the morning of 27 May, with headquarters having been moved unceremoniously from Arras to La Panne, just a few miles up-beach of Dunkirk, there was a meeting in the dining room of the Hotel du Sauvage where the British, among them General Adam (who was in charge of making sure Dunkirk's perimeter held) and Colonel Bridgeman (General Adam's Operations Officer, who had, some time back, made a thoughtful survey of Dunkirk's defences), listened to the order that had been wired in from the French General Weygand. The plan, they were told, was to thrust forward and eject the Germans from Calais. Instantly, the British regarded the idea as beyond nonsensical: had the French high command not been watching what had been happening over the last two weeks? And the coolness of their response – that of many of the French generals was not much warmer – made it perfectly plain to everyone that the one and only priority was evacuation. Abstract talk of defence lines and recaptured territory was akin to science fiction. And even if the thousands of leaderless men now swarming through the port town and on to the beaches were ready to launch such an attack, what would they do it with? Many had nothing but their Lee Enfield rifles. There were some other guns, but much equipment had already been discarded on the road back.

Adding to the disorientation – and it is something that takes an effort of imagination to visualise – the men, and to a very large extent their officers, had no access to communications equipment. There was virtually nothing in the way of radios and certainly no telephones, except at the makeshift headquarters at La Panne. Place yourself, for a moment, in the frayed, worn boots of a soldier who has made his way to the town harbour, milling with countless others, looking towards the mole, that jetty jutting out some half mile into the deeper waters, the view becoming obscured every now and then by the thick black smoke gushing from the town's bombed oil tanks. So many men, simply staring out to sea, wondering if, never mind when, the boats would materialise. There would have been nothing even in the way of rumour: how could there be in the midst of that crackling, scorching chaos?

Not that all the soldiers were inert; far from it. Even without an arsenal of weapons, there were ideas for at least holding off the enemy. There was a notion of getting kites aloft; these would in some way make life more difficult for incoming German bombers. But even with a number of kites extemporised from army kit and other material, the soldiers were thwarted by something beyond their control: the fine weather. In that breezeless air, kites – even if they had been of the slightest use – could not be launched.

Ferocious and brave rearguard actions were also being fought, notably by the 51st Highland Division, which as the German assault went on took up a line just south of the River Somme. Even as the general order to retreat to Dunkirk spread, these were among the soldiers who were doing their best to prevent the Germans from swallowing the Allies whole. They were also among those who would not get out via Dunkirk; their ordeal was to prove even more protracted and harrowing.

For Vic Viner, patrolling his stretch of beach, there was an element of the surreal about the evacuation. Here he was, a young sailor freshly landed on this alien strand, and being told that he was to be in charge of an entire column of men, keeping the peace as the enemy flew over. Mr Viner recalls the moment of dizzying realisation when he and his fellows – who had washed away the blood they had been sweating while rowing – disembarked on to the sands. They were handed revolvers. His lieutenant told him: 'The signal's come from the Vice-Admiral at Dover: You're to get order out of chaos.' They were to organise the soldiers into columns and make sure that those columns kept going. The lieutenant added: 'You're probably wondering why you've got the revolver. Well, the revolver is for anyone who tries to jump the queue. Or if anyone causes any other kind of problem, you're to draw your revolver and shoot them. That's the order that's come from High Command.'

The weight of it seems scarcely believable now; in an already fissile situation, the idea that a young fellow with a revolver would not only have the power to open fire on his own side at will, but would also have to make the quicksilver decision to do so, based on an effort to get ahead in a queue, is illustrative of the greater crisis. This was a world that rationality had already fled; for one young man to keep order might be conceivable for an hour, several hours. But at night? Among men who were already beginning to suffer from sleep deprivation, with all the consequent dissolution of quiet reason that that brings?

'I had to draw the revolver three times,' says Mr Viner. 'But I never did fire because the fella was just . . . It was an awesome responsibility. And I suppose – well, there must have been just a few casualties when our colleagues in the other columns had to draw their revolvers. So there we were, on the beach. That's when the bombers came to dive-bomb it.' Another young naval operative sent to try and keep order was Victor Chanter, who recalled: 'We commenced organising orderly queues, lines of soldiers for embarkation into small rowing boats and floats; lines which often dispersed quickly into the dunes behind the beach with the arrival of bombs and bursts of machine gun fire from German aircraft strafing the sands.'[2]

By now, it had become abundantly clear that a queue almost half a mile in length along the concrete and wooden mole was too slow a means of getting men on board ship. On top of this, the jetty was painfully vulnerable to German bombs; it had already taken a direct hit. 'So they got some planks as best they could to patch it up,' says former sea cadet Reg Vine. There had to be another method of getting the men safely off to sea. And this is where the little ships found their finest purpose. 'The bigger ships would lay out in the Channel, just offshore, and the little ships would take them. Some of the little ships – which were rather large – did the trips to Dover and came back again. Some went to Ramsgate. All those little ships – well,' says Vic Viner with feeling, 'there were very few that were manned by the owners of the ships. They were all manned by naval personnel. This is something we veterans get so cross about . . .' The idea that the boats were mostly manned by their owners, later a staple of popular depictions, is sometimes referred to as the myth of Dunkirk. In fact, says Mr Viner warmly, 'It was naval personnel doing the job.

'Back on the beach, I looked after three columns going out.' That is, three columns of men, with fifty in each column. Along with the practical concerns of food and water, Mr Viner found there were disconcertingly macabre moments. As well as the corpses in the surf, 'there were men in the water, just standing quite still, the water up to their neck.' And so it was that he tried to settle in, to find a point of stability. Over the course of the following few days, life on that beach would become progressively more harrowing.

For RAF signals operative Arthur Taylor, there was one other pressing element of jeopardy as he made his way into Dunkirk. It remained essential that no one discover that he was in the RAF. For, all around him, he could hear the chorus of bitterness, growing louder and more rancorous, about the failure of the RAF to take on the German bombers. There was a real sense, he recalls, that if his true status were known, he would have been beaten up, or worse. And so it was that even under that hot May sun, he resolutely held around him the long coat given to him by a sympathetic officer, and continued to tramp along in a pair of ill-fitting wellington boots.

'So I had the coat, the helmet and the officer's briefcase with all his maps in,' says Mr Taylor. 'And a rifle.' Plus, it seems, the comradeship of a dozen or so soldiers from other regiments, all heading in the one direction.

'In the meantime, we'd had no food or water.' As soon as they reached the smoky town, they somehow found a café that would open its doors to them. 'I marched in and said to the girl behind the bar, "Can you fill my water bottle with some water, please?" And she said "No, there's no water in Dunkirk – the Germans have blown up all the water-works. So there is no water – but if you give me your bottle, I'll fill it with vin rouge." So we all had red wine to take with us.

'And then,' Mr Taylor continues, 'we got to the edge of the beach and there was an officer or beach master – it might even have been Vic Viner – and he was telling us where to go. You had the option of going left or going right once you got to the beach. Turn right, you went to La Panne, where all the sandbanks were. Turn left, and that would get you to the queue to the East Mole.

'The queue was miles long. It took me thirty-six hours to get from the back of the queue to the front. And the queue was dive-bombed and shelled all day long. When the bombers came diving in, you spread out from there right to the edge of the water, so the target was wider and you were less likely to get shot or killed or bombed. And afterwards, you would look behind to see where the shells had landed and who had been killed. Or who in front of you had been killed. You were just lucky. If you got out of your place in the queue, then you had to go to the back.

'We had no water and no food – so we didn't want the toilet. You took sips of the red wine, to keep you going. Sleep: didn't have any. You couldn't. If you'd stepped out and lain down, they would just have walked past you. Plenty of energy though. I was only nineteen years of age.' Not that the thirty-six hours Mr Taylor waited, in that immensely long queue stretching from the sandy beach to the end of that rackety jetty, before evacuation were in any way so straightforward.

One soldier who turned right for the sands of La Panne was Bob

Halliday. The lack of food and drink swiftly became intolerable after such a long march. Despite the danger that he and his friend would lose their places in the columns they had joined, they thought they'd do something about it. 'So I was out scavenging with my pal – exploring broken down lorries near the town – seeing if we could get some food,' says Mr Halliday. 'Then there were three high flying aircraft, heavy bombers, which we assumed were ours. The bomber dropped a stick of bombs. And it lifted my friend and I across the road and we ended up in an open-fronted garage. Against the wall.'

There was a moment of blackness, and then Mr Halliday was able to open his eyes. 'I looked up and I could see . . . well, my friend was all right too.' Mr Halliday was perturbed by the persistent sense that his ear was not quite right, although he neglected to have a medical until some years later. 'So we made our way back, a bit shaken,' he says, smiling. 'Didn't find any food, and made our way back to the beaches, only to find that we were put to the back of the queue again because we had broken lines.'

All the while, the destroyers, the paddle steamers and the long flat-bottomed skoots were trying to load as many men on as possible. Jim Cockfield, with the 50th Northumbrian Division, had been among those who had just marched into Belgium when the Allies were forced into retreat. A footsore journey of some days had seen him and his friends pitch up on the beaches at La Panne, but they did some exploring a little further afield and found themselves a small rowing boat. Obviously their intention was not to row right across the Channel (though there were instances, a little later, when men made such declarations). They had seen, in the distance, a variety of different boats. Their simple idea was to make for one of those. They pointed themselves in the direction of one of the larger ships but it soon became apparent that their own craft was structurally unsound.

They swivelled a bit and came within view of a paddle steamer, the *Gracie Fields*. She had already performed sterling work; on a previous trip she had picked up 281 men and delivered them safely to Dover. And as Jim Cockfield's rowing boat drew up, the crew helped them aboard. A grateful Mr Cockfield went below deck to find the engine room, a handy place to dry out his sopping clothing. But a little later, there was a terrific explosion. The boat had been hit. It was the engine room that had taken the bomb. Mr Cockfield was unscathed; a few other men were not. As he recalled, there was steam everywhere. The steamer was now sailing round and round in circles, its rudder irreparably damaged – this at a time when there were 750 other soldiers on board. The *Gracie* was clearly going nowhere. Fortunately there were two skoots in the vicinity, and as the larger boat circled, the men were taken off and thence across the Channel in the more basic craft.

One of the skoots came back for the *Gracie Fields*; there was a chance that she might be towed and repaired. But the going was agonisingly slow; that night, under the moonlight and on the calm riffling waves, the paddle steamer began to fill with water. Captain Larkin – who had sailed her through peace and war – was taken off and the boat went down. But, thanks to J.B. Priestley, the *Gracie Fields* was later to acquire a form of immortality.

Another venerable pleasure craft, the *Medway Queen*, faced an unusual nocturnal hazard. On those warm spring nights, the sea was glittering with phosphorescence. As Sub-Lieutenant Graves, a member of the boat's crew, recalled of those night-time evacuations: 'Our paddles left broad twin wakes, and on two occasions German aircraft followed those wakes until their end and dropped bombs uncomfortably close. We were nothing if not resourceful about "The Medway Queen" and devised oil bags which were lowered over the bow . . . to break the force of heavy waves. This was most successful, our brilliant wakes disappeared.' But the boat threw up a new hazard – bright sparks streaming from the funnel like fireworks, caused by soot catching flame. As the boat sailed back into Dunkirk – the town itself bright and burning at night – there was what Graves described as a 'tragi-comic' scene, with buckets being passed from man to man to tip down the funnel to try and extinguish the blaze.

This in turn prompted a furious response from one man working in the engine room, who proclaimed: 'I do not intend to be f . . . king well drowned on the job!'[3]

The soldiers on that long jetty, in that wearyingly long queue, the flames of the town behind their back colouring the night sky, the ever-present German bombers flying overhead; there was little room for wider speculation. The immediate aim – to sit, to stand and wait, and keep a hold of one's nerve – was all-encompassing. How much was there, though, in terms of thinking of defeat? Veterans now say that in the midst of the hunger and confusion, watching men pile into the smaller boats or make the jump from the end of the jetty on to moving destroyers, there was little chance for anyone to focus on such ideas. Early on the following day, however, the news travelled down the line that the Belgian army had surrendered to the Germans. Everyone from Churchill and the War Cabinet to Admiral Ramsay, and indeed all those back home who were following events through the opaque announcements of newsreaders, now understood that the British army was on the brink of outright catastrophe.

10

'The Hour Is Too Solemn'

28 May 1940

For an invading land army, the line between aggression and brutality must always be dangerously thin; for any commanding officer, the job is to hold in check the triumphalist violence of his fighting men. And in 1940, the international conventions and rules attached to warfare that we know now were already in existence. The second of the Geneva Conventions, concerning the treatment of prisoners of war, had been ratified in 1929. Such prisoners were entitled to be treated with honour and respect. These things were understood very well, by the Allies and the Germans alike.

Yet out there in the field, after days of battle and bombardment, bloodlust was not so easily cooled. And in France, there were instances when, for no seemingly rational reason, German soldiers were impelled towards acts of savagery. Whether it was because these soldiers had been steeped in sadism in Poland – blooded, as it were – or whether it was a case of deliberate indoctrination, some German soldiers seemed to have become simply psychotic. One of the most notorious of these incidents is the Wormhoudt massacre of 28 May 1940, carried out by men of the Waffen SS. Strategically purposeless and brutal, it was indicative of a certain kind of insanity.

For all the British and French soldiers making their way to Dunkirk, there were also large numbers of troops attempting – with considerable bravery – to keep their escape routes open, and to hold off any further German advances. On the Wormhoudt road, a few miles south of Dunkirk, were men from the Royal Artillery, the 4th Battalion Cheshire Regiment and the 2nd Battalion Royal Warwickshire Regiment. Ammunition was running low, and the German forces were circling. Eventually – inevitably – despite efforts to obtain extra ammunition, they were overrun, their bullets spent, their position indefensible. They were disarmed, taken prisoner; obviously no one would have expected delicate treatment at the hands of the enemy.

But almost immediately, the conduct of their captors became unexpectedly homicidal. One soldier, wounded and unconscious, was simply shot through the head. Then, as the prisoners were ordered to march along the road, some men noticed other Germans from the same unit outside a small factory, with men lined up to be shot one by one. There seemed to be no frenzy about this; rather, there was something terrifyingly methodical about it. On the march were men with injuries of varying seriousness. Those who could not keep up with the pace were shot as they walked. There could have been little doubt in the minds of the other prisoners what these Germans intended for them. At gunpoint, and weaponless, there was nothing they could do.

Outside Wormhoudt, the captured company reached a simple wooden barn, not very large. One British officer, Captain Lynn-Allen, made a vehement and spirited protest to a German officer about the earlier shootings and the lack of consideration shown to the other wounded men. This earned him a screaming tirade of rage and abuse; then he and around 100 other prisoners – whether injured or not – were ordered by the Germans to walk into that small barn. Almost instantly, German soldiers threw stick grenades into the barn. There were shattered limbs, eviscerations, instant deaths; more grenades were thrown in, and astounding courage was shown by two Royal Warwickshire men – Sergeant-Major Augustus Jennings and Sergeant Moore – who threw the weight of their own bodies on top of the grenades before they detonated, absorbing the blast and protecting their comrades. Captain Lynn-Allen and one other soldier managed to escape as the Germans were taking cover from the explosions. But before Lynn-Allen could get any distance, he was shot in the head. After the blasts in the barn came machine gun fire to finish them off. Extraordinarily, a handful of men survived; some had been shot, though not fatally, and having lost consciousness were taken for dead.

The grimness of this episode remains intense; what is worse, perhaps, the British soldiers might not have been very surprised. During the Great War, each side had portrayed the other in demonic terms; and there were episodes on both sides of prisoners being murdered. From the point of view of young British soldiers in 1940, was this not exactly the sort of evil that one would expect from the Germans? The effect of such notions was to reinforce for all those other thousands of men picking their way towards the coast the desire not to be captured, for they were facing an enemy that could not be trusted to play by the rules. The flight to the sea was without exaggeration a matter of life or death.

None of these details were conveyed to the public back home. Indeed, the story of the Wormhoudt massacre took some years to emerge. The news in Britain on 28 May was dominated by that stunning body blow to the entire BEF: the capitulation of Belgium. Churchill's War Cabinet had met nine times that Sunday; the news of King Leopold's surrender added a new razor edge of stress. Talk around the Cabinet table was of the British 'making terms'; some would say the correct term was 'surrender'. Foreign Secretary Lord Halifax was of the view that a 'mediated peace' was desirable – that Benito Mussolini (Italy was still several weeks from joining the war) could be a diplomatic go-between; that the Third Reich and the British Empire could find a means of coexisting – even if it was also understood that such an approach would be a 'considerable gamble'. Churchill was horrified at the idea. He stated passionately that he 'thought the chance of decent terms being offered to us at the present time were a thousand to one against'. He then met other Cabinet members outside the inner circle. Hugh Dalton committed Churchill's extraordinary oration to his diaries:

> It is idle to think that if we tried to make peace now we should get better terms from Germany than if we went on and fought it out. The Germans would demand our fleet – that would be called 'disarmament' – our naval bases and much else. We should become a slave state though a British government which would be Hitler's puppet would be set up – under Mosley or some such person. And where should we be at the end of all that? On the other side, we have immense resources and advantages. Therefore, we shall go on and we shall fight it out, here or elsewhere, and if this long island story of ours is to end at last, let it end only when each of us lies choking in his own blood upon the ground.[1]

Yet that same day there was also evident a certain native genius among British politicians for getting snarled up in comically minor issues. In Parliament, a row took place about the BBC's output – a couple of MPs arguing that its vulgar entertainments and comedies were a disgrace at a time when the nation needed the moral uplift of great classical music. Another MP was bracingly rude about the Information Ministry's Harold Nicolson, and his 'fireside chat' approach to radio, regarded as patronising. Nicolson's superior, Duff Cooper was – when he made his own broadcast about the news of Belgium that day – sepulchral by comparison (although still inclined to a bizarre conversational style).

'I told you when I was talking to you a week ago of the danger in which our Army stood,' Cooper told the nation's listeners. 'That danger is very great tonight. At the same time, I said as strongly as I could that whatever the fortunes of war, even if the Allies lost this battle, we should not have lost the war. Final victory will still be ours. Well, we have not lost the war tonight, and assuredly we will not lose it.

'We can all remember the dark days of the last war,' he continued. 'The retreat from Mons when day after day our weary forces staggered down the roads of France with the German army pressing on their heels.' This image of retreat might not have been quite as helpful as he intended. 'The Belgian army are unable any longer to continue,' he went on. 'They have fought very bravely, they have suffered very heavily . . . this is no time for criticism or recrimination.' In fact, he continued, recrimination would now form part of the German master-plan – to turn ally against ally. What everyone now had to beware was the French turning against the British, and vice versa – not just out in the field, among soldiers, but also down at the pub after work. 'If anybody says to you "The French have let us down," proclaimed Cooper, 'you ought to reply: "Either you are a paid agent of Germany or else you are an unpaid one doing German propaganda for nothing. In either case, your mouth should be shut and silenced, because you are an enemy, and a most dangerous enemy to the Allied cause."'

There was a note of hysteria in Cooper's ringing phrases; even with civilians carefully checking themselves and others for signs that their words or deeds were damaging to morale, it is difficult to find saloon bars where those words were employed against those inclined to be rude about the French. But then perhaps it was intended as misdirection; for at the end of the broadcast came a chilling admission of the truth. 'The enemy has succeeded in forcing their way through the lines of the Allies,' said Cooper, 'and they have reached the sea . . . it will be necessary to do our utmost to withdraw the army.' But, he declared in conclusion, 'it will be an army whose courage is still high and whose confidence is still unshaken and where every man is still burning with desire to meet the enemy in combat.'

Every man? In Huddersfield, an MO diarist took the bus home in the late afternoon and witnessed 'a strapping young man . . . swaying drunk. When he got off, a man said: "Ten to one he's been called up – I don't blame him."'

Women were needed too. Advertisements placed that day in newspapers and magazines conveyed the urgency without too many giveaway details: 'An appeal is made for trained nurses to deal with Service casualties from France and Belgium who are being received in increasing numbers in emergency medical service hospitals which must also be prepared for air-raid casualties in this country.' To a generation that had grown accustomed to the continual sight of terribly wounded men in the streets, this would have had a chilling resonance. 'All trained nurses who are not already nursing in hospitals,' continued the ads, '[are asked] to offer their services at once. They are required for whole-time work in any hospital in Great Britain. £90 a year for trained nurses, £55 a year for assistant nurses, including board, lodging and laundry.' Incidentally, £90 then would be worth around £4000 today; £55 would be £2500.

Also being recruited were volunteers for the Women's Auxiliary Air Force (WAAF). They were 'required immediately for enrolment and training', said the adverts. And the types of position they were wanted for? Cooks; mess and kitchen staff; balloon fabric workers; teleprinter operators. Save for the last option, many women found there was not a great deal there that seemed particularly engaging. Which is why so many made the effort to learn the basics of Morse code; among some, the Wrens were the service to get into. The work (which included radio interception) was much more interesting. As a result of such preparations, it was now clear to all just how close to home the war had come. The plight of the trapped troops was one thing: the prospect that within weeks, the Nazis would be overrunning British towns all the sharper.

Many nurses found themselves working in circumstances that they had not imagined. 'At the start of the war, I was in the Queen Alexandra's Imperial Military Nursing Services Reserve,' recalled Josephine Mary Kenny SRN, 'and was drafted to the *St Julian,* a Weymouth–Guernsey ferry converted to a hospital ship. After a few weeks in Netley Hospital preparing, we were off collecting sick from French ports to hospitals in England. Then came Dunkirk!'

At first, the prospect, although daunting, did at least offer the comfort that she was on a clearly marked hospital ship; and surely the enemy would not attack such a vessel? 'It was a beautiful day, calm sea and hot sunshine, perfect for a cruise,' Mrs Kenny remembered. 'It was the birthday of Elspeth Abercrombie, my sister-in-charge so, with all the preparations completed, she and I sat on deck with some knitting.' This incongruously peaceful tableau was soon disrupted:

> Hearing a plane we looked up, preparing to wave, it was very low and heading straight for us. We saw the bomb doors open and two bombs fall out. We moved fast for the companion way just as the wireless officer's door flew open. It hit me on the side of the head and broke my spectacles causing a small cut near my eye. It bled of course and I arrived below deck, where four doctors and five nurses converged on me. I had the dubious distinction of being the only (if minor) casualty on board. How long the noise and terror lasted I do not remember but the plane circled round until it had dropped all its bombs. The *St Julian* was painted white with large red crosses on it and we hadn't even a catapult on board. So much for the Geneva Convention.[2]

After this outrage came the first batch of evacuated wounded. It required a particular kind of unflinching determination – in the face of what seemed like a non-stop attack from the air – to get wounded stretcher cases along the lengthy jetty and comfortably on board; a time-consuming and careful procedure. Josephine Kenny recalled the 'elation' as they successfully embarked a ship full of wounded men and sailed them back to Dover; equally she remembered the desolation when – thanks to fluctuating tides – the boat couldn't make contact with the mole, and they were forced to leave the injured where they were.

According to the Queen Alexandra's Royal Naval Nursing Service, this kind of care at sea was highly specialised. Because of the threat of bombs and torpedoes, and the possibility that their boat might sink, nurses would frequently wear bathing suits beneath their uniforms. There were patient survival tips that they had to learn: for instance, if a man had a wooden splint on his leg, it would have to be removed before he was evacuated into the water – otherwise the wood would float and the patient might be tipped head downwards into the water by it. Another (anonymous) nurse remembered vividly the ordeal of Dunkirk harbour:

> We sailed at 5.30 a.m. and arrived at Dunkirk at 8.50 a.m. We moored alongside the north east side of the Breakwater Mole. The quay was broken and on fire in places; the patients were embarked with no gangway, just lifted over the ship's side. The ship's officers and crew, stewards and RAMC personnel all acted as stretcher bearers and carried the patients up the length of the quay under machine gun fire from the air. The Naval Officer in charge on shore was so calm that one literally did not realise the aerial battle that was going on all the time. The quiet, when the firing ceased, was more noticeable than the continuous noise had been.

After the maelstrom, there was then the business of sailing back to Dover safely, negotiating a labyrinth of sea-mines, being swooped on by more machine gunners:

> We put the patients to bed as far as possible, and then made up beds on the floor. We did the dressings, which of course had not been done for a long time, and made them comfortable, and fed them. Then they slept all the way back. They were a little shaken by some bombs that narrowly missed us as we were leaving Dunkirk but they soon settled down.[3]

The fear was one thing (and a few of the patients on board such hospital ships were suffering from shell shock). But for the nurses, there was also the question of dealing with untreated wounds on board a ship that was always in motion, sometimes violently. This was more a matter of experience than constitution. The same was true of the haunting silence of so many of the men. One veteran recalled 'eyes filled with tears and gratitude, others with no "eyes" at all. While many without arms, legs and other parts of their faces and bodies, lay motionless, staring from behind their bandages.'

A variety of weapons of destruction were let loose upon the paddle steamers and the hospital ships. Particularly insidious was the acoustic mine – a submerged device that would let one or two vessels pass over it, but explode when it detected the vibrations of a third. Over the course of the next few days, the hazards that the hospital ships faced were to increase sharply; so much so that the bosun of the *Paris*, which before Dunkirk had successfully evacuated hundreds of wounded from Calais and Dieppe, had a premonition that the boat's luck was about to run out. On 2 June, and in spite of the vast and very clearly visible red crosses painted on to the sides of the vessel, denoting its status as a hospital ship, the *Paris* was bombed by Stukas and sunk. Survivors in the water had to be rescued by tug boats.

Former Teddington sea cadet Reg Vine saw both moments of comic incongruity and a stark horror that no one could have prepared him sufficiently for. Of the moment when he received the news in Teddington that they were to move down the Thames, Mr Vine says:

'There was a sub-lieutenant who simply told us: "We're going to the seaside." I said: "That's a nice trip."' The sub-lieutenant told him: 'We understand they need some boats over at Dunkirk,' to which Vine replied: 'Yeah, fine, when is this?'

'Tomorrow,' said the sub-lieutenant.

The sub-lieutenant continued: 'You'll have to get your parents' OK' As Vine recalls: 'Well, my dad would sign anything . . . We got aboard, left from Eel Pie Island (near Richmond) and we went down river with the rest of them – they used steamers, Thames launches, river boats. We all followed down to Ramsgate.' The sub-lieutenant said to him: 'Now don't come up on deck, stay down below.' Vine said: 'I'm all right, I've got my brother's HMS badge to put on my sea cadet's hat.' In those days, he explains, 'every ship was HMS. I kept down below. He came back. He said, "I've booked you in so we're all right, there's four of us and they'll put two navy men with us when we get down to the meeting points."

'So we got down there,' continues Mr Vine, 'and he said to me: "Here's your gun." We were being given five rounds for a .303 rifle. That's handy, I thought. "What's this for?" I said. "You'll be surprised," he said. I bloody was surprised.'

Possibly Mr Vine's commanding officer was surprised too as they put out from Ramsgate across the open sea – though at first the voyage was preternaturally quiet: 'Lovely weather when we sailed from Ramsgate. Early evening. We went out there and got there before dark. Couldn't hear a thing at first and that was surprising because it wasn't all that far away.' Then suddenly the deafening roar was upon them. 'You've got Stukas, machine guns and we're supposed to put them down with rifles,' says Mr Vine now, with some incredulity.

What followed next was a swift induction into the charnel reality of war. 'We had just been told we were evacuating some troops. That was all. Just evacuation of British troops. I was told on the way there, "You look after one lifeboat when you get there and Paddy will look after the other one." Right-o, I thought: lifeboats. When we got near the coast and you could hear the banging and the crashing and the screaming and hollering and god knows what – bodies and bits floating in the sea – well, I was as sick as a bloody dog. I couldn't help it.

'When I was a kid, I had been taken to a slaughterhouse by an uncle who showed me the killed pigs and bullocks and cut them all up. I saw bits and pieces like that. So now our captain said to me: "Just pretend you are back in your uncle's shop. And they're animals. They're not human beings. And they might unsettle your stomach so have a drop of this."'

Rowing their way through the occasional impact of a corpse's arm or torso, Mr Vine and his crewmates were able to make land near La Panne to begin the work of evacuation. 'We were collecting ammunition because the blokes' bits and pieces were lying on the sands,' he says. Mr Vine, in his youthful hotheadedness, tried to find German targets to aim for, including the planes screaming by above. His sub-lieutenant tried to calm him down. 'He said, don't shoot any more, because if you shoot, [the Germans] know who to have a go at. We were the other side of the mole. What was left of Dunkirk – hospitals, hospital ships . . . It was no good me firing – so I slung the rifle in the bloody sea because there were plenty of them floating about.'

In the space of two days, this sixteen-year-old had travelled from the willow-fringed peace of the Home Counties Thames to a screaming bloody pandemonium that blocked out any thoughts other than the immediate prospects in front of him. With the soldiers abandoning their weapons, Mr Vine and his naval comrades were now getting them through the shallow waters, trudging across the sandy seabed and on board the various boats that could at last swing round and take them back to Britain. There were the lifeboats, which Mr Vine was helping to row: 'We had two lifeboats towing and we could practically get up onto the shore.' But there were outbreaks of (perfectly understandable) impatience from the soldiers that this teenager was hoping to direct. 'What got me,' says

Mr Vine, 'was the fighting between the Belgians, the French and the British about who got on our boats.' Such men were inadvertently overloading the boats, and communication difficulties between the various nationalities exacerbated the frantic ill-will. 'I said to them, if you put twenty or thirty in this lifeboat, we'll never get off because we'll sink lower and lower. They understood.' And so a few men had to walk out into the water up to their waists before getting in.

That was fine; but Mr Vine claims to have witnessed rather uglier scenes – an effort by French and Belgian troops to ensure that they were not relegated to the back of any queue. 'They started fighting among themselves because we found that [the French] were stripping the dead bodies of our blokes, chucking their French uniforms away and dressing up as Tommy. And the Belgians too. Because our troops had priority, more or less. But they still let a certain amount of French in. But then there were British men saying to them, you should stay here and fight for your country – that's another thing that started the arguments.'

In the midst of the visceral confusion, it is astounding to hear some stories of how – even in the field – the most horribly injured soldiers somehow got proper medical attention. 'Old sweat' Harry Malpas, who had run away to join the army as a boy in the mid-1930s, was among those who had been near the front line when the German offensive began. He endured a harrowing few days of pursuit and hiding across the flat country. He and his Royal Warwickshire comrades knew that the destination was Dunkirk. But getting there looked impossible; every direction they moved in across country, they found themselves being intercepted by Germans. There were days and nights spent in narrow ditches, and in sewer pipes.

At one point, says Harry's widow Jean, he and his men found themselves in open country seemingly surrounded by the enemy. 'He couldn't see the field for German tanks everywhere. He said he and his comrades had to wait until it all went quiet – then they tried to make their way back to Dunkirk. But then they met this officer.

The officer asked the men who they were. Royal Warwicks, they said.' According to the officer, as far as he knew, all the other Royal Warwickshires had long managed to get to the coast. But while he had these men here, he would use them as a line of defence to try and slow up the enemy. Some others refused but Harry Malpas agreed to man a machine gun post. 'And he was on that machine post when he got his knee shot out,' says his widow. 'They blew the post up. He didn't remember what happened. But the other two with him were killed. And, he said, the next thing he was lying in the road and when he came to, he could hear a noise. German tanks were coming down the road. So he rolled in a doorway to get out of the way.'

Malpas must have been in extraordinary pain, his kneecap shot out and losing blood. But, says his widow, once he had come to, his recollections had a raw vividness. 'He said this big German soldier, must have been six foot odd, stopped the tank, got off it – and then picked him up, gave him a cigarette and threw him on the tank with their German wounded. And took him to a field hospital. He didn't know where.'

Clearly, Malpas was in no position to protest; he couldn't walk, let alone run. What happened next left him bewildered for the rest of his long life. 'They did his knee,' says Mrs Malpas. 'And that knee lasted from 1940 to 1990. They did a marvellous job. Well,' she adds, 'the Germans are good at engineering. Marvellous. The knee implant was a metal bar and it had hooks on. And Harry could run, walk, play football, do anything.'

More than that, the German doctor's handiwork became a wider source of wonder. 'He had to have it redone in 1990 because where it was joining the bones, it was wearing the bones away,' says Mrs Malpas. 'In 1990, Harry went to Bournemouth hospital. The surgeon looked at the knee on the X-ray and said "What's that? I've never seen anything like it." He wanted to know where he had it done, so Harry told him.'

'I must say,' the surgeon said, 'that the man who did this knee was a man before his time. Because it's a marvellous job.' The surgeon then said, 'Do you want it?' Harry didn't, so the doctor kept it to show it to students.

'Just think,' adds Mrs Malpas. 'A field hospital in 1940 too – a patch-up, not even the main facilities. And Harry was a British soldier. But to a doctor, you are just a body.' Of course, once the operation had been successfully carried out, the elation soon wore off; Harry Malpas – like some 50,000 others – was now a prisoner of war. 'They put him on a barge and sent him to Llansdorf, the main PoW camp,' says Mrs Malpas. But that was only the first step on a journey that would take Harry deep into Poland and a nightmarish life in the mines.

Back in Britain, at the time that Harry Malpas was wounded and captured, the absence of detailed news meant that distractions were still being entertained. There was the continuing row over football, and whether it was appropriate in a time of national emergency for this and horse racing to continue. But A.B. Clements, the editor of *The Sporting Life* newspaper – which carried daily horse-racing tips – was passionate. Those who would ban fixtures, he wrote, gave

> little thought for the conditions under which the masses of workers live. There is an enormous number of people in our industrial areas who cannot dig for victory, for they have no plot . . . and for whom 'talking it over at the pub' may not be all-sufficing. They may work 12 hours a day, seven days a week, but they still need relaxation besides sleep . . . it is conceivable that most working men could appreciate more refined enjoyments, but they must get their entertainment where they can . . . and for these, the football pools and the study of the day's racing programme are never failing tonics.

Clements in his anti-snobbery plea was on to something; for there was very little complaint about more middle-class pursuits. As the Dunkirk evacuation got under way, London's concert halls were still staging full programmes of classical music recitals; the Royal Academy in Piccadilly was pressing ahead with its annual Summer Exhibition. Nor had the dance craze abated; advertising her services as a tutor on 28 May in *The Times* was Margaret Clutterbuck of Marylebone. And as Clements averred, why not?

On the other side of the Channel, the bleak and increasingly obvious prospect was that there was a limit to the number of people who could be evacuated. And this meant that the wounded and unwounded soldiers obviously crowded out the ever-increasing numbers of civilian refugees who were arriving at the northern French coast. The boats could not have taken vast numbers of them, both for reasons of space and also to prevent almost intolerable chaos from descending yet further; for if it became widely known that there was safe transport to Britain, Dunkirk and the beaches might well be completely overrun. On top of this – and it may be that Reg Vine's memories count as a shocking exception – there was by and large no discrimination between British, French and Belgian troops. It was the uniform that counted; these were the men that were needed.

Coming face to face with these traumatised walking ghosts, recalled ship's cook Thomas Russell, was oddly haunting. Russell was on board one of the paddle steamers, working below decks to ensure that the men rescued from the mole would get at least some sustenance after what might have been days without food. He was concocting stew and dishing it out to sallow, silent men in an apparently endless progression. But keeping himself going, with the echoing thumps and metallic crashes from above, was something of an effort in itself. 'I swayed on sore feet, my head ached abominably, and my body was wracked with fatigue as up until then I had had no sleep for 72 hours,' Russell wrote. Then came a moment of eerie starkness:

> It was 4am – the end of a bandage was dipping in the mess tin which was held out to me, but I was unable to stop my robot-like dip-and-pour rhythm in time to avoid emptying a ladle of stew over it. Curiosity made me look up. The soldier was wounded in the head, his young face pinched and white under the blood-soaked field dressing . . . Our eyes met as, reaching out, he . . . heartily sucked the gravy from the end of [the bandage] before tucking it back into place. It was a savage gesture and I wondered when he had eaten last. He grinned at me as though it hurt his lips to stretch them.[4]

On another paddle steamer, the catering was similarly informal: while stew was once again on the menu, a great many of the men did not have mess tins. Some barely had their uniforms, having waded out into the waters while waiting for smaller boats to come. So in this case improvisation was necessary and the boat's previous incarnation as a pleasure cruiser came into its own: the stew was served to the men in pretty cocktail glasses.

There were other scenes of comparable absurdity. Some evacuees recollected the cheering incongruity, amidst the smoke and the constant bombing, of seeing naval commanders in almost supernaturally pristine white uniforms; or of senior army officers upbraiding young soldiers waiting silently on the mole for having long, untidy hair and beards. For other sailors and soldiers, though, there were no such glimmers of levity. A boat called *Bullfinch* drew up alongside the mole deep into the night with German planes howling down from the skies; the men on the jetty, and the sailors on the boats, were in no position to respond. It was psychological, as well as purely physical, terrorism. The soldiers climbed down a vertical ladder on to the boat and were thence directed into the unlit hold. Numbers of them continued to descend into that unfathomable blackness until finally the sailors could see dimly that the embarked soldiers were standing pressed shoulder to shoulder with barely any room to turn. At around 11 p.m., it was time to slip the moorings and the boat turned and made its way out to sea. The soldiers in the hold had no real idea of their destination, nor of how long it would take to reach it. All they had, after all that time in Dunkirk, was the darkness and the sound of the ship's engines. But just a few short minutes into the voyage, there was a series of vast explosions.

The soldiers down below understood that they were beneath the waterline; but there was no choice but to continue to stand in that impenetrable darkness, shoulder to shoulder. The captain sent word down via the younger sailors that the German bombers were following the ship's wake as it twinkled in the moonlight – the reasoning being that it was better for them to know something than nothing. Then, after a few minutes, the engines died, and the soldiers were standing in silence as well as in pitch blackness. They felt the faint movement of the sea and heard the deep thrumming of other passing boats. Again, the captain ensured that these men were told that they had problems with the engines, and that they simply had to stay where they were. Eventually, the problem was fixed, and the *Bullfinch* once more pushed forward.

Some hours later, under a silver dawn, the soldiers emerged from the hold, screwing their eyes up to see the port of Ramsgate. As they disembarked, they looked with disbelief around them at the friendly faces of the townsfolk who had come to help out with sandwiches and tea; the townsfolk, meanwhile, gazed with shock at the apparitions that shambled down that gangplank.

For some, the entire period from the surrender of the Belgians onward had a deeply hallucinatory quality; the bad dream in which your enemy will just not stop coming. Ernie Holden, conscripted into the Royal Artillery in 1939 as a twenty-year-old, had spent a rather pleasant few months on the border of France and Belgium. He and his comrades had been accepted into the local community – which Mr Holden compared to an English northern town in spirit – with great warmth. The suddenness of the German attack had awakened atavistic fears in the middle-aged villagers; the last devastation had of course been less than twenty-five years previously. The young soldiers, recalled Mr Holden, were simply blank with uncertainty. Rounded up by the officers, with no idea what to expect, they were first driven into Belgium, intended links in a line of defence, and then told just as quickly that they were now to retreat to Dunkirk. Mr Holden's journey back out of Belgium and into northern France seemed to him to take place in a trance: empty villages, deserted cottages, half-eaten meals, cows vast and bloated for want of milking. The dead lying on straw bales.

Then into Dunkirk, just as the evacuation was under way. Mr Holden recalled, dazed, walking through a town where flames spat through the cracks in the pavement; the power supplies were being blown out. He recalled being attracted to once-handsome hotels by noises within, and finding basements filled with drunken soldiers. Mr Holden himself was inexpressibly weary; like medic Charles Searle, Mr Holden had a supply of sugar lumps. But that was it. He made his way slowly to the beaches, where he found the spectacle of thousands of men in the dunes; then he decided to take his chances on the mole.

There were visible outbreaks of tension, he recalled, as he arrived there at twilight. If anyone struck a match to light a cigarette, they were fiercely shouted down: for weren't they making themselves a target for any bombers? A few Royal Marines patrolled the long straggling line, and Mr Holden soon found out why. He spotted an old friend a little further up the line and was suddenly desperate, after these strange days wandering, for a normal conversation. He stepped out of the queue and made his way forward – only to find a bayonet poking into his back. Mr Holden very quickly explained to the Marine that he was simply hoping to say hello to his mate. The Marine was implacable: back in line or the bayonet goes right through.

After what seemed to him hours, Mr Holden shuffled forward over the planks bridging the deep cavity left by an earlier bomb, and towards the large boat that had come alongside – the hospital ship *Canterbury*. He wasn't injured; but apparently he looked so terrible that he was none the less taken straight below. And from that point, he said, he fell into the deepest sleep; a sleep so profound, in fact, that he heard absolutely nothing of the bombing attack that was carried out against the ship after it drew out of Dunkirk harbour and set sail for Newhaven.

In the midst of all this, there were a few who had, by comparison, relatively tranquil experiences. Soldier Doug Dawes, who in the crowds on the beaches had gradually lost all his company, found himself alone in the dunes some distance from the harbour. He took himself down to the water's edge, gazed out at the wrecked hulls of ships partially submerged in that shallow water. He also looked out at a distant paddle steamer, and then he looked down at the waves. He noticed – and said that he only ever saw this once again – a curious phosphorescence, or twinkling, in the water, curling at the edges of the little waves. And it was at that point that he made his decision.

He removed his boots (for the first time in a week, he recalled). Then he stripped off all his other clothes and walked into the cold water. Dawes had calculated that, given the sand and the shallows, it would be possible to swim out to the paddle steamer; equally, if he got tired, it wouldn't take much to return. His effort was not entirely peaceful; bombers buzzed over, targeting the shipping, and Dawes said that he could feel the shock waves through the water after each blast. But he pressed on doggedly, apparently unconcerned; and eventually he was picked up by a large rowing boat, ferrying men to the larger vessel. Dawes recalled good-humoured jokes about his nudity; as the sailors manning the rescue boats recalled, it wasn't all that unusual. Either through choice, or through wear and tear, or simply as a result of bomb blasts, trousers had been lost on quite a wide scale. When Dawes was on board the steamer, a sailor got hold of a sack, cut two holes in the bottom corners and told him to make himself decent. He put them on, curled up on the deck and fell asleep. He was woken as the steamer sailed into Sheerness on the Thames Estuary; someone had placed an extra sack under his head to make him comfortable. He had slept for twelve hours, all the way through the voyage. Now he was safe back home.

Doug Dawes's story was unusually stress free. Nor did he seem concerned by the temperature of the water. Despite the warm spring weather, the Channel is usually shiveringly cold until July or August; even then, it is still very chilly. For soldiers who had waded out, sometimes to shoulder height, and who simply stood for hours waiting for rowing boats or little ships to sail in, the effect of the water, even in the shallows, was numbing. Soldier John Mulloy told David Knowles of his night-time wade to reach a lifeboat: 'I found the sea bitterly cold and when the water reached my stomach, I began to gasp for breath.' What was more, he added, 'I couldn't swim and was terrified of deep water.' The same was true for many of the soldiers. These were boys brought up in large inner cities, where such facilities as proper swimming pools were scarce and access to fresh-water bathing non-existent. Other veterans recalled how, on contact with the icy water, they panicked, went under, struggled ferociously, ended up doggy paddling. It was an additional psychological cruelty: the knowledge that if the Channel had instead been a bridge of dry land, it would have been possible to walk back to England in a day.

Elsewhere, one prevalent symptom among the unwounded, doctors noticed as the troops started returning, was an unusually high proportion of peptic ulcers. Possibly, they thought, this could simply be down to the terrible army food – and the subsequent lack of any food – augmented by a very heavy consumption of cigarettes. In fact, the doctors were forced to conclude that the men were suffering from 'war ulcers' brought on purely by psychological distress. In other words, the ulcers were a symptom of trauma. Many, especially in the following days, were to find that the symptoms went deeper still. The troops who were the first to return and disembark at Dover, Ramsgate and Newhaven, if not fortunate, were at least more blessed than those still left behind who, as the hours crept on, came to believe that they had been abandoned to the mercies of the Nazis.

11

'What Have We Let Ourselves In For?'

29 May 1940

'All your countrymen have been following with pride and admiration the courageous resistance of the British Expeditionary Force during the continuous fighting of the last fortnight,' read the statement from His Majesty King George VI issued on 29 May. 'Placed by circumstances outside their control in a position of extreme difficulty, they are displaying a gallantry that has never been surpassed in the annals of the British Army. The hearts of every one of us at home are with you and your magnificent troops in this hour of peril.' Lord Gort composed a suitably reassuring public reply from his makeshift HQ in France. It read: 'The Commander in Chief, with humble duty, begs leave on behalf of all ranks of the BEF, to thank your Majesty for your message. May I assure your Majesty that the Army is doing all in its power to live up to its proud tradition and is immensely encouraged at this critical moment by the words of your Majesty's telegram.'

Lord Gort's own telegram might have been counted a rare instance in those nightmarish days of a message getting through ungarbled. This was a landscape with no reliable communications or signals – little in the way of radio, practically nothing in the way of telephones – yet Lord Gort was remaining firmly in place at La Panne. His bland public message to the King was braver than it sounded. He and his subordinates had little way of judging either how close the enemy was to overrunning them, or how close to the precipice the remaining BEF – of whom there were still many thousands, exposed on those beaches – were edging. In Dover, Admiral Ramsay had issued an order placing the cruiser *Calcutta* at Lord Gort's disposal; a sure means of swift evacuation, which he might have thought would come at any second. But Lord Gort ordered that morning that the *Calcutta* should return to England with a full load of troops; he was staying put.

Any war is filled with counter-factual nexus points; and sometimes 'what-if's are far from being a parlour game because they help to bring us closer to the truly ragged, messy nature of events. Nothing is pre-ordained; there is no hand of destiny on any shoulder. And so was there the possibility, even by that stage, that the Allies might have staged a remarkable turnaround? Might they have reasoned that the Germans – stretched so far into France with their remarkable Panzer assault – had in fact overstretched themselves and were now curiously vulnerable? Just over two years later, for instance, Field Marshal Rommel – deep in the deserts of North Africa and seemingly with the British on the back foot – failed quite to see, as the British saw, that his supply lines had been sheared. Could there have been any chance of a similar reverse in 1940?

There were those on the French side who argued – and still argue – with some bitterness and vehemence about exactly this point. The British, the argument goes, were simply too quick to perceive defeat and go into retreat; although a defence line was maintained, the vast majority were too hasty in their abandonment of trucks and weaponry, the surfaces of village ponds strikingly steepled with the upward glints of discarded bayonets. Among a few of the French, there was the desire to try and launch counter-attacks. But they must have known that this was a question of psychology as much as a contest of numbers or even superior equipment. The Germans, in forcing the capitulation of Belgium, had administered a metaphorical stab to the solar plexus of the Allies; startling, disorientating, it also created an impression of utterly ineluctable power. The shattering relentlessness of the enemy impressed deeply, and is obviously still recalled vividly today.

There was to be no counter-offensive; yet for all of RAF signaller Arthur Taylor's apprehensions as he lay on the sands, still wearing the vast coat that disguised his true provenance, the soldiers around him were quite wrong to complain that the RAF had given them no back-up; indeed, as the vast majority of Allied troops had gathered around Dunkirk and on the beaches, the Spitfires in Kent were now at last in realistic range to provide solid defence. Some veterans recalled watching as Hurricanes and Spitfires came through those blue skies to take on the Stukas. There are other accounts of huge cheers as British planes brought German aircraft down; cheers that did not abate even as the men watched the German crews burn to death. Some later commentators took this as a warning chime of barbarity; but these planes had dropped bombs continuously, indiscriminately – it is difficult to gauge just how delicate anyone's moral sensibilities would remain when watching one's potential killer brought down. There were men who had seen their friends dismembered by the bombs. The noise of the planes was one of the few details reported with some clarity by the newspapers; an example of the German 'terror tactics' that 'had been used so successfully during the Spanish Civil War . . . Officers who have been taking part in the battles say that the din created by this form of attack is terrific. It is almost impossible to hear someone bawling an order a few yards away.'

The concomitant effect was that of sleep deprivation; exhausted and exposed on the sand dunes, all those thousands of men would barely have made it into the shallowest of slumbers without either being awoken by the unholy noise, or hovering near wakefulness in grim anticipation of it.

For such reasons the RAF could be only of limited help; even if Air Marshal Dowding had not realised that he needed to keep his fleet as intact as possible to face the battle that was to come, the point was that wherever they engaged with enemy fighters, the soldiers below were still pitifully exposed. In some cases, when bombs landed, even the lucky ones who lived received startling injuries; some from their own tin helmets, which had been made red-hot in the blasts. There were burns too horrible to think about – especially when, as one veteran put it, 'they were not only so close to the salt air but later found themselves having to enter the salt water.' There were men with raw, salt-exposed flesh – sometimes the flesh simply came away – who had yet to face the ordeal of entering the waves to board the boats. Meanwhile, the port of Dunkirk could not have been saved, nor could every single one of the vessels criss-crossing the Channel have been given covering fire. Just as the speed of the German advance had registered on the psychological level, however, so too the counter-attack by British pilots must at least have afforded a renewed sense of hope among men who had been standing helpless in the sand or on the concrete.

There was one tiny sliver of comfort in the type of weapons that the bombers used, recalled Royal Engineer Douglas Gulland. Having spent days defending the Escaut Canal to the south of Dunkirk, Gulland and his mates now found themselves on those wide expanses of open beach. The Germans, remembered Gulland, were using deep penetration bombs which only exploded when they were deep in the sand. If they had been using scatter bombs, he said, he and a great many others would not be around to discuss it. Even so, he added, once one of these deep penetration bombs went off, you knew all about it. 'It would have the effect of picking you up and hurling you several miles away, as it did in my case,' he recalled. 'But I was uninjured!'[1]

In Dover, where Admiral Ramsay and his subordinates within the operations room – now rechristened the Dynamo Room – had scarcely slept, there were fresh anxieties. A number of ships had been bombed; a horribly easy target, when milling around Dunkirk harbour, for the bombers to swoop at. This led to a supplementary concern about the harbour: there were reports that it was becoming choked with the wrecks of bombed ships; that other vessels were having to manoeuvre around the still-visible masts of the casualties. There were other obstacles too: guns; submerged trucks; khaki uniforms trailing in the waves and getting caught up in propellers; and corpses, blue and bloated in the water, similarly snarling up engines and rudders. In a signal sent on Wednesday 29 May to his trusted Captain Tennant who had sailed over to help, Ramsay declared: 'Evacuation of British troops to continue at maximum speed through the night. If adequate supply of personnel vessels cannot be maintained to Dunkirk East Pier (the Mole), destroyers will be sent there as well. All other craft except hospital carriers to embark from beach . . .'

Again there was frustration; Ramsay could not be sure if Captain Tennant had received the signal. He also sent a signal to Admiral Abrial (who worked side by side with the British in co-ordinating the evacuation of French troops) about the situation at the harbour and whether it was irretrievable, but again there was no response; no way of knowing if any of these communications were getting through. As others have acknowledged, however, the idea of embarking more men from the beaches was sound in any case; the vessels more spread out, the targets less concentrated. All that remained was the logistical difficulty of getting the men far enough out to sea that they could embark; and for that among the little ships there were several power boats, as well as the Thames Estuary cockle vessels, their young crews working under the guidance of naval personnel.

*

Back in Britain, there were further signs of cracks, of the tension climbing without anyone quite being fully conscious of it. At the Liverpool Chamber of Commerce on 29 May, for instance, Lord Derby made a startlingly intemperate speech concerning King Leopold of Belgium, who cannot hitherto have figured very much in the dealings of that association. 'Although the son of a brave man,' declaimed Lord Derby, 'his cowardice, his utter disregard for the welfare of his own country and for the safety of the Allies, when he himself called them in to help him, shows him to be a mastermind of perfidy and treachery. I wish I had stronger words to say what I think.' Or perhaps even a stronger drink to hand to amplify them further, given that he was defying Duff Cooper's admonitions concerning the apportioning of blame.

The growing tension on the Home Front manifested itself in a variety of forms. The poet and novelist Bryan Guinness, then with the Royal Sussex Regiment, happened to be in the centre of Cambridge when he witnessed a striking scene near one of the old colleges. 'I met the elderly historian G.M. Trevelyan in a gunsmith's shop,' he noted, 'buying a revolver with which to check the expected invasion.'

There were also further foreshadowings of the vast approaching social revolution; for with so many men away, it was now time for women to take over their roles in the heavy industrial workplaces. This had happened to a limited extent – for instance, in munitions factories – during the Great War. But now women were about to move into a much wider range of jobs, from railway signalling to steel smelting. 'We would certainly expect that more people would be put into employment,' Chancellor Sir Kingsley Wood stated drily in Parliament. But the unions were anxious to assure the menfolk that this revolution would not be permanent. 'The position is adequately safeguarded,' announced a spokesman for the Amalgamated Engineering Union. 'And we need have no fear that after the emergency situation has passed and we have to get back to normal, we shall have any difficulty in returning these men to those jobs that have been taken by women during the war period.'

The use of the phrase 'emergency situation' also hints at a continuing uncertainty about the exact nature of the crisis that Britain faced. Just a few months previously, many would have been forgiven for wondering if there was going to be any kind of war at all. Now the new 'emergency situation' lacked boundaries or edges.

The grip of Big Government was also finding pockets of resistance and outbreaks of passive aggression, a forerunner of the anti-bureaucratic spirit that was to find artistic expression in the post-war Ealing comedies. In Manchester, it was reported on 29 May, the new stricter system of rationing was being challenged by a substantial number of individuals and families all over the city. A newspaper editorial stated sternly:

> By Saturday, all applications for new ration books should be in the hands of the local food officer. For a week, the government has been reminding us and re-iterating the correct procedure in advertisements and radio announcements. Yet in Manchester, more than half the population has done nothing about it. 5,000 of those who have sent application cards have failed to enter their identity card numbers and hundreds have left out their names addresses and signatures, or even with the card cut in two, with the result that a section of the food office has to waste all its time and energy in attending to the deficiencies. Such behaviour is hard to explain except in terms of sheer laziness and thoughtless indifference.

But, despite the harrumphing, there was another explanation; a great many families were trying to avoid registering their children for evacuation. Despite the arguments of the authorities that big cities such as Manchester would be seriously targeted (as indeed it and Liverpool were), huge numbers of parents had cooled on the idea of sending small children away to live among complete strangers in remote parts of the country. In order to evade the notice of officialdom, housewives would of necessity try to obfuscate their household rationing needs, claiming the proper amount without actually numbering their children.

This also appeared to be the case in London, where it was reported that an unusually high number of people appeared simply to have 'lost' their identity cards. Possibly among them were a few – foreign nationals – who were candidates for internment. The process of identifying and interning 'aliens' had begun with German and Austrian women and children. On 29 May 1940, 1365 such people were sent sailing over to the Isle of Man where they were to stay 'billeted' in boarding houses in a holiday resort. It was dutifully reported in the press that the location was a delight, and that the internees would have access to the sunniest beaches and the local golf course. That same day began a system of curfew for those 'aliens' not interned; this restricted their hours of outdoor movement, meaning that they had to occupy their own lodgings from 10.30 p.m. every night until 6.30 a.m. the next morning. And if any should happen to be staying with a friend, for example, that friend would have to notify the local police station, in writing. So if, for example, such an 'alien', that very evening, fancied seeing John Gielgud's opening night as Prospero in Shakespeare's *The Tempest* at the Old Vic, also starring the young Jessica Tandy, they would have to catch an early performance in order to be sure of returning from Waterloo in time. In addition, they were forbidden from owning aircraft, 'sea-going craft', motor vehicles or bicycles. In time of war, all perfectly understandable; but the outcome is that everyone else, in seeing these announcements, would also feel the screw tightening, feel the grip of a conflict that had now arrived. It would have made itself apparent even in the cancellation of the Royal Horticultural Society's annual summer show, which was to have been held on 4 and 5 June.

It is perhaps sadly inevitable that in the midst of such restrictions, quotidian crime went on, as it had when the blackout first descended. 'Two men threatened a crowd in High Road Streatham with crowbars while a third threw a coal hammer through the plate glass window of jewellers James Walker,' reported one newspaper. The thieves got away with two trays of rings then worth around £300. What made the case noteworthy – apart from the fact that such things were still happening even at a notional period of national crisis – was the macabre modus operandi. In order to disguise themselves, the thieves rather ingeniously used the eyepieces from gas masks. Perhaps they were feeling a confidence not shared by the rest of the population; for did they stop to wonder how much use their fenced jewellery would be in the event of a Nazi invasion?

There were signs elsewhere of a certain comical insouciance. An amusing cigarette advertisement of 29 May depicted an RAF officer, seated in front of a map, with a glamorous WAAF operative standing behind him; both were smoking. The caption bubble read: 'Tell the Air Marshal I'll show him round in 15 minutes. Explain that I'm just enjoying a Churchman's Number One.'

Meanwhile, very quietly, stories of the return were starting to seep through into the mainstream press; nothing overdone in terms of headlines but the essence of what was happening none the less clear enough. 'Officers of the RAF and French officers who arrived by hospital train at a town in the North Riding yesterday described the pitiless bombing by German airmen of British wounded as they were being embarked at a port in the north of France,' ran one report. Readers might have found themselves wondering why French officers were there as well. 'They paid high tribute to the gallantry of the Navy in embarking the casualties under an almost continual rain of bombs.' This was a serpentine means of suggesting that the evacuation was confined to the wounded. 'In some cases, the men had to walk into the water to reach the ships,' the report continued. 'Many had to set off in small rowing boats and in fishing boats and they were afterwards picked up at sea.'

Even this skilful elision seemed to smack too much of defeat, though: a more jaunty detail was needed. 'The work of a famous Scottish regiment in covering the embarkation aroused great admiration among the men,' the report added. 'A walking casualty told of a young German officer who jumped out of one of the huge enemy tanks and shouted in perfect English: "You may as well surrender before it is too late!" They promptly replied with all their guns and the tank was put out of action.' It is possible that the wounded officers who carried this story back to Yorkshire might have somehow got the details a little muddled. None the less, there were true accounts of soldiers from Highland regiments marching around Dunkirk port and piping furiously on bagpipes as Junkers threw down more bombs and local dogs went mad, crazed with fear and hunger, and the smoky air became difficult to see through.

For those families still awaiting news from loved ones in France, the first suggestions of these stories may well have amplified anxieties. Veterans such as Charles Searle, Arthur Taylor and Reg Vine remember that clearly there was no way of getting word from Dunkirk or La Panne; the first their families knew was when, a few days later, they managed to make it home from barracks for very brief periods of leave.

Those who lived in Dover, Ramsgate, even as far along the south coast as Bournemouth, could see exactly what was going on, though; they watched the haggard, haunted men trooping slowly and carefully off the boats and being transported by bus to the nearest railway stations. The directors of Southern Railways were also fully aware of the situation; their timetables would have to be completely overturned in order to be able to cope with the massive influx.

There were some – in a foreshadowing of the general mood – who looked at these returning soldiers with remarkable insouciance. Young ambulance attendant Margaret Saunders of north London was hoping to do some 'PT' at her local gymnasium. 'We found we had been turfed out of the YMCA as it was full of French and Belgian soldiers,' she wrote. Her response was an amused shrug.

Instead, she said, she 'went to play tennis with Sandy. Played rather badly, so we drowned my sorrows at the Spaniards Inn.'[2]

For others less blithe, the frustration of not being able to know exactly what was happening across the Channel prompted a thought-provoking reader's letter to *The Times* on 29 May, not about the evacuation but about other operations. As E. Inwood of N14 wrote:

> Whether it is possible to see the effects of an explosion in Belgium from the heights of north London I do not know. Looking south east, from Trent Park, Cockfosters, over Epping Forest, at midnight last Sunday, I can say that I saw the sky in the black-out lighted by the reflection of an orange glow which appeared to come from below the horizon like the rising of the harvest moon. This happened consecutively on three occasions within a minute. Next morning I read the RAF had bombed oil dumps in Belgium.

This striking image – an entirely dark night sky briefly illuminated – was an echo of those stories from the Great War about the vast guns and cannons on the slaughter-fields and how they could be heard, even muffled, on watery nights back in England. That sense of grateful distance, yet also of macabre proximity.

And still the destroyers and the hospital ships and the little tugs beetled back and forth. One of the more unusual little ships, *Tigris I,* the old Great War submarine chaser renovated by the boat-owning Tough Brothers of Teddington, was now a fully fledged pleasure boat, and it usually carried around 350 passengers. On 27 May, Douglas Tough sent it downriver with two young Thames lightermen on board, Harry and Warren Hastings, accompanied, for the offer of a day's pay, by another lighterman called Bill Clark. Young Mr Clark had known nothing of what he was signing on for; he assumed the boat was being used to evacuate children from

London, and that he would be home that evening to his wife. The further down the Thames they got (having received more detailed instructions about heading for the estuary at Westminster Pier), the clearer it became that this wouldn't be the case. When told that they would be needing rations for three days, Mr Clark still could not quite believe it; he laughed and told the officers emphatically that he really did have to be home for his wife. It was only when they reached Southend Pier and received instruction from another officer that the nature of their mission was fully revealed. Bill Clark was enthusiastic. 'They should have said,' he recalled.

The acrid haze that heralded Dunkirk was one thing; more amazing to Mr Clark's eyes were the multitudes of men on board the great naval destroyers sailing away from the town across the Channel. 'They all waved to us,' he said. Then he gradually became aware of the extraordinary spectacle on the sands of La Panne – 'columns and groups down to the water's edge'. Mr Clark recalled that he had never before in his life seen such a gathering of people; 'not even at big football matches'.[3]

In a curious way, the unceasing roar of planes, guns, bombs and returning fire seemed not to invade his consciousness as much as it might. Perhaps it was something to do with the incongruity of the exceptionally fine, warm sunny weather and the almost preternatural calmness of the sea: rich blue, scarcely moving (an extremely unusual state of affairs for the normally grey and churning Channel). As the *Tigris* made it very close to the sands, Mr Clark became suddenly aware of a rather more comical incongruity – all the pleasure boat's signage: 'This way to ladies toilet', 'Gents toilet', 'Watneys Pale Ale'. What he might not have known is the intensity of relief that these signs triggered in men desperate for comfort and familiarity.

Mr Clark remembered calling to Harry his crewmate: 'God, what have we let ourselves in for?' as the bombs started splashing and exploding and violently wrenching the boat. The vessel just about touched the sands in that shallow dip into the sea, ladders were put down over the sides and, as Mr Clark recalled, all the men close by let out a great cheer; but he also noted the naval operatives walking up and down with revolvers. One of these young men would have been Vic Viner, who was there on the beaches right until the harrowing end.

In remarkably orderly lines, the men started wading out into the water towards the *Tigris*. As the first of them came aboard, Mr Clark recalled a rather startling absence of gratitude. 'Thanks mate,' the first soldier told him. 'We've been waiting three days and nights for you – and where's the air force we've been hearing so much about?' Other men were crestfallen when they learned this was merely a ferry boat to take them to a waiting destroyer; they were yearning for a simple sail back to the safety of home. There was also a terrific amount of argument when the crew of the *Tigris* insisted that the soldiers get rid of their rifles. It was a matter of precious space on board, but equally for the men it was a matter of the training dinned into them; that there could be nothing more terrible than losing one's rifle, still less deliberately throwing it into the sea. Then, when the first load of about 250 men were aboard, Mr Clark recalled with piercing clarity the boat casting off from the sand and the visible distress of the men left on the beach, who looked convinced that rescue would never come. For the men on board – now sprawled out or lying in the saloon that normally would have played host to day-trippers – the initial ingratitude gave way to its opposite: suddenly, as if in some kind of ecstasy, they started offering Mr Clark and the crew their cigarettes. The captain, all the while, was having to steer the craft through a maze of other little boats, all milling around on that millpond ocean before the bigger ships, occasionally bashing into one another, necessitating leak repairs.

Mr Clark and his crewmates went back to the beaches many times over, working into the night, ferrying men back and forth under moonlight. There was little in the way of rest or comfort, though there was good strong tea and corned beef. After a few runs, Mr Clark recalled his surprise the next morning when a naval officer gave them fresh orders: they were to pick up French troops only. This was greeted with bafflement: were they not there to save their own? And why would the French troops even want to leave their own soil? The lightermen were told crisply that these were orders from the Prime Minister himself. They did as they were told. The sight, if anything, was even more haunting: many of the sallow-faced soldiers cried openly as they were ferried to the destroyers. These men knew, Mr Clark said, that they were leaving their families behind. And leaving them to what?

For, by now, the news could not be suppressed. British and French and a smattering of Belgian troops were being transported by the thousand back to Britain. Though France had yet to declare surrender, the whole thing surely was the most miserable, humiliating – and frightening – defeat. If the German army could reduce Allied forces to this level in a little under three weeks, what would it mean for the rest of the war? Surely this was a harrowing moment, the proof that British fighting forces had not an ounce of the thrust, discipline and skill of the German army? Yet somehow, in the days that were to follow, everyone – seemingly spontaneously – seemed to grab hold of quite the reverse idea. From almost out of nowhere, the people of Britain began constructing quite a different kind of story out of the Dunkirk retreat. With no prompting either from the government or newspapers or newsreels or the radio – rather, simply what they were saying among themselves – the people of Britain colluded in summoning a national myth which remains with us today. And they were doing all this while the many thousands who yet remained on the beaches and in the port witnessed scenes of impersonal butchery that spoke of a quite different narrative.

12

'I'll Come Looking for You!'

30 May 1940

The German communiqué, reported on 30 May 1940, was crisply triumphalist, and perhaps with good reason. 'The great battle in Flanders and Artois is drawing to a close with the annihilation of the British and French armies,' it read. 'Since yesterday, the BEF also is in complete dissolution. The British troops are in headlong flight in the direction of the coast, leaving all their incalculable [sic] war material in German hands. Swimming and in small boats, they try to reach the British ships . . . the German Air Force has attacked these ships with devastating results.'

All of which was indeed the case. In the simplest psychological terms, however, this did not appear to be how people in Britain were seeing it. 'There is a pretty irony,' wrote the *Manchester Guardian*'s correspondent, 'that . . . hope was inspired by a German official communiqué. Its flamboyant and boastful account of British transports off Dunkirk . . . was taken with the usual weary unbelief as to details.' The correspondent noted the effect of the news in London. 'London's mind seized on the main point, the admission by Berlin that British soldiers were being taken off by ship. It squared with certain rumours that ran like wildfire through the House of Commons lobbies yesterday and have spread through the town today. They said that the evacuation of the BEF had begun, and not too badly either.'

Operation Dynamo was still largely the stuff of rumour and gossip, even in Parliament – and this before government exhortations against idle talk became widespread and incessant. Not that the indications weren't already there; but this was the delicate point at which the full weight of the defeat had to be faced, and dealt with in a way that was not only palatable but also not treacherously pessimistic. The Manchester correspondent continued:

> It has been obvious, of course, for more than a day that the BEF has pinned its hopes on the chance of fighting its way through to Dunkirk and withdrawing by sea. It will have to sacrifice all its heavy material but that is a small matter; an aroused England can make that up better and faster than any other nation could. One's aching anxiety has been for the magnificent men. If the men are saved, the nation can go on with a good heart to the heavy task which is before it.

So what precisely had led to these magnificent men being trapped and almost wiped out by an unstoppable army? Very few seemed willing to give the question much time. Perhaps there was an unspoken feeling that the BEF had had no business being in France in the first place; that the overriding interest was the defence of their own realm.

Whatever the case, Lord Gort – still in his makeshift headquarters at La Panne – chose this moment to release the news of those men who had received honours. There was a range of decorations, from DSOs to Military Crosses, for valour and courage, all of which were undeniably richly deserved; many officers and men had done their utmost to hold the lines of defence, firing at the enemy across the narrow space of a canal, or ensuring – under heavy fire themselves – that bridges were effectively destroyed and rendered impassable for tanks. These were men who knew that they were fighting for the survival of the BEF; that the longer they could hold out, the greater the chance that those thousands would be evacuated.

'The series of magnificent rear-guard actions, which will be inscribed in gold in the annals of British and French arms, continued yesterday,' reported *The Times*'s embedded correspondent. But intriguingly, the correspondent was also now free to start describing the more compelling story, and to take it beyond the realm of baseless pub gossip. 'What so many people in this country have seen with their own eyes has now been announced – namely that under cover of these actions, troops not engaged in the fighting line have been evacuated. The perimeter around Dunkirk has narrowed and both on and outside it, a number of fierce, more or less isolated fights are raging . . .'

An official government announcement also confirmed what people living along the south coast had known for days. 'The wounded and a large number of other elements have already been safely withdrawn,' it read. 'These operations are being conducted ceaselessly by day and night with coolness and determination in the face of fierce opposition . . . The spirit and conduct of all concerned are beyond all praise.'

On the beaches of La Panne, that coolness and spirit might easily have been interpreted as a form of trauma. 'Well, I got three parts cut,' confesses Reg Vine with a laugh. As one of the youngest lads in the evacuation operation, on board a Teddington cruise boat, sixteen-year-old Reg didn't need a great deal of grog to make his head swim. There was a tricky question of authority, though, as he tried to usher troops on to his boat. 'What annoyed me was that all the troops were arguing with me as they got on the boat. I was directing them – "Up there, and up there, OK that's enough, can't take no more."' One soldier, when the boat had reached capacity, demanded that Reg let him on board too. When Reg refused, the soldier threatened to yank him overboard and leave him in the sea. Reg responded, rather darkly: 'You might chuck me in – but I'll get out and I'll come looking for you and I know your face. Now bugger off and wait your turn for the next trip.' The soldier in question might only have been a few years older than Mr Vine, and his desire to get away was hideously understandable. Not only was the bombardment almost ceaseless; the smell now rising from the beach was extraordinary.

Reg Vine had seen with his own eyes how some of the men were trying to turn the charnel house to their advantage as more bombers came over: 'The falling bombs kept blowing up the same body parts in the sand, and the bits and pieces were getting smaller. A lot of blokes, what they were doing – I thought it was a bit sick but then it seemed like common sense – they were putting dead bodies on top of their own to protect them, like a shelter. You find three or four dead bodies, normally you would decently cover them up with sand but these men were pulling them over like a dugout, getting underneath them.'

In this atmosphere, it would have been psychologically impossible for peace to prevail. While the boat ferried back and forth from the sands, Mr Vine saw a great deal more as he occasionally glanced past the mole. 'Knives, punch-ups. I even saw blokes shoot themselves. And drown themselves – they would just walk into the sea and disappear. They must have been really mental and upset and thinking, there's no chance for me. Because there were so many waiting. It was the waiting. And that mole was always jammed until it broke in half when they got it with that direct hit.' More fighting broke out as the queue became increasingly disorganised. 'It was like a football match gone mad. A riot at a football match. The officer would start saying something, then suddenly the officer's gone down. Someone's pinged him and done him in.'

Young Vine was not particularly conscious of his own tiredness as the hours and the crossings stretched on. There was that sense of existing in a fugue state. 'We were going back and forwards to the destroyers and any ship that was big enough to take off our lot,' he says. But as the situation grew more frantic, the captain of Mr Vine's boat and naval officers allowed it to take an even more active role. 'We towed out lifeboats behind us right across the Channel with more lads in them.' Deliverance was one thing, but this left everyone hideously exposed to the air attacks, which were being stepped up still further. It was a particularly gruelling experience for the men huddled in the lifeboats; the planes did not even have to scream – the constant turbulence from bombs exploding in water exposed enough raw nerves. Like so many of the soldiers, Mr Vine started to complain loudly about the apparent absence of the RAF. 'I said, why can't Churchill send some bloody fighters out? And the answer came back, "We can't afford them, we're saving them." They were saving them for the Battle of Britain.'

The hours that it took to get back to Ramsgate with the open lifeboats in tow seemed to pass for Reg Vine like a bad dream. Incredibly, despite the never-ending attention from the bombers, he did occasionally find himself drifting off in the boat's wheel house. They managed to snatch a little sleep elsewhere too: 'It was only a small boat but we had a place where we did the cooking and we more or less took turns to fall asleep from exhaustion rather than anything else, so at least you got two or three hours. We didn't get a lot.'

He at least had the psychological comfort of those structures around him. The soldiers they were towing did not. 'I've never seen blokes cry so much,' says Mr Vine. 'And shout out for Mum. "Help me!" It goes through your mind. It's a frightening thing.'

Those first few men who had made it back were now being observed from a number of angles as they travelled in incongruous style.

'People living in houses beside the railways in some southern suburbs of London have been watching a stream of troop trains bringing men back,' reported *The Times.* 'Many of the trains are made up of dining cars. Through the windows, tired out soldiers, some with several days' growth of beard, can be seen sprawling fast asleep, their heads on the dining tables.' Commuters such as south London shopkeeper S.J. Carty had started to notice the changes made to regular services. At his Surrey station, on 31 May, another traveller asked the station-master the reason for the delay of their train; he 'got his head bitten off'. The idea that it was down to 'movement of troops' was still 'rumour'.[1]

But the people of Ramsgate had a grandstand view of the extraordinary spectacle. Those lucky soldiers who felt well enough waved at residents sitting in upstairs windows as they themselves clambered aboard buses and were taken along the seafront to one large restaurant, which had been turned over entirely to giving them much-needed food and drink. There were barriers in the streets to hold curious crowds back, and to prevent the buses being impeded in any way. The people who gathered behind the barriers stared silently – the lack of noise was felt by some to be a sympathetic greeting. In another light, it might be interpreted as a silence of horror. But keeping the mood aloft, the Salvation Army – normally at the service of destitutes and helpless drunks – had swung into action with a platoon of mobile vans loaded with tea and scones. There was a handful of Belgian officers, happy to offer their views. They were, they said, 'astounded' when the order had come from the Belgian army to cease fighting. There were some French troops too; either they did not offer their views on the Belgians and the British, or these were not relayed to a wider audience.

Certainly, these first evacuees were starting to talk, if in the barest terms – understandably, after the days and nights that they had been through. The men who were quoted had been specially selected; many others found that they were told, upon arrival back at Dover, that they should refrain from saying a word to anyone, especially the press. This was presumably to do with the need to keep morale high; also to prevent an outbreak of blame, with the anger being focused upon the French. 'It has been simply hell,' said one soldier. 'Believe me, the Nazis don't love you. Their planes are everywhere.' Another soldier said: 'All of us were almost naked, and we have had no food since yesterday at midday and no sleep for three days.'

An unnamed private from Liverpool told how he had received a machine gun bullet in the foot and, with no time to have it seen to, had had to march thirty miles a day for several days in order to reach the coast. A sergeant from Whitley Bay said: 'Although we have come back wounded, we have given them plenty to remember us by . . . column after column was mown down by our Bren guns.'

Such quotes, put out for public consumption, together spoke of endurance, courage and defiance, along with a spark of undimmed humour. But at this stage, it seemed as though hardly anyone was in need of subtle prompting; the undercurrent strongly detectable in so many accounts now is simply one of profound relief.

Nurses up and down the country later bore witness to uniforms filled with sand and dirt, and to missing limbs and burnt eyes. Mary Cope recalled that she was careful that above her surgical mask, her own eyes were 'smiling'; that way the patients would not guess at the true horror of their wounds. According to Myrtle Paton, who worked at a cottage hospital in Surrey, one day the soldiers – English and French alike – received a secret visitor. With not a word to the press, Queen Elizabeth turned up, charmed the French soldiers by speaking to them fluently in their own language, and gazed upon the shrapnel and bullets that had been removed from their flesh. French troops were being given the option to stay in England, to join what would become the Free French forces; but among the unwounded, great numbers wanted to return.

The *Manchester Guardian* came closest to addressing what was actually taking place. 'We must be prepared, as Mr Churchill said, for hard and heavy tidings,' their correspondent wrote. 'Whatever the measure of success that attends the withdrawal now going on –

the question which above all today possesses our anxious thoughts – the losses in the recent fighting must have been grievously severe.' Indeed, the *Guardian* was prepared to go further and use a word that no one else had uttered – defeat – at the same time eliding it with some convoluted logic to do with national character:

> The grave defeat which we have suffered has, however, offered us a lesson which once and for all we must have learned by now . . . This vast battle of the last three weeks has shown that, however much we ourselves may have been sure of it before, the British soldier – patient, enduring, unbreakable – will win any battle if he is given the indispensable weapons.

It is difficult now to unravel the exact meaning of the 'lesson' to which the newspaper referred: was the entire debacle simply the result of the British soldier being insufficiently well armed? Was it a Churchillian plea to the Americans? But in another sense, the editorial swerve was understandable; there was hardly any need for a Ministry of Information to keep a careful eye on what newspapers were printing, for the newspaper editors had to keep an even more careful eye on the feelings of their readers. And the feeling was not one that their loved ones, these young men, had been utterly humiliated. The blame lay in quite a different direction, as the reporter went on to suggest: 'It is strange to read long exhortations to the people of this country not to reproach the French for errors committed at the beginning of this war.' Ah! The French! Perhaps the Belgians had absorbed their own fill of responsibility. 'But who reproaches [the French] and what time is this for reproaches among those who are bound together, to live or die, in a most sacred cause? Let us assume that the French have learned their lesson and let us see to it that we ourselves, while there is yet time, learn the bitter lessons that the war, daily, is telling us.'

In an era of ubiquitous news feeds and sources, it is important to remember just how restricted the conduits of information were back in the spring of 1940. Newspaper readership – from low brow to high – was at an all-time peak. But the newspapers themselves were cramped not only by their readers' sensibilities, but also by greatly decreased pagination, which left little room for detailed accounts of what was fast becoming a dizzyingly complex war. In terms of broadcasting, there was the BBC, with its mix of classical music, inoffensive comedians, and talks given by retired brigadiers and popular writers such as J.B. Priestley. The alternative was to rotate the tuning dial to foreign stations; which is how the infamous Lord Haw-Haw (the alias of Nazi sympathiser William Joyce, broadcasting from Germany) became almost what one would describe as a cult hit: his taunting bulletins, featuring tantalising local details of broken church clocks in small market towns, in order to spread fear of espionage, were the source of illimitable conversations in the pub. Listeners tuned in simply for the sheer variety; Margaret Saunders of north London twiddled the dial after her evening tennis games. In general terms, as the official news of Operation Dynamo began to break – preceded as it would have been by excited eyewitnesses on the south coast telling what they had seen – this was also the moment at which the myth, at first as fluid as mercury, began to solidify.

And those who turned to *The Times*'s editorial on 30 May 1940 would perhaps have found their own feelings reinforced by a stirring piece that focused on the unquestioned sea-going triumph of the operation itself:

> It grows more and more certain that in the supreme struggle of the French and British armies, hemmed in against the north-eastern coast of France, the world is witnessing one of the grimmest and most glorious feats of skill and steady gallantry in all military history . . . The shrouded valour of the troops is the more stirring because it rests, and must rest, simply and selflessly on duty and discipline . . .

The editorial writer added, getting to the heart of his argument:

> it should never be forgotten that the real struggle is for dominion of the sea. The very magnitude of the effort which the enemy has exerted in his drive towards the Channel Ports shows he is under no illusions about the chief obstacle to his ambition of world domination – the sea power of the Allies, of which the backbone is the British Navy.

Remaining nameless, however, was the man who at that moment was the backbone of the navy. Admiral Ramsay and his team had been working without stint, juggling dizzying logistics, calculating which ships would be best deployed in what sort of role, but also judging the crews of those vessels; after two or three round trips from England to France, picking up men, sailing back again, how close were those crews to the brink of exhaustion? Would they need to be relieved and another ship sent in their place, or was it possible that they could manage just one more foray? The captain and crew of the *Canterbury* were in such a position, pleading that the civilians on board needed to stop. Admiral Ramsay impressed upon the captain exactly how much the urgency of the situation was escalating. The crew, on hearing this talk, gave it a couple of hours to recover their energy and spirit – and then headed back out across the water.

The English Channel is – and has always been – a furiously busy stretch of water. During those long, calm spring nights, under warm cloud and glimpses of moonlight, when the normally frenetic waves merely rippled and sucked at their hulls, lines of boats, following the three routes, back and forth, continued to plough through the darkness. Some twenty destroyers acted as ferries, carrying hundreds of men, in tandem with the great minesweepers, the old converted pleasure steamers; meanwhile, bobbing along that long elegant ribbon of northern French beach were the flat-bottomed Dutch skoots and the simple lifeboats. There was very little, if anything, in the way of radio communication between these craft, or with Admiral Ramsay back at base. They were all simply pointed in the direction of the job that they had to do. Similarly, these vessels had no way of radioing the columns of troops on the beaches to let them know what was going on. Soldiers would stare into the distance, see the small boats that seemed either to be taking their time or not to be moving at all; for the many men who chose to wade out into the waves to wait, the weird calm of the sea made it possible for them to stand like eerie sentinels, often up to their shoulders in the cold water.

All shipping was vulnerable, the destroyers as much as the luxury Thames cruisers. For the exhausted men on board, each falling bomb, and the possibility of the ship being holed, would test whatever strength they had to unknown limits. There was the terrible tragedy of the minesweeper (and paddle steamer) *Waverley*. The crew had managed to get 600 soldiers on board, and it had swung round as it was making back for England. Soon after, disaster came shooting from the sky; a direct hit which resulted in the boat sinking very fast. Out of those 600 soldiers, just over 200 were rescued from the water by a nearby destroyer. But for the other 400, almost unable to move after so many days without food, the currents were too strong. They drowned. In the case of another fatally hit boat, the *Crested Eagle*, fire was an additional horror. One soldier recalled how the bomb first went through the engine room and how, incongruously, there were 'spuds, carrots, meat everywhere – the bomb hit the provision store as well'. But then came the explosions and with them, the all-engulfing flames. Those who jumped for it into the waves had, moments before, witnessed others horrifically injured by fire; but they in turn were then mercilessly targeted by machine gunners in low-flying planes.

One victim on board the *Crested Eagle* was Vic Viner's older brother, who had originally been on board the destroyer *Grenade*. When that got hit by bombers, Mr Viner's brother abandoned the fast-sinking craft; the vessel that plucked him from the water was this paddle steamer, too tempting a target to overlook. Mr Viner only learned of the tragedy later: 'She was dive-bombed by twelve bombers,' he says quietly. 'As she was going out towards the open sea, she was bombed. Everyone involved was burned to death.'

The menace not only lay in the skies above; it prowled through the waters beneath too. One U-boat, lurking on the edge of the northern route, lay in wait for the returning destroyers *Wakeful* and *Grafton*; in the silence of that night, the torpedoes struck and the boats were sunk. Back in Dover, Admiral Ramsay knew that he had the weight of the entire British Army on his shoulders; and he also understood very well that if Operation Dynamo should fail, and huge quantities of men either perished or were taken prisoner by the Germans, then the repercussions would be incalculable. A nation stripped of so many fighting men, not to mention the vast majority of its materiel, would surely be forced at some stage to seek humiliating terms with the enemy.

Before Dynamo, Admiral Ramsay's letters to his wife had been epics; pencil-written efforts covering many pages, on some of which the blank margins had been filled in with extra, vertical words. As the crisis took its course, understandably, his communications became terse. 'Just a few lines,' he wrote on the night of 29 May:

> The tempo is frightful and ever-increasing. You will know by now what my task is: the most colossal ever undertaken of its kind, and in circumstances without precedent. Everyone is stretched to the limit, doing magnificently, but flesh and blood can't stand it much longer. Officers and men cannot continue at this pace but all are doing their best. No-one can foresee what tomorrow will be like. Perhaps it's as well. But we must keep a brave heart and trust that we shall be able to stabilise and retain our position against what is to come.

It is not too presumptuous to imagine Admiral Ramsay in his cave office, overlooking the Channel, in the small hours of the morning, the sky above him velvet blue, and watching that sinister orange glow from across the sea; seeing how very close the enemy was. And imagining, with so many soldiers rounded up, that enemy standing on the French shore and looking back across right at him. He would have understood very well that this bizarre flotilla, the mighty destroyers and the cockle pickers, had to push on ceaselessly. If they failed, then from where would he be writing his letters to 'darling Mag'?

Some – especially in the aftermath – elected in their accounts to minimise any idea of overwhelming carnage and focus on spirit. One such, understandably, was Private D. Warren of the 2nd Battalion Hampshire Regiment. Though, like everyone else, he and his men faced a black night of bombing, the embarkation was recalled as more of an atmospheric adventure:

> Although there was no moon, an unwelcome illumination was afforded by a blazing oil tank at the end of the beach. In the flickering light, we stood at the water's edge, surrounded, almost enveloped, by dark groups of men, so silent, yet effervescing with excitement at the unbelievable prospect of seeing England again. In front of us was a hastily constructed yet very efficient pontoon composed of a string of lorries driven into the sea and covered with boards, thoughtfully constructed in order that a few of us could get aboard in comparative comfort. We were among a few of the fortunate ones to use it.
>
> Waiting their turn were a queue of Tommies and a queue of Poilus side by side . . . we were so concentrating on retaining our balance that a constant barrage of shells whistled unnoticed around us. In such circumstances, one always finds the wit, and such remarks as 'Pass along the car, please' and 'Any more for the trip around the light-house' were being shouted out . . . One sailor nonchalantly remarked that he had been on this job three days and two nights.[2]

For those trying to get a sense of these events back in Britain, *The Times*'s correspondent chose to highlight an aspect of the French crisis that very few English readers would have thought about: 'Evidence continues to come through of the courage with which French civilians have faced danger and in many cases death itself in the performance of their duty during the invasion. The telephone operators stuck to their posts as long as their services were required . . . many women were killed at their switchboards.'

Suddenly all sorts of measures were being enforced at once. The Royal Automobile Association followed the lead of the Automobile Association and placed its network of roadside emergency telephone boxes (even before mass ownership of motor cars, there were hundreds of these all over the country) at the disposal of local Home Defence Units. This meant that they could be used not only for relaying messages swiftly but also for instant use in the case of enemy parachutists being spotted. On the same day, 30 May, Lord Reith of the Ministry of Information announced that a much-discussed plan to remove signposts and blank out direction indicators was going ahead. This was now a nation on red alert.

And in a wider sense in those hours and days, Britain's industrial base, spurred on by various Whitehall ministries, began to drive itself into a frenzy. A seven-day week was implemented, with rest periods for workers now the subject of special negotiation. Instead of weekends, shifts would be more strictly, mathematically compartmentalised. The Minister of Supply, Herbert Morrison, unveiled a new slogan (again, proving that government and crude advertising spin are pretty vintage bedfellows). The phrase, 'Go To It!', was printed on posters – 115,000 of them – which were stuck up on factory noticeboards, property hoardings and all over outside walls. South London shopkeeper S.J. Carty commented wryly: 'I admire the designer. At first glance, I thought it was for "Gone With The Wind". I asked several people what they thought of it. Replies were stupid, rude, or a vacant grin.' Meanwhile, the Trades Union Congress and what was then the Employers Confederation (its modern equivalent is the CBI) met with government officials to discuss how wages would work in this new system; would the workers receive pay increases to reflect the disappearance of holidays and the huge amount of overtime? Or was it in the national (and more pressingly, economic) interest to keep wages where they were?

Julian Huxley, brother of novelist Aldous, was a member of the Children's Nutrition Council, and the very idea of workers' wage restrictions filled him and his fellow committee members with horror. 'There have recently been references to the need for "equality of sacrifice" by all classes to avoid inflation,' he and other members of the council wrote. 'There are, however, a large number of families already so close to the margin of their physiological needs that further sacrifice might deprive them of the means to satisfy basic needs for food and warmth and so endanger health.' We were all in this together: the political landscape of Britain had changed dramatically since the First World War. And in the factories (and even within top secret radio interception establishments like Beaumanor Hall in Leicestershire), the unions had a surprising amount of traction, certainly with regard to conditions. By 1940, the working man had a stronger voice; and among those being evacuated from northern France were soldiers who recently had been working men. Army life had not brought about a change of political sympathies.

George Orwell had been deep in discussions with his friends Dr Borkenau and the literary editor Cyril Connolly about the disposition of the working man, and the possible effect of the Dunkirk evacuation. Was it really possible to detect, as Dr Borkenau insisted, a tang of revolution in the air? In his diary entry for 30 May 1940, Orwell wrote:

> Last night, a talk on the radio by a colonel who had come back from Belgium . . . contained interpolations put in by the broadcaster himself to let the public know the army had been let down a) by the French (not counter-attacking) and b) by

> the military authorities at home by equipping them badly. No word anywhere in the press about recriminations against the French and Duff Cooper's broadcast of two nights ago especially warned against this . . . Borkenau says England is now definitely in the first stages of revolution. Commenting on this, Connolly related that recently, a ship was coming away from northern France with refugees on board and a few ordinary passengers. The refugees were mostly children who were in a terrible state after having been machine-gunned etc etc. Among the passengers was Lady —, who tried to push herself to the head of the queue to get on the boat and when ordered back said indignantly: 'Do you know who I am?' The steward answered 'I don't care who you are, you bloody bitch. You can take your turn in the queue.' Interesting if true.[3]

Class tensions found other, more curious outlets. As the internment of German women on the Isle of Man continued, the Labour MP for the East End district of Bethnal Green, a Mr Thurtle, raised the issue in Parliament of a different sort of foreigner: the waiters who worked at the upmarket Savoy hotel. Was the House aware, Mr Thurtle asked, that the Savoy was staffed with anti-British Italians? One might wonder quite why a Labour MP representing an area quite a long way from the Savoy would suddenly find himself so concerned about this particular establishment. It is not unreasonable to suggest it had something to do with the widespread suspicion among deprived East Enders that London's wealthy and powerful were continuing to enjoy huge, rich meals at the Savoy Grill. As it happened, they were. Perhaps Mr Thurtle's question was a purely subconscious effort to sabotage the hotel. The restaurant was at the heart of the political and artistic establishment. And indeed it prided itself on being so – which was why, in response to the accusation that it was teeming with potential enemy agents, the Savoy issued this severe response:

> Italian waiters are not peculiar to the Savoy. Every first class and most second and third class restaurants have Italian staff, though often British born. It is therefore obviously unreasonable to single out one hotel as though that was the only one with Italian waiters and it is especially absurd to quote the Savoy whose staff is over 80% British and whose ownership and direction is 100% British.

Two weeks later, the Italian manager of another luxury London hotel – Claridges – was fired and interned and there was a nationwide round-up of Italian waiters, from all classes of establishment.

This seemed to be a time to insist on unity. In Broadstairs, on the Kent coast just a few miles from Ramsgate, where troops were being disembarked, the Under-Secretary of State for Air, Captain Balfour, gave a strong address which hinted at the past complacency of the nation, expressed his distaste for the power of the unions, and foresaw the struggles to come:

> It is a critical hour as regards the position of our forces overseas. Perhaps we had needed some tremendous upheaval in our lives, like this trial, to bind us together as one community, instead of all of us leading our sectional [sic] lives. Perhaps we needed the war to make us simple and to purge us of our prejudices and over-developed material ambitions . . . from these sacrifices and tests we should come out a simpler people with that nobility and purity of character which is possessed by our people collectively.

George Orwell, by contrast, was a little sceptical about the idea that the nation could be electrified with inspiration:

> Still no evidence of any interest in the war. Yet the by-elections, responses to appeals for men etc show what people's feelings are. It is seemingly quite impossible for them to grasp that they

> are in danger, although there is good reason to think that the invasion of England may be attempted within a few days . . . They will grasp nothing until the bombs are dropping. [Cyril] Connolly says they will then panic, but I don't think so.[4]

Connolly was only mirroring the thoughts of a great many civil servants and politicians in Whitehall. Yet against Captain Balfour's call for purging and purity and Orwell's somewhat sardonic view was a rather more energising message from an unexpected source: the United States. The White House, of course, as yet preserved its strict neutrality (the Americans would not enter the war for another eighteen months or so). But the US media proved to be unapologetically rousing, and the nature of this support would start to filter back. Indeed, it was the American press that began to forge the legend of Dunkirk in terms more radiant than Churchill or the army would have wished. The *New York Times* stated of the Dunkirk evacuations:

> It has become an epic of bravery and endurance. An epic of hundreds of thousands of men, pounded on all sides by land, blasted by maddening attacks from the skies, probably short of food and ammunition, but still fighting desperately to keep an escape open to the sea . . . They have fought like tigers, no matter what the odds against them. They have kept their discipline, their coolness, and their courage. Those who survive will bring stories of individual and regimental heroism that may live as long as bravery is honored among men.

Again, it seems as if history is being rewritten on the spot: a crushing, humiliating withdrawal is portrayed almost as an episode of Homeric triumph. As the newspaper's correspondent continued:

> Those who never return will have left a memory that will inspire the Allied Peoples for generations to come . . . There has never

> been any doubt, since the surrender of King Leopold, about what the outcome must be but never the less, the American people have never been willing to give up the hope that some miracle might occur.

As these words were written, over 100,000 men were still stranded in France, some on the edge of delirium with lack of sleep and food deprivation. They were now in the most urgent need of that miracle.

13
Remote in Some Dream of Pain

31 May 1940

'Those men were desperate,' says young naval recruit Reg Vine. 'This is what killed some of them: the seawater. Seawater can kill anyone if you drink enough of it. Probably some of them drank it deliberately, some of them did it because they couldn't help it.' The thirst, for some, was that bad; the German attack on Dunkirk had been so assiduous that many men on the beaches were now too tired and weak even to find the scant supplies of fresh water they so badly needed. 'The Germans knew that,' says Mr Vine, 'that's why they kept on bombing Dunkirk and the little villages up there so they couldn't get supplies.'

Elsewhere, Vic Viner found his experience on the beach, trying with a revolver to keep the men in some sort of line, increasingly dizzying as the days went on. 'When I first went out there, I was fighty, all clean. I had not gone through what these soldiers went through to get to Dunkirk. I just landed on it. But then I went through the bombing, the fact that food was very scarce, and water was very scarce. And I didn't change and didn't wash for six days. I had a job to do.' It is quite remarkable that he survived those six days and is able to talk about it today. Like other veterans, there is a suggestion that he entered a form of fugue state; perfectly conscious, almost hyper-aware, and yet with a sensation of time passing in a different way. Mr Viner now also remembers very clearly the miracle of the weather:

'One day, at four o'clock, the surf stopped and the sea became as flat as a table. And it stayed like that for six days. All you get in the historical reports is that the sea had an abnormal calm. Now, two years ago, I got talking to a weatherman and I said "Can you explain to me how that sea became so calm? And how, since then, seventy years on, that sea has never gone as flat as that again."'

The weatherman said, 'What do you think it was?' Viner replied, 'Well, if you ask veterans who were there, then there is only one answer. Some power above. Some power did that.'

Mr Viner continued to patrol a column of 150 soldiers with his revolver (he had no idea at the time that his older brother had been lost with the *Crested Eagle*). 'The men were frightened, they'd been shattered, they'd gone through all that. And all they were saying was: "Let me get home, let me get home". Now,' adds Mr Viner, 'I *knew* I was going to get home. I knew that I had no worry that I would be taken captive.'

He also muses on the seemingly infinite elasticity of youthful endurance, insisting now that no matter how relentless the bombardment from above, it somehow never really troubled him. 'You just stayed there. If you could get into a sand dune, the bomb would blow up the sand and blow up the bodies of anyone who was in it. But we all laid down and just hoped the bombs and the strafing wouldn't come our way. If you had a couple of hours' sleep in twenty-four, you would have been very lucky. Just lying on the beach, in the dunes. My area of the beach was all bombed to death.

'We were running on adrenaline. Food was just now and again. A little French lady, if she saw me, would call out "Sailor! Sailor!" and give me something to eat. Where she got the food from, don't ask me. Now and again you got a lorry coming in from the front which may have had something on it. But there was no food as such. Of course, as the troops came in and we gradually put them aboard, they probably would have had something on the way down. But those who were waiting – there was nothing. The average time they waited on the beach would probably be two and a half days. A long time. With bombing all the time.'

For all of Mr Viner's preternatural calm, the cumulative effect of the flight to Dunkirk, plus this prolonged agonised wait, resulted in some truly haunting scenes. There were minds that slipped their moorings completely. 'The number of deaths with the bombing . . . there's no figures ever been given. They can't be sure. And the other thing: suicides. They just walked into the water.

'You don't hear about that now,' says Mr Viner quietly. 'But they flung their rifles – if they'd got any arms – took off their rucksacks, walked into the sea.'

Mr Viner said to one sergeant: 'Where are you going?' The sergeant answered: 'I'm going home!' Viner said: 'We'll get you on board as soon as we can.' 'Oh I can't . . .' said the sergeant, 'I'm going home, I know where England is.' Viner asked: 'What are you going to do?' And the sergeant said: 'I'm going to walk there.'

'You'll drown,' said Viner. '"Oh no, no . . ." And I watched him drown.

'And that's what happened to quite a few. In my little part, my estimate would be a good fifteen who just walked away. I did know in my area, when we were able to talk to different lots of beach parties, of two or three who had been walking in and their minds had gone.'

So much for those who could walk. By this stage, there were many others who could not. 'Some died on the beach, they didn't get any further, because the medical supplies were so limited,' says Mr Viner. 'I only saw one ambulance and four medics. And they didn't get to the beach – they were taken prisoner by the Germans. The medics elsewhere did as best they could.

'The only thing I knew was that I would be killed by the bombing. It wouldn't be anything else. It would only be the bombing.'

Back in Britain, the narrative had now found its definitive shape in the newspapers and even perhaps among the wider general public; this remained more spontaneous sentiment than official urging, not least because it also involved the authentic voices of the women who now crowded around the entrance of Victoria station in London hoping to catch a glimpse of a loved returning soldier stepping off one of the troop trains; or those up and down the routes of Southern Railways who now made it their business to feed the shattered soldiers. For them, this was not a narrative of death, or delirium, or defeat. Instead it was a story of great men being forged in fire; laced perhaps less consciously with a particularly English streak of eccentricity that would find its artistic apotheosis in the later Powell and Pressburger films. As one unsigned journalist noted:

> Through one suburban junction near London, trainloads of the BEF have been coming at the rate of four an hour. There is always a few minutes' halt there, not long enough for an organised service of meals but long enough for such local folk as are allowed on the platform to express their pride to the grinning sticky unshaven men who hang from the train windows. One woman had set up a table on the platform early this morning and stocked it with all the bread and the cheese that she had in the house. When that was exhausted, she sent her neighbours shopping with the £8 she collected from station staff and volunteers . . . the policeman on duty spent most of his time cutting up the cheese. The district's best known publican sold out the station bar's stock of beer, taking it out in wash-basins to the men. The soldiers were plied with cigarettes, meat

pies and bananas and were asked eager questions about men they'd never known.

One man went a step further and bought up the local supply of picture postcards. He and his friends then wrote 'BEF' across them, handed them out to the soldiers in the trains, and told those soldiers not to worry about stamps but to write short notes to their mothers to let them know that they were all right.

Some veterans were startled by the passion of this reception. In a few small towns, returning troops were greeted with brass bands. They had assumed that they would be in disgrace for 'running away'; instead they were greeted with 'open arms and with every sort of affection'. 'It was quite ridiculous of course,' recalled one veteran. But he was also told to make the most of it while it lasted.

There were photographs that made it through to the newspapers, of the decks of destroyers packed with soldiers who seemed, against all conceivable odds, to be cheerful. The upbeat nature of the picture captions was equally determined. 'One of the many souvenirs brought back by men of the BEF – a German bugle,' declared one. 'After their magnificent resistance against overwhelming odds in Flanders, thousands of troops of the BEF have already been brought back safely,' declared another. Even the foreign troops were greeted with a cheerfulness that bordered on hysteria. 'Gallant comrades! Some French troops who have been brought over with the BEF from northern France enjoy a cup of tea at a London station,' was the uplifting image in one newspaper. Little was said of the scale of a disaster that could result in troops escaping from their mother country and abandoning it to the enemy. Nor were the newspapers or newsreels about to disturb this equilibrium.

The evacuation, declared Sir Arthur Salter of the Ministry of Shipping, was a 'heroic drama unsurpassed and in its kind unequalled in the history of the world'. Amidst the popcorn of these high sentiments though came the first real glimpse of the soul of the story. Speaking at the Royal National Lifeboat Institution,

Sir Arthur went on: 'Operations depended on men partly drawn from the seamen and fishermen from whom came the coxswains and the crews of the lifeboats.' The imagery of the 'little ships' had begun to flourish; and no matter how peevish naval figures would later become about the notion that these ships were crewed entirely by inspired amateur civilians, sailing courageously into the maw of hell, the fact was that those journeying back and forth included a significant number of non-naval personnel, whether under the command of trained men or not. It was the image promulgated in the 1942 Hollywood film *Mrs Miniver*, in a short sequence where the hardy captains of yachts and steamers answer the call and sail, as one, out on to a darkly twinkling ocean. In his speech, Sir Arthur Salter used the occasion for a wider warning, a lesson from the little ships: 'Civilians might soon have to face trials and dangers in which they would need to summon in themselves the same qualities of courage that have been daily shown by those at sea.'

A great mass of men, now almost bludgeoned into insensibility by the bombardment of the beaches, were still yet to be spirited back. One veteran – suffering the dizzying after-effects of bomb blast which had hit him as he foraged for food away from the beach – teamed up with a pal and moved further along the sand, where they fashioned a raft with drums. They knew that they could not use it to sail forty miles through mines and E-boats back to England. But equally, it was their chance to be picked up by a destroyer. They made the decision and paddled out into the waves, farther and farther from the shore, under the intense blue sky; a temptingly open target.

'We were in the water for several hours,' recalls the veteran. 'We waited and waited and waited. The navy were in charge. We just kept moving.' And eventually, they were taken aboard one of the larger vessels. 'When we got to Ramsgate, one of the smaller boats sailing beside us had some Guards aboard. And when the Guards drew up at Ramsgate, their sergeant major was pacing up and down and he was shouting. He made them march off as though they were on a Sunday parade.' Some men made light of their dampness, the veteran recalls: 'The rest of us were sodden-trousered. Just as well I didn't smoke. The cigarettes would have been in the water.' Indeed, the veteran adds, this was a source of terrific annoyance among some of the men on board who finally, after all those hours and days, had found a moment where they might have a relaxing smoke, only to find that their fags had disintegrated. 'But those Guards. The discipline must have been terrific. You expect them to run everywhere – but they did what they were told. And they were trusted.'

'Railway stations serving the Channel ports have for two days been pouring out great numbers of soldiers returned from the fighting front in Flanders,' proclaimed an editorial in *The Times*, swiftly settling into the line that what had happened was no source of ignominy. 'They are tired and battle stained. But they carry themselves proudly and cheerfully for they are not the remnants of a beaten army but men who have played their part in an achievement that will be memorable in history.' Indeed so, but how did *The Times* reason this out? It continued:

> There is no more difficult or perilous operation of war than the rear guard action of an outnumbered army. It has become vastly more difficult in the age of mechanised warfare and bombing from the air . . . the embarkation has been carried out under a constant rain of bombs and very largely upon open boats . . . What is supremely important is that the men now being brought to England are not fugitives from a lost battle but unbroken units . . . their discipline forged to a steely edge by experience of war.

The women who were turning out beside the railway tracks to hurl fruit through the windows of passing troop trains scarcely needed any prompting from the newspapers, though; theirs was a spontaneous reaction, one that spread quickly. Largely unspoken was the relief that men were now back to defend their own soil; that a German invasion was imminent seemed to be broadly accepted throughout the country. Psychologically it was important not to focus on the harrowing defeat the army had just suffered, but on ensuring that no such defeat happened again.

Signs that civilian tension was rising were found in many different areas. Down in Portsmouth, locals were gripped by the case of a 42-year-old woman, Marie Ingram, who was accused with two men of trying 'to obtain information about tanks from a member of the Royal Tank Corps and had said that she knew how to get the information across to Germany'. The charge of espionage was one thing; the double shock came with the views that Ingram had allegedly expressed: that England would be 'invaded by the Germans in three weeks' time', and that 'the Royal Family and members of the cabinet would be publicly executed'. In their place, 'Oswald Mosley would be made ruler of England.' Ingram even allegedly saw sinister significance in the arming of the Local Defence Volunteers; rather than using guns on German parachutists, she allegedly averred, they would instead use the arms to help the invaders as they led the spearhead assault on the nation. She was accused of declaring that 'our boys had not much heart for fighting and Hitler would not negotiate with anyone but Mosley'.

Any fascist sympathisers were delusional. What though of those from the opposite end of the argument? In the spring of 1940, there was a small 'Stop the War' movement, run by the Peace Pledge Union. This was a continuation of a previous 'Stop the War' flurry back in February, when a Labour councillor in Southwark Central had given up his seat to fight for re-election under that banner. The councillor had received support, funds and footwork from local Communists; they had printed 130,000 items of anti-war literature, and some three thousand volunteers helped with the campaign.

The councillor belly-flopped in the actual poll; none the less, the embers glowed bright. In late May, two young men from west London – Albert Rowland, a 21-year-old window cleaner from Paddington, and John Adkins, 20, from Harlesden, were arrested after a scene when they were handing out leaflets in Westbourne Park Road. The leaflets had the phrase 'Stop the War' printed prominently on them. One passer-by told the two men that they 'ought to be ****** well shot'. The magistrate who later heard their case judged their behaviour to have been 'seditious and subversive' and they were each sentenced to five weeks in prison. Perhaps the previous autumn, such noisy dissent might have been tolerated and accommodated; not now.

Indeed, at such a time, anything other than a custodial sentence would have been unthinkable; for even though newspaper photographs determinedly showed the cheerful faces of unwounded returning soldiers, it was obvious what so many thousands of them had been through, and were still going through; peace protests would have damaged morale by suggesting that such bravery had been futile.

For those returning, the very ordinariness of Britain had a rather dazzling quality. Charles Searle of the Medical Corps had reached Dunkirk and taken his chances in the great queue on the mole. A naval destroyer drew up but could not risk stopping. The tide was fairly low and the men had to embark as best they could, with a gap between the jetty and the vessel of about a yard, and the ship moving steadily forward. That meant making a fairly bold leap for the deck.

'I had to jump, we all had to jump, because if you missed the boat, you went into the drink,' says Mr Searle. He was at least unencumbered by weaponry. 'You'd thrown all your equipment away anyway. I only had a couple of things, my own personal stuff. Of course, if you had any luggage, that was someone's place you were pinching. So you had to chuck it. As soon as the destroyer got to the end of the mole, the boat was full up. It revved its engines.' And off they sailed. Though it sounds reasonably straightforward, Mr Searle found especially harrowing the plight of the civilian refugees, some of whom had also managed to get aboard. For a trained soldier to have seen such things was one matter. For these frightened, helpless people, sailing away from their own homes, it was another.

'We were all refugees ourselves. And there was no chance to treat anyone.' But, he adds, by and large, 'those who did get on the boat, there was nothing wrong with them – they weren't injured. Those who were injured were left on the beach or at the hospital there. But those who got on the mole and on to the boats were the able-bodied people – and they could be used again as squaddies.' The atmosphere on board was one of determined calm, although even without the threat of bombers, the circumstances were still nerve-racking. 'They gave us cups of tea and a few biscuits. And every rivet on that boat was chattering, it opened up its throttle.' Then, after several hours, on a fine spring day, there was a moment of sublime relief. 'When we saw the White Cliffs, when we came into Dover, yes . . . And of course when we got there, all the trains were ready. The authorities knew what was happening, there was 300,000 troops to get rid of.

'We were bumped on to the train, then the train was steaming off – wherever it was heading. I've got a Bible here,' he adds, reaching for a shelf, 'which someone gave me at some station we stopped at. These religious people,' he laughs. 'The Salvation Army, they were ready with buns and tea wherever we went.'

In fact the Salvation Army were in serious competition with the Women's Voluntary Service (WVS) – although, as noted by the Service's historian Charles Graves, when the first wave of soldiers started to come through, it was thought by those who didn't understand what had been happening that what the ladies could most usefully provide was their skill with darning. When it quickly became apparent that it was more than just uniforms that would need serious attention, the organisation's chair Lady Reading ensured that her volunteers did all they could. The mayor of one coastal town recalled the scenes as the soldiers started pouring in off the boats: 'We showed them into cinemas, churches and halls. As they came in through the doors, many of them fell asleep straight away.' That much was expected; what the mayor had not anticipated was the quiet dedication of the women who then looked after them:

> You should have seen them . . . rolling them [the soldiers] into lines, removing their equipment, their boots and their socks, washing their feet as they lay there. And then taking their socks away to wash them, returning them later. I went round and watched them and I thought how much the men's feet had bled. But I looked again and saw that it was not stale brown blood but fresh red blood that came from the women's hands.[1]

Back across the Channel, young sea cadet Reg Vine had had to go to extra lengths to impose his authority on often traumatised men. The strain he was under himself was quite immense: 'I didn't go daft. But I could have gone daft. If I had done a day longer there, or much longer . . .' He witnessed tragedy more than once. 'You'd get this lot of soldiers on to a destroyer. I saw one boat going down. I said to the skipper, we just put those blokes on that bloody thing. I said to him, look, they're gone. The skipper said to me, "Don't worry, Reg, don't worry – we're still here." That was his expression.'

Eventually, it was Mr Vine's turn: 'We sailed back into Ramsgate.' And initially, the arrival was too brisk, too efficient, for him to realise how many civilians were looking on. That was to change. 'We were told to get a train, and see you back at Sea Cadets when you feel like coming back,' he says now with a laugh. The train journey, like all those undertaken by the returning soldiers, had an element of pot luck about it. 'You didn't hang around waiting for a particular destination. You got on the first train and patiently went where it took you.' Mr Vine, based on the outskirts of London, remembers his journey vividly. 'We got cheered when we eventually got off. The whole train was full. Blokes that were rescued, together with the rescuers. It felt more or less as though we had a victory instead of a defeat. Luckily for us, we came from Ramsgate and the train went round and got as far as Richmond – so we only had to catch a little train from Richmond afterwards. Troops from the 1st East Surreys, well, they lived in Richmond, so we piled in together and we got a big cheer. People were on the platforms – they were allowed on, no tickets or nothing. And there was WVS with all their sandwiches and tea. What a homecoming. I'd only been out there for a few days.

'The people were so pleased – of course, so many had relations out there,' Mr Vine continues. 'All wondering, all asking – have you seen so and so? I said to one person, look, I've seen thousands, how can you describe a face or even a photo – even if you showed me a photo I wouldn't remember because we were all just dirty stinking English.' That wasn't a metaphor; the men were caked. Washing had proved impossible, though not for want of trying. 'Some of them hadn't had a bloody wash because they wouldn't wash with the salt water – well, you couldn't. Soap doesn't go with salt.' It was a minor concern. 'Fifty per cent of them had given up the hope of ever getting back. Yet they got back. What cheered them on was all the little boats out there.

'Well, I was back at Sea Cadets after about a week. The skipper said to me, don't tell many people what you've seen and I said, no, it's one of those things.' The experience had been haunting, and Mr Vine did not mind admitting to his skipper that if he had known what he was letting himself in for, he would have thought twice. 'If I knew it was going to be as bloody as that, I wouldn't have gone, I told him. Honestly, because it was such a horrible sight. And the skipper said to me, yes – but don't forget there's thousands who never come back so we've got to look at it that way – we saved what we could. He then went on to say we could have saved a lot more if we'd had more help from the Royal Navy. He blamed the navy because they wouldn't bring any back from Gibraltar or anywhere because they were all under convoy duties.' It made a change from the opprobrium aimed at Air Marshal Dowding and the RAF.

*

The spontaneity and generosity of the civilian response was also triggered by old memories; it was just twenty or so years since trainloads of troops had returned from northern France, and countless families had felt themselves within the shadow of that trauma. There must have been a shudder not just of sympathy, but of foreboding too. What had these young men seen?

The railway stations of Kent and Sussex were, like the main Victoria terminus in London, filling with people who wanted to help in some way; this was everyone's war now. 'My heart went out to them,' said Winifred Thorne, who had been on her way to visit her husband, stationed in Canterbury, but found herself stopping on the platform at Gillingham when she saw a troop train. 'The people on the station, the WVS and ordinary people like myself were giving out refreshments, so I thought that I must do something as well.' Her original plan had been to take some treats to her newly enlisted soldier husband; it was swiftly abandoned. 'I got the pork pie, sweets, biscuits and cakes . . . and handed it all to the troops,' she said. 'They were so grateful one of them even kissed me. I'll never forget it!'[2] Some of the soldiers then asked her 'what the news was' – cut off from any communication, they had no way of knowing how many men had been successfully saved or indeed how close the Germans were to invading.

They weren't the only ones with no idea. In the Kent seaside resort of Margate, the local police and council had initially simply been told by the authorities to be on the highest alert as 'something had gone wrong in France'. Instead of anticipating the arrival of British soldiers, the people of Margate thought that this meant the invasion was about to begin. The jetty was fitted with explosives, ready to destroy it to deny its use to Germans. Only a little later, when the first of the little ships began to appear, did it become clear what was happening. And then Margate, like so many other small resorts, suddenly found itself in the midst of a different kind of crisis. It was not just food and drink these soldiers needed, but also, in a great many cases, clothes: some were wearing tatters, others had had their clothes blown off by blasts. The townsfolk hastily looked out every available spare blanket, shirt, trousers, boots, underwear. Further down the coast at Folkestone, WVS volunteer Phyllis Knott remembered that the men were 'wet, bedraggled, some with hardly any clothing . . . Amazingly they were all mainly quite cheerful but I suppose that is because they were all so glad to be back home.'

Those impossibly weary returning troops, slumped against the train windows, drawing deep from greatly appreciated cigarettes, might have glimpsed trains filled with children whistling past in the opposite direction. That last weekend in May, the evacuations were on again. Boys and girls who, since the previous September, had returned to their parents and their London homes after experiencing the strangeness of rural life, now found themselves being packed up again. On top of this, children who had been sent to stay in Essex, Kent, Suffolk and on the south coast were themselves now being told to pack up; they were going to be sent to what the government called the safer areas of the Midlands, and to Wales too. The reason was that an immediate German bombing campaign was feared, if not a full-scale invasion.

London was steeling itself; the anxiety could be heard even in the small ads in the smarter periodicals. The Eccleston Hotel in Victoria, for instance, described itself as 'London's safest' without venturing further information on how this might be. Another hotel, the Mayfair in Berkeley Street, was more insouciant. It offered special terms for 'Officers of Her Majesty's Forces' and was so confident – or careless – of security that it also offered 'Dancing to AMBROSE and his ORCHESTRA, every evening until 2am. Cabaret.'

Rather magnificently, even at this moment of national suspense, the spectacularly left-wing Labour MP Emmanuel Shinwell – later a greatly influential, much-admired figure – gave a speech on how victory would only come if the government paid closer heed to the working classes. Or, as he put it, 'making the necessary changes in our industrial structure in spite of all traditions and interests'. Again, we hear forward echoes of the post-war settlement to come. 'I have the utmost confidence in the Labour members of the government,' said Mr Shinwell, 'and have no doubt that the Prime Minister and several others will stand by them – but we are still saddled with some members of the old gang who are mainly responsible for the present position.' The future held little room for unreconstructed squireocrats. Others preferred to keep the enemy across the water in view.

But the cost of the operation was already being felt, and it was by no means over. Of forty-one naval destroyers which played their parts in Dynamo, six were sunk outright, and a further fourteen were damaged badly by bombs. Rear Admiral W.S. Chalmers later illustrated the additional hazards that the crews had to face. They were there not simply as a cross-Channel ferry service; they had to be ready to rescue sailors from other stricken vessels, or indeed help with navigation on routes that were now becoming obstacle courses dotted with wrecks. The crews were also hampered; for when a vessel was filled with soldiers from the beaches and came under attack from the air, it was much harder for the sailors to manoeuvre with their guns in among the crowds of weary men on deck. On top of this, according to Chalmers, the destroyer captains were lucky if they managed to grab two hours' sleep in every twenty-four. He cited one such man who, having safely brought his destroyer and the rescued men into Dover harbour, almost instantly slid down the bridge ladder and fell asleep at the bottom. The destroyers would, in the end, bring back about 96,000 of the evacuated men.

But Admiral Ramsay was also keenly aware of the brilliant work done by what might be termed the 'amateur' vessels. He ensured that they were mentioned in dispatches. 'Of the civilian manned craft,' he wrote in one report, 'one of the best performances was that of the London Fire Brigade fire-float "Massey Shaw". All the volunteer crew were members of the London Fire Brigade or

Auxiliary Fire Service, and they succeeded in doing four round trips to the beaches in their well-found craft.'

Admiral Ramsay was even more impressed by the courage of the crews of the Thames Estuary cockle boats, all six of them; one of the vessels, *Renown*, never made it back. He wrote:

> The conduct of the crews of these cockle boats was exemplary. They were all volunteers who were rushed over to Dunkirk in one day. The boats were Thames Estuary fishing boats, and only one of their crews had been farther afield than Ramsgate before. In spite of this fact, perfect formation was maintained throughout the day and night under the control of a sub-lieutenant RNVR and all orders were carried out with great diligence even under actual shell fire and aircraft attack.

If anything, that was an understatement. Crewing the cockle boat *Resolute* was another member of Leigh-on-Sea's Osborne family, 19-year-old Eric, together with his cousin Horace and a naval rating. On one sailing, when they got to the Dunkirk beaches, the tide was too far out for them to be of practical use to the soldiers, who would have had to wade and swim a huge distance. So they piloted the vessel round to Dunkirk harbour. In the pale orange glow of the burning town, they manoeuvred past the mole – where again, the tide was too low and having no ladders on board, they could be of little use to the men high above them – and steered into a dark body of water thick with oil and debris, mechanical and human. A steamer was on its side and sinking fast, a German bomb having shot down its funnel. The cockle boat was piloted up against one of the pier ladders; some of the soldiers above, looking down at the tiny vessel, were quite vociferous. No matter how desperate they were to get away, they were not about to risk going all the way back to England in a boat as ridiculously small and impractical as that. Eric and Horace Osborne clambered up the ladder and, as Eric said, made contact with French soil, largely to be able to say that they had done so. Then they argued their case and managed to persuade a number of soldiers to join them on board *Resolute.* At that point, Eric Osborne recalled, the Germans on the outskirts of the town renewed their bombardment; and in among the blasts and the lethal shrapnel, he and his cousin, plus a quantity of soldiers, got down the pier ladder in an instant.

Amid the pandemonium, lessons from the last war were being heeded. 'The deeds of the three fighting forces are already such as to place the civilised world under a debt of gratitude that can never be written off,' wrote Rear Admiral Charles Beadnell. The hyperbole was a necessary prelude to one of the less palatable consequences of the past week. He himself, he wrote, had in 1918 taken personal care of men with severe cases of shell shock, at a time when such things were not understood so well. These ranged, he wrote, 'from headaches to states of certifiability'. He was not questioning the courage of the BEF; instead he was finding a way of reminding everyone that trauma was to be expected.

By now, it was being estimated that three-quarters of the BEF – plus a sizeable chunk of French forces – had been successfully evacuated. This somehow only turned the screw on the brave rearguard fighters left behind, struggling with ever greater desperation to halt that final German push to the Dunkirk coast. It was upon those last days that both Herr Hitler and Mr Churchill now understood what their forces were opposing. There might have been some on both sides who anticipated that the British would now seek a way of making peace; that there might be a way that Britain's empire, and Germany's spreading realm, might find ways of coexisting. Instead, something hardened; not just around the Cabinet table of Number 10, but in the national psyche. There is evidence that many people were very glad that the British seemed to have dropped their obligations to France. But it wasn't just that. It was something more perverse. Military equipment lay in ruins in the fields and rivers of a foreign country; soldiers were (largely) back home, filthy and haunted; it was understood that the enemy had all the lightning power of modernity on its side, new technology that Britain had only just started trying to match. And yet, in those first few days of June, the nation as one seemed to say: 'Fine. So that's how it is.'

14

'Beyond the Limits of Endurance'

1–3 June 1940

For those left behind, the immediate prospect had the quality of a nightmare. It was not just the idea of being at the mercy and the whim of the enemy; it was also the fearful uncertainty of what that enemy intended. Many thousands were marched to confinements in conditions of great harshness and cruelty. Harry Malpas, who had encountered such unexpected and generous skill from a German field doctor when his knee was shot out, then had to experience the bitter contrast of the aftermath. Thanks to his knee, he was sent on via barge to the Lansdorf PoW camp. Meanwhile, captured comrades in the Warwickshires had to face hundreds of miles of hot, dusty roads, suffering all the while from hunger and thirst. (There were stories of locals leaving buckets of water by the roadside to at least give the prisoners a drink; but the German guards kicked the buckets over.)

'Harry's PoW number was 50745,' says Mrs Malpas. 'And they

made him speak German. Many years later, whenever we went abroad on holiday, there would be Germans and we would get into conversation with them. First they would ask Harry about his leg, why he was limping. And Harry would tell them it was a war thing. Then they would say to him, your German is excellent, where did you learn the accent? The fact was that he picked up that and many others because he worked with Russian and Polish prisoners at the main holding camp. They were in working parties. Harry was sent to a farm in Poland. Well, he escaped from there, twice. The third time they put him in the coal mines instead, telling him that he wouldn't escape from there.'

Farm work at least held out the offer of sunshine, no matter how back-breaking it might be. The mines were a prospect of dread; a moral underworld, patrolled by men who themselves seemed to have come from that darkness. Here, extremes of violence and sadism were somehow part of ordinary life. 'They worked twelve-hour shifts, seven days a week,' says Mrs Malpas. 'That is, until they met their quota. Because if they didn't meet that quota, they would have to work on until they did, with no clocking off.' Harry Malpas was working with a range of different nationalities; there were even Russian women working there. Malpas told his wife that the local Polish people were very good to them, exhibiting rare outbreaks of kindness and altruism in an otherwise sordid world. 'Sometimes there was a sandwich smuggled in to the prisoners in the top of a helmet.' They needed the extra sustenance. 'The rations were barley soup and black bread. And what you could steal. Potatoes for instance.'

Harry Malpas was deep in the forests of an unknown land, engaged in work that could have killed him, and with no sense at all of when – or if – deliverance might come. And other than the whip-wielding brutality of the guards, there were macabre local mysteries too. 'When Harry came up from the mines after fulfilling the daily quota, he said he never knew what that foul smell in the air outside was. Until a working party went out one day and came back and told everyone else, there's a camp down there and everyone's wearing pyjamas.' They were not to know that Auschwitz was just a few miles away.

In its unrelenting daily grimness, says Mrs Malpas, life took on a certain level of pitch-black humour. 'The commandant went round the camp every night with his dog, an Alsatian. Well, one night, the dog was off its lead and it went into a hut on its own – and it never came out.

'Harry didn't know who did it but his fellow prisoners already had a big pot with stew going.' There was no question where the dog had ended up. 'These men used to trap birds for the stew as well. Harry would describe how they used to get a bit of string, a stick, a net. And then how absolutely everything they caught used to go in the stewpot. So the commandant's dog went in. Eventually, they were all called out for a special parade, they had to stand on the compound and not move until anyone admitted that they knew the circumstances under which the dog had gone missing. No one told and the commandant gave up.'

There were also episodes of rough extemporised justice. 'There was an officer with a riding crop and a brass lamp – he was called Panic,' says Mrs Malpas. Panic's particular penchant was for lashing the Russian women with his whip. 'Now, everyone was working with these little shovels. When Panic set about this woman, another prisoner hit him from behind with one of the little shovels; Harry said they had an edge like a razor blade. They buried this officer deep in a hole. Once again, they were all called out on to the parade ground – but once again, no one told.

'Harry was in the mines for four and a half years. When he went in, he was fifteen stone. When he came out, he was seven stone.'

Although this is only one story, the broad experience of those captured near Dunkirk was grim: the forced marches, the thin soups of withered vegetables and decaying meat, the lack of fresh water, the steady loss of strength. To be taken prisoner of war in this theatre was a dehumanising process. Many veterans recall the lupine aggression of the young German soldiers, giddy and cruel with triumph and adrenaline. Among the prisoners was a lot of unarticulated bitterness; not merely the frustration of being caught almost before the conflict had begun, but also the sense that they had been up against a technically far superior enemy; that they had been let down by a certain level of complacency as regards arming the troops. And of course there was the terrible sense of vanishing into oblivion, with – at least temporarily – no way of letting loved ones back home know where or how they were.

Lord Gort had, quite properly, waited until the last possible moment before leaving France. By Saturday 1 June, he was back in England (angrily, against his wishes, but at the orders of Churchill), with defiant words: 'We shall meet them again,' he announced, 'and the next time victory will be with us.' After a debriefing in Whitehall, Lord Gort made the short journey across St James's Park to Buckingham Palace, where the King invested him Knight Grand Commander of the Order of the Bath.

It seems startling now that just a day beforehand, Prime Minister Winston Churchill and his deputy Clement Attlee had flown out – their plane high above besieged northern France – to Paris for a war council meeting with Premier Reynaud and his deputy Pétain. The meeting, as reported, 'reached full agreement regarding all manoeuvres which the situation called for . . . the Allied Governments and peoples are more than ever implacably resolved to pursue, in the closest possible concord, their present struggle until complete victory is assured.' The fine words are in dazzling contrast to the increasing sense of desolation on the French side, and the firm resolution on the British side that neither should drag the other down. Days before that meeting, Churchill had told the Cabinet in his Commons office: 'M. Reynaud wants to get us to the conference table with Herr Hitler. If we once got to the table, we should then find that the terms offered us touched our independence and integrity. When, at this point, we got up to leave the conference table, we should find that all the forces of resolution which were now at our disposal would have vanished.'[1]

That Friday in Paris, Churchill, accompanied by General Hastings and General Ismay, listened to M. Reynaud's complaints that more English than French troops were being evacuated from Dunkirk. Churchill told him that he would try to ensure that the balance was rectified. It was also at this meeting that one of the French officials raised the possibility of France suing for a separate peace with Germany. He was immediately told by British military officials that Britain would have to respond by blockading France and more particularly, the French ports that would have fallen into German hands.

So by that first weekend of June, the patterns of the shaken kaleidoscope seemed to have settled into their new configurations. The Prime Minister was perfectly adamant that Britain would fight on, no matter what. By contrast, the scenes of refugees packing cars and leaving Paris told their own grim story. And in the meantime, on those wide beaches in the north, rearguard soldiers were finding it ever harder to beat off the surging confidence of the Germans. As reported by Douglas Williams for the *Sunday Times*, 'the position of the troops remaining on the beaches became more and more precarious this [Saturday] evening as German shelling and dive-bombing increased in intensity.' He related how many men were now being forced to swim half a mile in 'oil-scummed water' to the ships that were forced by tides to wait offshore. For reasons of delicacy, there was one detail he omitted; the water was now also clogged with corpses. A Guards officer interviewed at Ramsgate – his uniform still soaked right through – told that after he had swum out to a destroyer and got on board, the vessel was bombed four times from above. There was also the story of the defenders' courage – an anecdote concerning Black Watch men who had been fighting desperately, and who asked 'When is the next boat?' Not for two hours, they were told, at which their commanding officer said: 'Well boys, you might just as well go back and do a bit more. It's no use wasting time here.'

The Ministry of Information was still careful about which soldiers and officers were permitted to relay their stories; many veterans recall that their commanding officers had given them strict orders, upon return, that they were to tell no one – including family – of what they had been through. But again, the Ministry was running behind the popular mood. Families would have seen soon enough when their fathers and brothers came home what sort of experiences they had been through. And the strict censorship of the press continued to be matched by a huge amount of self-censorship. Editors had no wish for their readers to turn against them for printing demoralising material.

But what they consistently did was – accidentally – to highlight the peculiar contrast between the mighty events across the Channel and the relentlessly whimsical nature of some corners of English life. One reporter was beguiled that Saturday by games of cricket being played in small Kent villages under the sharp, warm blue sky, the clicks and the applause held in counterpoint by the music of peaceful birdsong.

The incongruity was sharp for military and civilians alike. Deptford shopkeeper S.J. Carty encountered some soldiers on the trains. 'Going home, sat next to a Major – a 3rd class carriage too,' he wrote. 'A Tommy came in, battle stained . . . [he said] when they got away, the sky was black with enemy planes . . . he was wearing the trousers of a pal who had been killed beside him. He fell asleep at the finish of his conversation.'

One man living near Waterloo station on London's South Bank recalled seeing 'three young men . . . in stained and crumpled denim fatigues'; two of them were 'barefoot', they were all sunburnt – and one was casually swinging a German helmet. 'They looked glad to be alive.' The eyewitness could not recall seeing any other evacuees and mused that these had somehow escaped the regimented return to makeshift barracks; they also brought home 'the reality of war'.

Yet the reality was still multi-faceted. In his diary on 2 June, George Orwell gave a brief yet vivid portrait of London life that odd, suspended weekend:

> The usual Sunday crowds drifting to and fro, perambulators, cycling clubs, people exercising dogs, knots of young men loitering at street corners, with not an indication in any face or in anything that one can overhear that these people grasp that they are likely to be invaded within a few weeks, though today all the Sunday papers are telling them so . . . Yet these people will behave bravely enough when the time comes, if only they are told what to do.[2]

The repeated phrase 'these people' might seem today as comically patrician as any grand announcement from Whitehall. Orwell was quite clear-eyed, though. In the newspapers, some correspondents were putting out the flags to an unbalanced degree.

One such, a special 'naval correspondent' for the *Observer,* was keen to let readers know that there had been not one iota of ignominy in the evacuation. 'I was on the bridge of one of our destroyers packed from end to end,' he wrote. 'As I stood there, it occurred to me that there are retreats and reverses that are things of splendour.' He forbore to mention any notable historical precedents that he might have had in mind. 'It may well be that the triumphant extrication of the BEF may prove [a] turning point in this war.' For of course, at that stage, few would have even guessed that Britain was merely at the start of it. The proud naval correspondent made light of the bombing, relating that one explosive which detonated in shallow water had resulted in a geyser of grey mud that spattered uniforms up and down the deck and resulted in a great deal of laughter. That much sounds rather too glib to be the entire truth. But, the naval correspondent concluded:

> this was no army in defeat. They looked in magnificent fettle, ruddy and burly, and wearing full equipment . . . they settled down quickly on deck like a well-behaved school treat . . . They were not just undaunted. They talked like victors. But for the German superiority in aerial bombers, they knew themselves the masters of the enemy. They were not braggarts. They knew, that was all.

Later, when newsreel footage of Dunkirk carried a similarly larded, excessively sweetened voiceover, cinema audiences hooted with mirth. Stirring patriotism was one thing; treating the public like daft children was another. Despite all the efforts of the Ministry of Information, it was quite plain what had happened; there would hardly be 300,000 men back on these shores for any other reason. Nor indeed was this sort of propaganda candy-floss necessary in the first place. Rather like the Home Office psychiatrists who predicted that a Blitz in London would lead to an outbreak of mass psychosis and the complete breakdown of civic society, the authorities were misreading the mood of the general public. 'Everyone seems to think that we are making the best (an excellent best in its way) of a very bad job at Dunkirk,' wrote ambulance attendant Margaret Saunders, prior to a bout of sunbathing. And the larger point was not that their loved ones in the BEF had behaved with leonine valour and supernatural discipline, but that they were now back to defend their own shores.

The troops were now scattered all over the country; some posted back to their original barracks, others sent to seemingly random ad hoc camps. Charles Searle, for instance, found himself far from his native Bow bells in a bell tent outside Bristol. Others were met trying to work out which train connections to catch from a remote stop in Derbyshire, where a shoal of evacuated children from Southend had also pitched up, being given milk by local volunteers and looking around with bewilderment. 'We come from the Thames,' said one child gravely, staring with apparent awe at the louring hills in the distance; something he would never have seen in his native estuarine abode. The young soldiers were sympathetic; probably many of them had never ventured this far into the wilderness of the north before either.

The *Manchester Guardian*, meanwhile, reported the arrival of hundreds of men, 'including many of the wounded'. These soldiers were apparently a source of curious trepidation. 'People were able to see something of the strain that had been put upon soldiers,' the reporter wrote. 'They came out from the temporary billets in schools . . . they still looked tired . . . some clothing was still improvised and not quite a uniform . . . They would be seen in cafes and in the streets and on all sides one could hear words of admiration from civilians, anxious but too restrained to speak to the men.' Doubtless, too, the men were under orders to say as little as possible, though one wounded man on a stretcher was heard to exclaim: 'Fancy coming home like this and never having seen a German.'

Young RAF signalsman Arthur Taylor was numbed by the time his deliverance from Dunkirk arrived; a mix, he said, of the hypnotic percussion of the bombs with the red wine that was his only alternative to fresh water. 'I didn't even know that Churchill had become Prime Minister until we got on to the beaches,' says Mr Taylor. 'Someone had a radio and we heard then that he was PM. We thought, oh, we're all right now. Chamberlain didn't really inspire and at our age, we didn't bother really. So, I was on the beach with red wine: just taking sips every now and then. It didn't make us giddy. The tide was coming in and going out. I can't remember much about the queue, apart from dispersing to water's edge when the bombers came over.'

There was of course the continuing difficulty of his RAF status; he had witnessed a Spitfire pilot, who had been forced to ditch in a parachute, arrive at the mole and join the queue only to be thrown off it by a group of furiously resentful men who believed that the RAF had abandoned them to their fates. However, he says now with a laugh, 'We eventually got on to the mole and you were shoved around. You waited your turn and there was an officer or one of these blokes counting you off, and said, right, 163 men. You lot get on that fishing trawler the *Lord Gray*. Well, I got on and lay down and slept. I woke up and first thing I remember, we were halfway across the Channel. The water was as calm as that table top there. I just turned around and went to sleep again until we got to Dover. And that was it. Don't remember the trip across at all.

'But we were lucky really. There was one soldier with us who – just a few hours before in Dunkirk – was out in the water. He was up to his chest, with the tide going up and going down. And what upset him most,' laughs Mr Taylor, 'was that the pack on his back was full of cigarettes.'

It was only as they disembarked at Dover that it became clear that Mr Taylor was with RAF signals; at this point, it only mattered so they could allocate some part of the country that he might get sent to. 'They sorted air force, army regiments, everyone. Of course the Guards marched off. And we got on the train. And there were the ladies with buns and tea and everything you could eat. We were starving. Shoved in a carriage, on a train, and off to London.' Once they got to the main London terminus, 'we were waiting for a coach. So we all went to this little bar on the station and there were drinks all round. From everybody.'

In London, there was no dallying on the Underground for Mr Taylor and his RAF colleagues; instead, a motor coach (possibly diplomatically wise – the idea of a handful of RAF men travelling in confined tube compartments with tired and emotional soldiers might have been explosive). 'We got on to the RAF coach to Uxbridge.' Now a busy suburb, Uxbridge was then a small town on the fringes of west London. These days, one might expect that the priority for the authorities would be that the men received high quality rest and recuperation. Back then, things were a little rougher and readier. When they got there, 'the Station Warrant Officer took us up to our billet and said, "This is where you can sleep tonight. We'll give you something to eat now. And in the morning, reveille on this camp is 6 a.m. But since you came from Dunkirk, you can lie in until 7 a.m."

'We went straight to sleep, no pyjamas,' adds Mr Taylor. And certainly, he says, there was 'no counselling. An hour extra in bed. That was it.'

Very shortly afterwards, he did get a short time off. 'I went to see my mother. I told her I'd been at Dunkirk. "Oh, she said, I thought you'd been in the south of France." I said, what gave you that idea? She said, "I don't know." So she hadn't been worried! We got a few days off. And then back to camp and back on guard duty.'

Curiously, he says, given the exhaustion of the previous few days, it did not take long for their body clocks to readjust – like jetlag, though in some ways not even as extreme as that. 'You go to sleep the next night, and the next, and you gradually pick up.' On top of this, there was activity. 'Guard duty, no time to think.'

Mr Taylor and the men were quickly marshalled back into a tight military routine. There was a very good reason: the crisis wasn't over. Indeed, it was perceived to be just beginning. 'And of course I still had no uniform,' says Mr Taylor. Anything he had – from the outsize mackintosh intended to disguise his service, to the other pieces – was either back in France, or in no fit state. 'I was walking around and people shouting, where's your hat? So we had to be completely re-kitted. Everything. Brand new. Then we were put on guard duties, guarding cars.' Not just any cars, of course. 'These were old cars that had been driven on to airstrips and into fields to stop the German paratroopers from landing. Because the invasion was on.'

In essence, Mr Taylor and his comrades were now taking over – properly armed – duties that had until now been handled by the Local Defence Volunteers. Again, the very idea of this must have been psychologically soothing to anyone who saw the military come in: the idea that the nation was defended. Mr Taylor, from here, was shuttled to the north, and eventually found himself at Liverpool

Airport, where 13 Squadron were reassembling. 'That's the very first time I saw 13 Squadron personnel – after all that time.'

Similarly, for young Glaswegian Bob Halliday, deliverance had come with eye-rubbing speed, and what happened afterwards was in its own way just as disorientating. He and his friends decided they were going to make their own luck. 'We decided that with the amount of abandoned lorries near the beaches, we could use their power-drums, and other parts, and build a raft,' he says. 'We were going to get the non-swimmers simply to sit on the raft – and the swimmers were going to push it. And one man was going to swim out to sea and see if there was any enemy about.

'A chap from High Wycombe was going to swim out – he was a big hefty swimmer – but when we went down to the waterside with this big craft, we met the navy – and they said, "Look, the boats are out there and the small boats will be coming to pick you up. But you must file out. Leave the raft. Drive those lorries into the sea." So we filed out into the water and waited and waited. And gradually, three men in a lifeboat came, and they dragged us out of the water and took us to a Dutch skoot called *Ahilda*. It was used for going into shallow waters. So we went on board – and as soon as we had done so, they asked for volunteers to go back and bring some of the other men back.

'But I didn't,' says Mr Halliday. 'I'd had enough.'

Bob Halliday and his friends were transported safely back to Ramsgate, and rushed on from there. 'We went on to a place in Oxfordshire, an officers' training camp.' Like so many other soldiers, they found themselves subject to a strict clampdown. 'When we got there, we were locked in. We weren't allowed to go out, we were a mess. We had to try and tidy up as best as we could.' It was clearly crucial for public morale that the public should not catch more glimpses of traumatised troops than could be avoided. But after a short period of confinement to barracks, says Mr Halliday, 'they sent us on leave.' He returned to Glasgow and found the slightly strange shyness of a young hero's welcome; a community looking at him with admiration yet not quite feeling that it could broach the questions that it wanted answered.

'For three nights then they sent us home. We got a nice welcome home. As soon as it was known that I was back, all the families and all the other lads gathered. There were a lot in the same boat as me.' But there were still, heartbreakingly, families waiting for news: while Bob Halliday was there, many others were absent. 'Mums, sisters, came rushing up to me to say, did you see John?' It was a forlorn hope in among hundreds of thousands of other troops. 'But,' says Mr Halliday, 'you could understand.'

In the midst of the great movement of men, there were lighter moments. One major and his men had been picked up by a Thames barge, bedraggled, their uniforms practically shredded, but essentially unhurt. As they neared their port destination, they were thrilled to see the grand reception that awaited them by the quayside; the sheer numbers of eager faces. Among them were the lady mayoress and a press photographer. It was only at this point that the major and his men realised that they didn't have any trousers between them; with some speed, they improvised rather badly with curtains from the boat's portholes.

On the trains, too, were to be found moments of satire. John Thornton recalled being jammed on to such a train after having landed at Dover just before dawn on 1 June. 'We were going very slowly through a station some miles north of London,' he told the BBC, 'when we saw an RAF airman and his wife or girlfriend standing on the platform. Some wag shouted "Good Lord, we've got an RAF after all – there he is!" and everyone on the train jeered. I ought to point out,' added Mr Thornton honourably, 'that the Luftwaffe had dominated the skies over France . . . although I later learned that the RAF had suffered very heavy casualties unseen by us.'[3]

Sometimes, after these train journeys, the disorientated soldiers would find themselves not in barracks, but in makeshift camps, like refugees. In Leicester, a number of soldiers were marched off the train and through the gates of a local park. For a little while, they were left there, sitting on the grass, as arrangements were made. Local schoolboys – gripped, but also slightly timid about these bedraggled figures – approached and asked if they might have any souvenirs of war that they would be able to keep. A few of the soldiers, with smiles and heads shaking, produced small items for the boys. One lad remembered some years later the remorse he felt when he finally learned what these men had been through. But was such contrition necessary? Possibly, after such an ordeal, a friendly question from a kid would have been the life-affirming proof to the soldiers that they were safely home.

Back at Dover, there were other nameless arrivals from the French port, whose destiny was rather darker than those of the soldiers. 'They were nobodies . . .' ran the rather moving newspaper report. 'They had been abandoned in the ruins of Dunkirk and they had fled to the human companionship of the crowded beach.' This was the extraordinary postscript to the story of what had happened to the frightened dogs – maddened by the non-stop bangs and crashes – in the midst of the siege. 'Terrified by the noise of shellfire and by the sense of death, they had trotted with the troops to the ships or swum out to the nearest little boats. Now setters and spaniels, shepherd dogs and mongrels stood patiently on the dockside waiting for the RSPCA wagon that came to take them to be destroyed.' This was not random cruelty; rabies was a real problem on the continent, and the very last thing that Britain needed. The report continued:

> There is no one to pay for their six months of quarantine and the free dogs' homes are full of dogs that belong to penniless refugees. Most stood quiet, suffering the petting of the soldiers, but some were shell-shocked, cowering into corners and trembling. One little fox terrier bitch trembled incessantly and jumped whenever a bus went by. One only of the wretched pack has been saved. A whole boatload of British soldiers has

undertaken to pay the ten shillings a week for six months that will keep through its quarantine a minute black puppy.

The report was also a shrewd form of misdirection, removing some of the focus from shell-shocked, trembling soldiers. It artfully neglected, too, to mention that at other ports, the bewildered dogs were perfectly happily taken in by such organisations as the PDSA, and served out their quarantine before being farmed out to new English homes. Some troops remembered the almost hysterical laughter on board as they realised that these sweet animals only understood French, and stared blankly when addressed in English.

None the less, the animal stories were important. At such a time of national emergency, one might imagine a shut-down of all avenues of escapism, but this was emphatically not the case. If anything, the claims of culture were being pushed harder than ever. After a short interregnum, the Sadlers Wells ballet company announced on 1 June that it was resuming performances. Indeed, during wartime it seemed to find a fresh lease of artistic life. Elsewhere, in terms of popular fiction, that crucial weekend also saw the publication of several juicy new spy thrillers, many involving Nazis as the villains. *Introducing Mr Zodiac*, otherwise a standard espionage shocker, featured an astrological theme and contrived to involve a monstrous cameo from Hitler himself in Berchtesgaden. The big bookstall bestseller was a thriller called *Faked Passports* by a young writer called Dennis Wheatley; later better known for occult fiction, he was shortly to immerse himself in the dark arts of British counter-intelligence.

One might think that, that weekend, there would be a sense of shutters being brought down, of lowered voices, of quiet tension. Instead, the Bishop of Rochester, Dr Chavasse, went on the offensive with a sermon so inflammatory it was reported as news. 'The last war revealed tragically and rather unexpectedly to those of them at the Front that a war, however righteous, opened the door to sensuality and materialism,' he said. That same door of sensuality was, he said, swinging open again. 'The licence that infected the population like an epidemic occasioned after the Armistice a general collapse of moral standards from which we have only recently and painfully emerged,' he continued. 'Unless we take precautions, we shall have to tread the same downward path again . . . Alcohol should be regarded as the Fifth Column, the enemy within our gates, sabotaging government output and damaging morale.' Yet the drinks industry, quite naturally, regarded this as a time when teetotalism would snatch comfort and relaxation away from those who needed it most. One brand used the young actress Pat Kirkwood – much rumoured to have enjoyed a romance with Prince Philip – as the acceptable face of alcoholic refreshment in magazine advertisements that week. They quoted her as saying: 'My exacting work on stage and screen makes great demands on energy and fitness. I find an occasional glass of plain Martini Vermouth a light and pleasant stimulant which undoubtedly helps to keep me at the top of my form.'

It took another of the theatre's more notable figures to point out, that weekend, the sort of jeopardy that the country now faced, and what best to do about it. Playwright and novelist Patrick Hamilton – whose work would later be filmed by Alfred Hitchcock – wrote a letter to the *Manchester Guardian* suggesting complete evacuation of all mothers, children and 'useless mouths' from cities, and for the remaining men to make ready. 'Who can deny that a man will fight better, whether in the Army, in a government office or in a factory, if he knows his children are in safety?' This was also an interesting prefiguring of a theme that Churchill – perhaps subconsciously – would touch on a few days later; an idea that a Nazi invasion would not be resisted merely by conventional military forces, but by all men, civilians as well as soldiers; and that the battlefields would be the urban spaces. No more trenches, no more no man's land; instead, every house, every garden, every factory, every railway line would now be the front line. There would be no liminal spaces for sanctuary.

So there is an element of bathos to be found in the 'situations vacant' columns on that first week of June 1940; the sheer numbers of grand houses advertising for parlour maids and cooks and manservants and chauffeurs. 'Wanted end of June, Butler, over military age, for country house. Wages £70–£75.' That position was in Devon. 'Useful Lady's maid, about 35, required; hairdressing essential.' That was for a townhouse in smart Knightsbridge. 'Good, plain cooks' were required too, all over the country. Yet already, the age of servants was over, without the upper classes having quite realised it. Even men too old to serve in the military had more important things to be doing now, either in factories, offices or indeed on roofs in the middle of the night, watching for fires. The women, even more so, had a calling rather higher than that of domestic maintenance. There was a scramble to get into the Wrens; equally, there was burgeoning enthusiasm for storming the gates of the factories, and indeed heading off into the country to help work the land.

The upper classes might have thought in June 1940 that difficulties in hiring staff would dissolve after the war. Yet this war – and the months before it – had already changed the landscape irrevocably. The soldiers of the BEF were coming home to a land that was, paradoxically, beginning to mould itself more to the wider will of the ordinary people, just as the government demanded greater and greater efforts and sacrifices from those ordinary people. The vortex of the Dunkirk escape, that intense release of mass emotion, was an element in cementing the sense of the primacy of the ordinary man and woman.

The landscape of Britain was, by that weekend, changed physically too. Everywhere, all road signs and mile stones had been grubbed up and removed. In many cases, street signs had been painted over. England, declared one observer, was 'now a maze'. Those much-anticipated German parachutists would be flummoxed by such a labyrinth. Meanwhile, the Automobile Association and the Royal Automobile Club had been semi-militarised – their motorbike patrolmen now wore steel helmets and their bikes were camouflaged.

As the last few hundred Allied troops – more French now than British – were helped aboard the little cabin cruisers and flat-bottomed skoots, Duff Cooper, the Minister of Information, had flown to Paris. There was already a sense of darkness falling across the city and yet remarkably – perhaps betraying a further element of denial – in the British efforts to keep the French in fighting spirits, Cooper made a BBC broadcast from Paris, having earlier been caught up in a dramatic bombing raid that curtailed his lunch. 'My visit . . . has coincided with the most important air raid yet made on Paris,' he told his listeners. 'Perhaps the Germans heard how beautiful Paris is looking and determined as they are to stamp out beauty in the world, thought Paris was a most desirable objective on this June morning.' But there was to be no sense of defeatism:

> The French are now fighting for their lives. This is not the first time. The French people are different from us and are sometimes difficult to understand, but there is one thing they have in common with us. They have a love for their own country and they have the courage to die for it. So long as our countries are solidly united, there is no cause for fear.

Paris was to fall just seven days later.

In any case, had Cooper misjudged what the British public might fear most? The scenes of open jubilation as tired men came home on leave spoke rather of a sense of release occasioned by the fact that the two countries were no longer bound together, with British troops helpless on foreign soil. British destiny did not appear yoked to French.

*

In the letters pages, a new mood of Blimpish bellicosity could be heard. One missive, addressed from 'A Kentish Parish', declared:

> There are a very few whimperers and panic-mongers still among us. We know them. Would it were possible, since nothing will quiet them, to ship these people away to the safe place – wherever it is – that their watery bowels yearn for; leaving in our island only the true children of its soil who will work and fight as of old in silence and in God's name.

Fine – if sinister – words; but elsewhere in Kent, there was one man at the very edge of physical and mental exhaustion who had a rather more nuanced sense of the children of Britain's soil. Certainly, over the last eight or nine days, he had seen extraordinary courage from the most ordinary quarters; but he had also seen what the enemy was capable of doing. Admiral Ramsay, working day and night on a balance of experience and instinct, had co-ordinated the fiercely complex to-ing and fro-ing of so many hundreds of different vessels, using the keenest instinct of all to gauge when crews were passing beyond their limits.

The non-stop sailing was one thing; the non-stop jeopardy was another. By the weekend, daylight sailings had to be suspended; despite all the efforts of the RAF, the German fighters were simply becoming too accurate and the rate of attrition both for the navy and civilian shipping was sickeningly high. It was not enough that the captains and their crews must turn from a safe harbour and head back out when all limbs ached and the eyes could barely stay open. It was knowing they did so with every chance of being hit, and sunk, and left flailing in the waters of the Channel.

But it wasn't over; there were still a few thousand men stranded. On the evening of Saturday 1 June, Admiral Ramsay sent to all the boats that were bobbing around under his command the following signal: 'I fully appreciate the demands which are being made on the endurance of officers and men but the situation makes it imperative that you should make one last effort. I am sure that you all realise what is at stake.'

Ramsay's deputy Captain Tennant meanwhile had signalled from his position at the mole, supervising the evacuation from the French side. He sent his boss this admirably direct communication, the tone of which suggests a great deal of easy mutual respect: 'Things are getting very hot for ships; over 100 bombs on ships here since 0530; many casualties. Have directed that no ships sail during daylight . . . If perimeter holds will complete evacuation tomorrow, Sunday night, including most French.'

There were still 6000 British and 50,000 French troops awaiting rescue from Dunkirk; the oscillations between hope and despair were wild. Admiral Ramsay was, in the meantime, surveying a fleet that had been battered and pummelled almost to a standstill; almost but not quite. The sheer scale of all that they had achieved was a spur to inspiration, for that one last mighty effort. On the Sunday, Ramsay sent this signal to all ships: 'The final evacuation is staged for tonight, and the Nation looks to the Navy to see it through. I want every ship to report as soon as possible whether she is fit to meet the call which has been made on our courage and endurance.'

So began one final sortie, an extraordinary blend of logistics and bravery. Since no boats were now sailing under the bright spring sunshine, there was a gaggle of vessels now gathered at all the ports; Admiral Ramsay saw to it that their departures, in the gathering royal blue twilight of that early June evening, were spaced carefully, so that they would not all be bunched together at the Dunkirk mole. The rescue was lickety-split; by 11 p.m., the destroyer *Winchester* found a mere 152 British soldiers to take back. And so it was that, half an hour before midnight, Ramsay's deputy Captain Tennant was at last able to signal back to Dover: 'BEF evacuated.' Yet even after huge numbers of French soldiers had been embarked, it was not over. There was the matter of the 10,000 or so French troops who had been fighting desperately just four miles away to try and ensure that the Germans did not break through. 'I hoped and believed last night would see us through,' said Ramsay in a signal to all craft. 'But the French . . . were unable to send their troops to the pier in time. We cannot leave our Allies in the lurch and I must call on all officers and men detailed for further evacuation tonight to let the world see that we will never let down our Ally.'

After so many round trips, the crews of the destroyers would almost have been hallucinating with exhaustion. Ramsay himself seemed to be bumping up against his limits. Though his secretary, a man named Cull, later emphasised his superior's apparent tirelessness, he admitted that by this stage, he did 'begin to show the strain a little. I remember him saying to me there must be one final lift but the ships remaining were few . . . and scarcely fit for service, the men tired and exhausted.' Cull recalled that Ramsay agonised over whether he could call on these men for this extra effort. And indeed on the early evening of Monday 3 June, Ramsay sent a signal to his superiors in the Admiralty telling frankly of 'immense strain' among crews, the ends of tethers being reached and fresh tests 'that may be beyond the limits of endurance'.[4] In other words, they would be able to pull off the feat once more, for just one more night; but if any further evacuations were needed after that, fresh teams would have to be drafted in. The Lords of the Admiralty understood perfectly and agreed.

And so it was, in the scant hours of midsummer darkness, that the last spectacular effort was made. There was very heavy shell fire from the Germans in Dunkirk port; but the French troops, plus a great many refugees, had a glassy-eyed stoicism. That night, some 26,000 people were borne across the Channel into England's safe harbours. Three thousand of them sailed on board *Tynwald*, an Isle of Man pleasure steamer constructed to convey Lancastrian mill workers to their summer holidays. That night, too, Admiral Ramsay and the small workforce around him took their turns to grab a couple of hours' sleep on the mattresses that lined some of the corridors, before wakening again swiftly and, without any pause, plunging straight back into the work.

Operation Dynamo officially came to an end on Tuesday 4 June 1940 at 2.33 p.m. Of course, there were still thousands of British troops scattered elsewhere in France who were to try and make it out from other ports, in the frenetic days to come. But the legend of what Ramsay and his team had pulled off now began to develop fast. The evacuation itself was a feat of endurance and sharp organisation combined with the will, shown by all, to somehow not give way to panic or hysteria. The story of Dunkirk, as it would be told and retold, was to take on mythic proportions; perhaps it is modern Britain's core creation myth. And the very telling of all these stories in 1940, on both sides of the Atlantic, was to produce a spiritual updraught thanks to which the British were psychologically prepared for that summer's battle for survival.

PART THREE

15
The Spontaneous Legend

June 1940

As a speech, it is not only quoted to an extraordinary degree, but also replayed with some frequency; certain of its more distinctive phrases are still used by our more weaselly contemporary politicians. It has been said of Churchill's rhetoric that the real key to his genius was his deliberately antiquated vocabulary and cadence. Rather than trying to adopt modern terminology, Churchill instead would deploy phrases that might have come from the eighteenth century. As well as being stirringly theatrical and emotional, this might also have had the double advantage of fogging his precise meaning. For there are passages in his speech of 4 June 1940 – best known for its phrase 'we will fight them on the beaches' – that now leave one unsure as to the Prime Minister's exact intentions on that day.

Nor does the popular memory of Churchill's soaring speeches always tally with the response they originally received. Contemporaries recall that the passages held by posterity to have been the most stirring were sometimes greeted with indifference or even slightly shifting impatience in the House of Commons. The address that Churchill gave to MPs on 4 June 1940 has lived on – and will continue to do so – by virtue of its rousing conclusion, which we will examine. But the words that immediately preceded it speak now of an interesting vulnerability. When it came to evoking the legend of Dunkirk, Churchill had surprisingly little to do with it. It was not simply that he was anxious that the British public was being lulled into a false sense of victory; it seemed also that he needed everyone to know what he had most feared – just how close the nation had come to the edge of the precipice. And indeed how close it still stood. As the last of the British troops shuffled off those bullet-riddled boats, General Montgomery made plain his vehement opposition to the idea of a ribbon being created to mark the event. 'If it is not understood that the army suffered a defeat,' he said, 'then our island is in grave danger.'

It is difficult not to analyse Churchill's 4 June speech as though it were Shakespeare, a passage from *Henry V*, a text wrought with codes for certain influential people to hear. Was it the Prime Minister's way of preparing the British public for the ignominious fall of France? Was it some crafty lateral appeal to American politicians and the American public for more active aid? The famous passage where Churchill suggested that we would 'fight them in the streets, fight them on the landing grounds' drew cheers. But why? The imagery was that of desperate guerrilla warfare. An army forced to fight the enemy 'in the hills' was an army that had lost; its resistance could be no more than a defiant gesture. Which is why it is worth pondering now the idea that this is what Churchill really believed; that Hitler's forces were poised, barely thirty miles away, to swoop and to conquer before Britain's shattered and bewildered forces could mount any effective defence.

Just before Churchill rose to the dispatch box that afternoon, his deputy Clement Attlee had been answering questions on everything from taxation on profits to soldiers on bicycles. The Prime Minister, when he began, took a while to settle. He was intent on giving a full and proper account not only of the evacuation, but also of the episodes of valour, and the perfidy and weakness of the Belgian King for capitulating. 'The German eruption swept like a scythe around the right and rear armies of the north . . . it severed our own communications for food and ammunition,' he intoned dolefully. There was the irresistible insult thrown at the German army that came 'plodding' behind the 'armoured and mechanised onslaught': 'The dull, brute mass of the ordinary German army and German people, always so ready to be led to the trampling down in other lands of liberties and comforts which they have never known in their own.' But the Prime Minister also confessed that the Allies none the less had been comprehensively outmanoeuvred. 'When a week ago today I asked the House to fix this afternoon as the occasion for a statement, I feared it would be my hard lot to announce from this box the greatest military disaster in our long history,' he said. 'I thought – and some good judges agreed with me – that perhaps 20,000 or 30,000 men might be re-embarked.' In other words, not even 10 per cent. 'The whole root and core of the British army', upon which the larger armies for the future would be built, 'seemed about to perish upon the field or be led to an ignominious and starving captivity.' (In fact, even as Churchill spoke, many hundreds of British soldiers were about to be subjected to that very fate.)

Yet despite the 'pitiful' surrender of Belgium, the British forces had resisted an enemy which fought with 'great strength and fierceness'; and the Royal Navy 'had to operate on the difficult coast . . . making trip after trip across the dangerous waters'. There was no mention of the very core of the Dunkirk legend: the little ships. Churchill acknowledged the 'countless' merchant seamen who had taken part with such enthusiasm. No nods, however, to the paddle steamers and the Thames yachts. It would take another great rhetorician to see – the very next day – how in fact it was this element of the story that made it so beguiling and ultimately redemptive.

Churchill even acknowledged his own theatricality when he

declared: 'Suddenly, the scene has cleared, the crash and thunder has for the moment – but only for the moment – died away. A miracle of deliverance, achieved by valour, by perseverance, by perfect discipline, by faultless service, by resource, by skill, by unconquerable fidelity, is manifest to us all.' In the House, there were calls of 'hear, hear'.

The address then went on to touch the subject that was clearly closest to Churchill's heart: the air force. The courage of the fighters sent his rhetoric aloft once more, going so far as to invoke the Crusaders and the Knights of the Round Table – images from antiquity, yet following the theme of young men 'going forth every morn to guard their native land'. There was nothing evasive in this high language; Churchill was quite frank about the devastating loss of equipment, and the fact that Britain's war effort, up until that point, had been inadequate in terms of production keeping pace with events. But even here was a glint of heroism: 'Capital and Labour have cast aside their interests, rights and customs and put them into the common stock.' He spoke of the seven-day weeks, the extra hours. None the less, he went on, 'our thankfulness at the escape of our army . . . must not blind us to the fact that what has happened in France and Belgium has been a colossal military disaster.'

In 1940, there was no broadcasting from the chamber of the House of Commons. The way that many people would have first absorbed the essence of the speech was through reported quotes, spoken by the newsreader, on the evening's radio broadcasts. The next morning, newspapers printed the entire speech. (Unlike subsequent occasions, Churchill did not go into a BBC studio to give the speech again; the first time he repeated it was for a 1949 recording, intended for posterity.) None the less, despite not having heard the leader actually utter the words, there were many at the time who recalled a near-religious feeling; a sense of being transfigured by the events of those days, a sentiment, in that crystal June sunshine, of irrational optimism. So that when we consider now the most famous passage of that speech, we see how Churchill's plea for steely determination and watchfulness might have been transformed into a rather more powerful emotion. 'We are told that Herr Hitler has a plan for invading the British Isles. This has often been thought of before,' he declared, making reference to Napoleon. But this cheery growl of defiance was followed by altogether chillier, less reassuring imagery, and it is worth going back to the reporting from the Commons chamber to hear the first response to it:

> We shall not flag or fail, we shall go on until the end, we shall fight in France, we shall fight on the seas and oceans, we shall fight with growing confidence and growing strength in the air, we shall defend our island whatever the cost may be, we shall fight on the beaches, we shall fight on the landing grounds, we shall fight in the fields and in the streets, we shall fight in the hills, we shall never surrender.

At this point, there were 'loud cheers'.

> And even if, which I do not for a moment believe, this island or a large part of it was subjugated and starving, then our Empire beyond the seas, armed and guarded by the British fleet, would carry on the struggle until, in God's good time, the New World, with all its power and might, steps forth to the rescue and the liberation of the Old.

Again, an interesting moment of vulnerability: if he did not believe for one moment that 'this island' would be subjugated, why mention it? What seemed more calculated was the echo of John of Gaunt's speech in Shakespeare's *Richard II*, particularly the phrases involving 'this sceptred isle' and 'this little world/This precious stone set in the silver sea'. The Commons chamber was, as soon as Churchill finished, filled with 'loud and prolonged cheers'. Other MPs now weighed in; not with questions as such, but, like the

Keighley MP, who wished to tell the Prime Minister that he 'was glad the PM had told the nation in the plainest terms the efforts it would be called upon to make'. No one listened. There was, according to reports, some impatience in the chamber with the very idea of anyone trying to follow such an address.

And despite the cheers, there were others who claimed that it filled them with gloom. Labour MP Emmanuel Shinwell later declared that 'we were very much depressed as a result of the events that led to him making this speech, and all his oratory could not remove that depression'. Possibly it was never intended to do so.

Because, of course, the speech was only marginally intended for domestic consumption in the first place. Churchill knew that his words would be instantly relayed to German High Command. If France was to fall, it was vital that Hitler should not consider that the British would fold as well. Perhaps more pertinently, Churchill knew that his words would be reported widely across the United States of America, where the drama of the last few days had fired the passion and imagination of journalists seemingly to a greater degree than their British counterparts. Churchill knew that this speech would be studied with great precision in the White House. President Roosevelt had already, through quiet channels, sought to ensure that if Britain were to collapse in the face of a Nazi invasion, its naval fleet would be scattered across the world in time, to Canada and South Africa. If that were the case, then America would have no hesitation in joining the struggle.

But Churchill's patience was finite; his references to the crippling lack of materiel were pointed and pleading. His signal to the President that Britain had no intention of making terms with the Germans was also crucial; even at the genesis of what has too glibly been described as the 'special relationship', Britain was very much the supplicant: tragically eager to please, desperate for help. Those close to Churchill at this time recalled the deep contrasts in his emotional state. He had only been Prime Minister for just over three weeks. Before he made that speech, he is reported to have said to Duff Cooper (who then repeated it to MI5 operative Guy Liddell): 'The end is very near. But there will be no surrender. We will go down fighting.'[1]

The phrases were already forged. The sparseness of the repeated imagery in that speech – of men fighting in the streets and in the hills – calls to mind a final noble stand, a gesture of bravery before subjugation. Yet there is also perhaps a tinge of passive-aggression, a message for the US Congress; that if forced to stand completely alone, then Britain would have to fight in the most desperate and despairing way – and there would be weighty economic and geopolitical consequences for the US too, not least because of the power of Britain's presence in the East. No nation could be isolationist now; the threads that connected them were becoming sharply visible.

Back home, Duff Cooper's Ministry of Information sought out responses to what the public had gleaned of Churchill's address. 'The grave tone . . . made such an impression,' it reported, 'and may have contributed in some measure to the rather pessimistic atmosphere of today . . . some apprehension has been caused throughout the country on account of the PM's reference to "fighting alone".' In other words, there was anxiety about how much longer France would remain a steadfast ally. But as mentioned, balancing this are many accounts of women and men feeling invigorated and almost giddy with relief; noticing the brightness of the spring colours, and with an irrational sense of rising confidence. One voice – this time heard on the BBC, as opposed to being merely reported – arguably did more to produce this reaction than any other. The hugely popular playwright, author and broadcaster J.B. Priestley had had a vision quite the reverse of Churchill's. His were the words that set in iron a nation's view of itself that persists even today.

Priestley's talks – his 'Postscripts' – came just after 9 p.m. On the evening of 5 June 1940, his Dunkirk theme focused not on the might of the navy or the precariousness of Britain's position with the Nazis poised across the Channel, but crucially upon how the amateur spirit had saved the day:

> Here at Dunkirk is another English epic. And to my mind what was most characteristically English about it – so typical, so absurd and yet so grand and gallant that you hardly knew whether to laugh or cry when you read about them – was the part played in the difficult and dangerous embarkation – not by the warships, magnificent though they were – but by the little pleasure steamers. We've known them, and laughed at them, these fussy little steamers, all our lives. We have called them 'the shilling sicks'. We have watched them load and unload their crowds of holiday passengers – the gents full of high spirits and bottled beer, the ladies eating pork pies, the children sticky with peppermint rock . . . There was always something old-fashioned, a Dickens touch, a mid-Victorian air about them . . . Yes, those 'Brighton Belles' and 'Brighton Queens' left that innocent foolish world of theirs . . . to sail into the inferno, to defy bombs, shells, magnetic mines.

Here was on the face of it a sentimental appeal, but actually there were subtleties; Priestley was turning the old-fashioned paddle steamers into a wider metaphor. They were fussy and antiquated – 'even the new ones' – and were part of an innocent, foolish world; but compared to the steely, soulless, blank metal modernity of Germany, did they not encapsulate the spirit or soul of a nation? Here was absurd dignity combined with a certain self-deprecating humour; and yet, when it came to it, a bulwark determination and stout bravery in the face of terrifying crisis. Priestley was encouraging his listeners to identify with the silly yet doughty boats; that was who they were too. 'Some of them – alas – will never return,' he said:

> I tell you, we were proud of the *Gracie Fields* . . . And now never again will we board her at Cowes and go down into her dining

> saloon for a fine breakfast of bacon and eggs. She has paddled and churned away – forever. But now – look – this little steamer, like all her brave and battered sisters, is immortal. She'll go sailing proudly down the years in the epic of Dunkirk.

Although Priestley also talked on other occasions of the excellent and courageous services, in this talk he pulled off the more resonant achievement of domesticating the war. This was not like the fields of Flanders in 1918, with a helpless population waiting for news from the front; this was new. The silly paddle steamers that served as a synecdoche for the British national character had also, brilliantly, shown the Germans that no matter how whimsical the British might look, there was iron there too.

On top of this, crucially, in seeing the poignant humour – the brilliant and deliberate conjuring of Gracie Fields – in the situation, Priestley hit upon the core emotional response that seemed to echo along every railway platform, and in every small town and village that received homecoming soldiers allowed out on leave; and that was the powerful laughter of relief. After all those days of suspense, which had in their turn followed weeks and months of uncertainty, there was at last catharsis. And it was accompanied by a sense of incongruity that the hideous Nazi war machine – so ineluctable, so merciless – had been thwarted by something so ostensibly frivolous. The humanity and humour of the British versus the robotic advance of the Nazi future; this is what Priestley conjured and it is this imagery that remains so enduringly powerful now.

For Vic Viner, the twenty-three-year-old who had stood keeping order for six days and nights with a revolver, the return home and the reception his comrades received was the subject of much discussion. But, he says now, it was really about one thing: 'The civilians realised that they had got their boys back again.' And defeat? 'There was one person said to me at the time, "Look at it as a victory for the navy as opposed to a defeat for the army." I told them we all recognised the whole thing was a defeat. If the army hadn't have come back, well . . . It's recognised as defeat. The only good thing that came out of it was that we were able to bring them back.'

But the war was now starting in earnest and there was little time for dwelling or philosophising. 'Afterwards, you thought to yourself, did I do all of that? Was I partly responsible? But I thank God I was able to do it. I'm just lucky that I was able. I was given the job to do and I did it. Years later, a general said to me: "Don't you think that you could forget some things?" I said, "Sir, you don't forget that experience." That's the only answer. You can experience your career in war but no one knows what it is like to have experienced Dunkirk unless you've been there.'

However unforgettable his experience, Mr Viner had very little breathing space before his next venture into France, this time on a mission entailing very different sorts of jeopardy. Indeed, years later, when reluctant to talk about those days and nights on the beaches, he was more than happy to think back to the subsequent adventure. 'The only part of France that I did speak about was the job that I did after I came back from Dunkirk,' Mr Viner says now. 'I had just over six days in Chatham. Then after a while longer some of us went back to France – to Cherbourg. And the job there was sabotage. Because that's what I had been trained to do beforehand. I'd been trained in torpedo detail, I'd been trained in mines, I'd been trained in mine disposal, sabotage and that's why twelve of us went over to Cherbourg.

'We were there to blow up anything that we could,' Mr Viner continues. This, in essence, meant that following the evacuation of more British troops through the port, Mr Viner and his colleagues would try to destroy as much abandoned materiel and vehicles as they could find before the oncoming German forces could acquire them.

'I had fourteen days in Cherbourg,' says Mr Viner. 'We did all sorts of things. We were blowing up vehicles, we were blowing up bridges. We got a signal to go to Cherbourg dockyard to do what damage we could do there. Then we had another signal and the lieutenant said to me, "This is bloody silly, we're being told to blow up Cherbourg arsenal. If we do that, we'll blow ourselves up."'

The lieutenant continued, 'I've got two jobs for you. There's one of the dock bridges to blow, and a light cruiser. What we want to do is render the cruiser unsafe. We won't blow her up. We'll do some damage to her. What do you think?' Mr Viner responded, 'We'll blow up the stern so that the rudders and the propellers are wrecked.' When the job was complete and they were safely out of the dock, his colleague said to him, 'You realise what the name of that ship was? *Joan of Arc* – you've blown up Joan of Arc, Vic!' Mr Viner's response: 'Don't tell a Frenchman, for god's sake.'

After the tense but essentially static ordeal of the beaches at La Panne, this fresh new life of mayhem – involving fleet-footedness and brazen nerve – was not merely welcome but exhilarating. The destruction also brought with it a sense that a tangible blow was being struck against the enemy; psychologically, this was completely different to huddling down as the Germans relentlessly attacked.

'The last job we had was on the main jetty at Cherbourg where there are six big gantry cranes,' says Mr Viner. 'They had to be destroyed. We were using a new explosive. We'd been taught what to do, and we blew the first five – but the sixth one, which was nearer the entrance, didn't blow. Meanwhile, a navy destroyer had come in to the port to take us back – we were due to go back to Portsmouth that day – and the tide at Cherbourg is eighteen feet, so the destroyer was getting lower and lower and lower. When we'd realised that the sixth gantry crane hadn't blown, we called out to the commander.' What they hadn't realised was that the German tanks were not merely advancing, but were now just yards away from them. The destroyer's commander was admirably brisk. Mr Viner recalls that he shouted to the young man and his comrades: 'Lay down flat, I'm going to open fire – there's a Panzer coming along the jetty.'

'So we lay flat,' says Mr Viner, 'he fired, destroyed the Panzer. Then he told us: "Fix your fuse because I'm going to slip. I can't stay moored any more." We could see he was going. We ran along the jetty and actually jumped aboard her as she was going out of the harbour.'

For the second time in just a few days, Mr Viner found himself sailing back to the safety of England, but this time, the adrenaline coursed through his veins with something akin to delight. The relief of being back mingled with the everyday Pooterishness of the instructions they received from their superiors. 'We got to Portsmouth, and they said, "Right, you're going to catch a train to Waterloo, then to Chatham and you'll have something to eat on the train." So we were sitting in the compartment, and John next to me says: "Vic – down the back of your serge jumper, you've got a wide black mark. That wide." I said: "So have you."'

The officer told them, 'You know what happened, boys – that's when the destroyer's shell went over the top of you. The heat as it went over the top of you – burnt your serge.'

Mr Viner now talks of such things lightly. But obviously, in a wider sense, for some very young, and not extensively trained men, the events of those last few weeks had a more serious impact. Not just on the soldiers on the beaches, but on the sailors ferrying back and forth, as well as those who had been manning the minesweeper operations. A fascinating secret memo, sent just a couple of weeks later by the Chief Medical Officer at the Dover base, listed the conditions that he had come across in the Dover Patrol at that time. Parts of his memo seem as harsh and unsympathetic as Great War attitudes to shell shock; the problem was in part 'a lack of discipline'. None the less, this was a serious attempt to study the after-effects of what had been the first full shock of the war, knowing that more such shocks were certain to follow.

Compiled with the help of a surgeon lieutenant who had 'psychological training', the report stated that 'undoubtedly, "Fear Complex" has been a major problem at Dover, particularly during the past two months'. The memo continued: '122 cases are mentioned in the accompanying reports; this out of approximately 700 men is a high rate, especially when it is remembered that the mildest cases and obvious malingerers are not included in this total.' The causes of this sickness rate? 'Arduous and hazardous employment . . . Indiscipline . . . Lack of rest . . . Bad Example' were among the top of the list.

But what were the symptoms of this 'Fear Complex'? How did it manifest itself? There was a condition simply and chillingly labelled 'Psychosis' – 'it must be detected early and sent to hospital'. There were also 'Anxiety States'. Simply sending the man away for a rest, averred the medical officer, was not good enough in these cases; hospital once again was required. 'Hysteria' was less serious; it could be dealt with by means of a short period away. More prevalent was 'Physical Fear'. 'It is often brought on by waiting about and apprehension,' wrote the officer, 'it is also highly infectious and may result from bad example, particularly in a senior. These cases are open to reason and should always be returned to their place of duty, great care being taken to differentiate from true Anxiety Neuropsychosis.'[2]

The doctor also had some cures to hand: 'Instruct skipper . . . in the importance of keeping their crews smart and cheerful; and impress upon them the necessity of always showing a fearless bearing themselves; Senior Officers can help by explaining the great importance of the duties which have to be performed.'

But there was no glibness here; a closer study of the men of Dover Patrol, facing the ubiquitous dangers of U-boats and E-boats, had thrown up other conclusions about the repercussions of war, and at a time when psychiatry was still a relatively young discipline. As psychiatrist Dr Gerald Garmany wrote:

> The high incidence of unconcealed and uncontrolled fear among the . . . men is in accordance with the views that Officers in charge of trawlers have expressed in conversation. Namely that these men are taken from civilian life where they were

milkmen, tailors, farmhands etc and after a period of training, often as short as two weeks, are put into trawlers to work under very exacting conditions. Their team spirit is but ill-developed and their sense of discipline very poor in some cases.

This lack of preliminary training seems in these men to leave them in their own hands, some option, between say, fighting with a gun, and scurrying below which they later explain, without any sense of dishonour, by some such phrase as 'my nerves went to pieces.'

Garmany's tone seems less that of an understanding psychiatrist and more the martinet Great War commander. His answer to such 'scurrying', and to cases of nerves being dealt with in the sick bay, was for doctors to give an uncompromising declaration to their patients that the work simply 'must be faced up to'. 'A too obvious sympathy increases in the man his belief that he is being asked to do something beyond endurance.' In many senses, this is undoubtedly right; how can a war be fought otherwise? Yet there was also a dilemma in the first great shock of conflict; how to communicate with barely trained men, fresh from sedate civilian lives? How did one reason with a man who had – perfectly understandably – been driven to the edge of frenzy by constant bombardment, or by the sick anticipation of the boat beneath him being torn to pieces by mines and torpedoes and bombs?

As elsewhere, the wider public seemed to have a better instinctive understanding of such things; fathers, for instance, who had experienced and witnessed the horrors of the last war, and wives who had to live with such trauma. 'One of the boys who managed to get back [from Dunkirk] is all shaking with nerves,' wrote one Birmingham mother, not without sympathy. 'He said they can stand anything bar the bombing.'[3]

Though a good proportion of the BEF had been returned, many tens of thousands were still in more southerly areas of France. On neither side of the Channel was there any breathing space, any respite. Having got his hold on France, Hitler was seemingly poised to make his assault on Britain. The invasion might come at any moment. That was certainly the widespread assumption at the time; despite the ecstatic and near-transcendent visions of a burgeoning summer, of all those blues and whites and pinks coming into bloom, that one now reads in diaries and letters, there was behind it all the sense that the desperate hour was at hand. For those soldiers still in France, who knew that the Germans were now well placed to swing through to Paris, there was no chance for reflection or consideration. The emotional repercussions of Dunkirk, however, were to prove startlingly profound.

16

'Very Well – Alone'

June 1940

The popular crime novelist Marjorie Allingham – who had, in May, been in the depths of pessimism – was among the many who found themselves oddly transfigured by the Dunkirk evacuation. Writing shortly afterwards, she said: 'In those weeks in May and June, I think 99% of English folk, country and town, found their souls, and whatever else it may have been, it was a glorious and triumphant experience.' Elsewhere, Mass Observation diarist Nella Last had found herself moved to an extraordinary, almost religious degree: 'This morning I lingered over my breakfast, reading and re-reading the accounts of the Dunkirk evacuation. I felt as if deep inside me there was a harp that vibrated and sang – like the feeling on a hillside of gorse in the hot bright sun or seeing suddenly, as you walked through a park, a big bed of clear, thin red poppies in all their brave splendour . . .' Vita Sackville West found herself transfixed not by the voice of Churchill, who did not of course start broadcasting his own speeches until a little later, but by the account given of his 'beaches' speech by the BBC. 'It made me shiver (though not through fear),' she wrote to her husband Harold Nicolson.

Elsewhere, Winifred Cullis – although, as head of the Women's Section at the British Information Service, she was not necessarily the most impartial observer – said: 'I know the English woman to be happier than she has been in a long time. She has learned the joy that comes from sharing responsibilities . . . [the] conviction that if she suffers without complaint now, victory awaits the end of the struggle.'[1]

'Passions are thoroughly roused now,' wrote Sheffield clerk Arthur Collins. 'Looking back over the last nine months, it seems we have been wasting time.'[2]

Among the surprised witnesses to this bubbling up of energy and enthusiasm were the 100,000 or so French troops – the *poilus* – who had been successfully evacuated alongside their British counterparts. Like the British, they were disembarked and taken almost immediately to the nearest railway stations; from there, they were dispatched to destinations largely in the south-west of England. French troops received just as much in the way of generosity as their British counterparts, both upon arrival in the port towns, and then in Devon and Dorset, when they were sent to towns and villages close to Plymouth and Weymouth. It was not just a question of ceaseless sandwiches, pieces of fruit, chocolate and tea. These men also received haircuts and had their boots polished. They were billeted in local schools, but also with local householders. If there had been any more general tension between the French and the British, it seems it was not felt by these troops.

The wounded were, of course, taken care of in hospital; those who were uninjured found their time in Britain short. Just four or five days after landing, the great majority of the French troops were re-embarked, this time setting sail for Cherbourg (that is, just before young sailors like Vic Viner were let loose upon the harbour charged with causing as much damage as they could). This brief, though sweet, reception in England was remembered by many French troops as the period that made up for the rising tensions on the beaches at Dunkirk; the high feelings caused by the idea that they were being abandoned by the British. It should also be remembered that there was a multitude of French vessels involved in that rescue. Just days after 4 June, when the evacuation was over, this great sense of fellow feeling was to be crushed instead under a weight of horror and sympathy.

As to the British troops, dispersed to all corners of the country on sometimes epic train journeys, there was a general sense of surprise at the continuing enthusiasm for their return. In some villages, extra flags had been put out to mark the return on leave – however short – of young soldiers. A few veterans recalled that the heroes' welcome was actually rather embarrassing; they knew fine well that they were not returning victors, but soldiers who had been beaten by an enemy many times more proficient and better prepared. But the point is that the cheering civilians knew that too. No one was under any illusion. The great majority of civilians up and down the land would have realised both that Britain's part in the conflict would stretch on and on, and that the mighty force that had caused the return of their beloved sons and husbands was even now poised just a few miles across the Channel. Instead, this nationwide expression seemed one of relief and of catharsis; the first real moment, since the war had been declared the previous September, of a kind of positive mass emotion. Veterans remember that there was a feeling of coalescence; the sense that Mr Churchill's belief in fighting on was the correct one. Almost immediately this would lead to a concomitant heaping of scorn and rage on 'the old gang', namely the former Prime Minister Neville Chamberlain and those of his colleagues who had been such enthusiastic proponents of appeasement. For all the jaw-jutting sense of sinewy determination, there was also an aggression that found ugly outlets.

Nor was the public in any mood to be treated as fools. Pathé newsreels – which, other than the radio and the newspapers, were the main source of news for millions – showed footage of the returning boats, dubbed with a soundtrack of stirring, madly upbeat martial music, together with a montage of healthy looking soldiers grinning at the cameras. The narrator gave an account so relentlessly positive and jingoistic that, according to Mass Observation, the cinema audiences reacted with sarcastic running commentaries of their own.

Among those audiences, indeed, were some of the very men who had been rescued from the beaches. One veteran recalled how he got a pass to leave his camp in a town in Kent and went along to the cinema. Already the town was in very buoyant mood; the soldier remembered how, when his troop train had arrived there just a day or two previously, it seemed that the entire town had turned out to greet them – from the elderly to very young children. More important than the votive gifts of oranges and chocolate was the sheer wave of celebration. In that town's cinema, just before the programme started, there was an announcement from the management for the benefit of the civilian audience: the management was pleased to see members of the BEF in the house. This announcement brought a loud cheer from the rest of the audience. There then followed a newsreel entitled – as the soldier recalled with tongue firmly in cheek – 'The Glorious Retreat from Dunkirk'. It must have been surpassingly strange to see the events of the last few days projected in bright black and white with stirring music, though the soldier kept his thoughts to himself on the matter.

Meanwhile, there was a telling public plea from an unsigned corporal writing to the newspapers: he asked specifically for soldiers of the BEF on leave to desist from giving lethal souvenirs such as cartridges to inquisitive children. He also asked specifically that soldiers should not disclose where they had previously been posted in France. But, he added, he was very keen for the public to know that the military were extremely grateful for the 'wonderful reception' that they got – and were continuing to get.

The curiously high spirits were reflected in the letters pages of newspapers and periodicals. Even the prospect of imminent invasion invited a jest or two. 'Little do they know, poor devils,' wrote one correspondent of the anticipated German paratroopers, 'that the moment they land upon this enchanted – and now uncharted – island, they will find themselves up against our own secret weapon – namely, the total inability of the English yokel to tell anyone the way, even if he is willing to do so.'

And very quickly – with no prompting either from Churchill's oratory, or indeed from the carefully funnelled news items put out by the Ministry of Information – the legend of the 'little ships' was burnished. A poet signing himself only as 'WCR' contributed this stirring verse to *The Times* just a couple of days after the last of the men were brought ashore:

Small ships, tall ships
The call went forth for all ships
Craft of every class and rig came crowding to the shore
Long ships, strong ships
Scarcely worth a song ships
All came sailing gladly in flotillas by the score
Old ships, bold ships
Heart as good as gold ships
Their historic moment, like the fabric of a dream.

A curious and striking way of putting it; yet perhaps for everyone in Britain under that hot June sky, every day, and not just in that 'historic moment', had the texture of a dream. It was curious how normal life continued – the shopping, the cleaning, the children playing, the factories and steel furnaces working at full pelt and sweltering, while men in uniform quietly assumed the duties so proudly carried out until now by the Local Defence Volunteers. There was the odd little yip about the tightening of rationing but, as one newspaper editorial sighed, almost with contentment, 'the joy of having something to complain about is too obvious to need mentioning to English readers.'

The cult of the little ships continued to spread remarkably fast. Those elegant Thames motor yachts that had played their gallant part came sailing back up the river on 9 June; at first, amid the bustle of river traffic in the east, they were not noticed. But when the flotilla of boats sailed past St Katharine's Dock and under Tower Bridge, on what was after all a quiet Sunday lunchtime, they were spotted. As they processed westwards through the City, each subsequent bridge – London, Southwark, Blackfriars – boasted more and more onlookers. Some had come to wave; some were there to cheer. Word spread fast through the town. So much so that when the boats reached Westminster Bridge, about a mile further along, there were serious crowds ready to greet them with a hullabaloo of noise. 'Greetings were exchanged' between the public on the shore and the boats' small crews. An especially loud roar was set up for a returning London fire boat, which sailed in among the other smaller craft; had it really been two weeks since it had set off into the darkness of the estuary, and thence to the seas beyond? 'The volunteer ships which helped to evacuate the BEF from Dunkirk,' wrote one commentator, 'have won deserved glory.' Another reporter became slightly over-enthusiastic about the Thames spectacle. The crews, he wrote, were 'nearly all stripped to the waist, showing bronzed and muscular torsos'.

And so it was that the little ships were slotted neatly – and unconsciously – into the national story; the island which had triumphed at sea against Philip II of Spain in 1588, and against Napoleon in 1805, had now scored another unique maritime triumph, this time involving volunteers whose bravery far outweighed their experience. Those battles of distant history were always taught as narratives of great men; the narrative of Dunkirk, right from the start, was a seagoing triumph for the age of the common man.

*

The news from France grew more ominous by the day; the evacuation of Paris, those motor cars with ubiquitous mattresses tied to their roofs in the hope of thwarting German bombers, went on at speed. Yet there were still desperate flutters of the old life; women's journals in Britain, for instance, in early June 1940, carried a few photographs of the latest from the French fashion houses, and gave their predictions of the forthcoming trends; those fashion houses desperately trying to signal that no matter what the next few days brought, this most integral of French exports would carry on as it had before. A vain hope.

Frantic dialogue continued between French military high command and their British counterparts; the same applied to the higher reaches of government. In the days after the troops had been returned, plans were formulated, debated, became nebulous, forgotten. There was an idea, discussed between French and British generals, that a number of troops could be immediately returned to France, that there might be room for establishing a line in Brittany. It didn't happen; and there were still thousands of British troops in France making their way to the more southerly parts of the country to try and find escape routes back to Britain ahead of the relentless Wehrmacht. Churchill and the War Cabinet had no wish for the French to believe that they were being abandoned. Yet there were also suggestions that Churchill could not quite comprehend just how swiftly the French spirit was deflating. Part of his psychology would somehow not quite accept it.

Was the fall of France a shock to the people of Britain? The speedy collapse of morale certainly seemed to take Churchill aback. The Prime Minister was prone to reciting a couplet from Byron's *Childe Harold's Pilgrimage*: 'A thousand years scarce serve to form a state/An hour may lay it in the dust'. There are some who believe that Churchill in his darker moments was deliberately gloomy about Britain's prospects, the better to arouse defensive instincts. But to the French government and the military, there were not too many flames of optimism left burning. Even in late May, just as the embarkation of British and French troops was about to begin, a French under-secretary of state had been observing a meeting between Churchill and M. Reynaud and noted afterwards that 'England has already put on mourning for us.' On the last day of May, after a visit to Paris, deputy Prime Minister Clement Attlee had observed sadly 'the curious silence and almost deserted look of the city, which obviously had already decided to surrender'.[3]

Churchill, senior members of the War Cabinet and military high command met with their opposites – M. Reynaud, General Weygand – in France on 11–12 June. The French outlined the enormous losses that the military had suffered, all the divisions wiped out, rounded up, taken prisoner. Churchill suggested that Paris might be abandoned in order to allow the military to pull back and defend the south. He suggested too – as he seemed to have done in that speech to the Commons a few days earlier – that the French resort to guerrilla warfare. Weygand responded that this would have the effect of laying waste the entire country. Churchill asked again that the French fight on; he invoked the idea of appealing to the US, and President Roosevelt, for help. This was not just for the benefit of France; and Churchill was to make repeated pleas from that point onwards. Prime Minister Reynaud got his reply from President Roosevelt on 15 June: the US was not going to enter the war. In any case, Paris was now utterly lost; German tanks were rolling down the Champs Elysées. The government had been forced to retreat to Bordeaux.

By 22 June, capitulation was complete; Churchill's nightmare, that the French would not, before signing an armistice, send their naval fleet to British docks, was realised. It was striking that he thought there might be any chance of that at all. And so it was that young men like Vic Viner were sent quickly over to ports like Cherbourg on missions of immediate sabotage.

And for those other thousands of British troops? The ones who had not yet been taken prisoner? One story, concerning Richard T.

Clifford, who like Arthur Taylor was with 13 Squadron, and as such was part of an RAF unit embedded with the army, is very stirring and at least partially representative. In late May, and completely cut off from the Dunkirk escape route by the encircling Germans, Clifford was forced instead to point himself southwards. Soon his unit disintegrated and his ordeal became one of extemporisation. At one point, he linked up with a group of fleeing refugees; they found a car and attempted to cross the border between France and Spain – but the Spaniards would not let them across. He then tried ports in the south of France. On one occasion, he almost managed to get on board a ship to North Africa – but at the last moment was denounced by a French couple who demanded to know from the authorities why an Englishman was being given this sort of priority. Clifford was captured, and found himself being marched by the Germans; yet the guards were so far apart that he somehow managed to give them the slip by leaping over a wall. Clifford's journey became an epic walk that involved, in that hot summer of 1940, many starry nights sleeping under the sweet-smelling half cover of orchards. He lived off whatever food he could forage, augmented by the kindness of strangers.

Now aiming for the Swiss border, some weeks later Clifford came within sight of barbed wire and sentry posts. Though it seems extraordinary now, he somehow managed to make his way through these obstacles and reach the sanctuary of Switzerland. On arrival in Geneva, this by now very thin and unkempt figure presented himself at the British Consulate.

Similarly, huge numbers of English soldiers, tens of thousands of them, used their ingenuity to get back to British shores; some wireless operators, with technically advanced equipment, were forced to flee at greater speeds to prevent both the technology and the knowledge falling into Nazi hands. There were escapes in cars and on motorbikes. Many managed to slip across the Spanish border, others managed to sail out from French ports.

The proper domestic response was of sympathy and certainly

the letters pages featured some piously expressed sentiments; but among MO diarists and others, there was more a sense of apprehension: if France, how long before Britain? Yet Dunkirk had sharpened and crystallised a certain nationwide bullishness. On 18 June, the *Evening Standard* published what is now one of the most famous cartoons of the twentieth century, drawn by the man who had, throughout the 1930s, been a cause of real and continual grief to Hitler: David Low. His previous work – vehemently anti-appeasement – had portrayed Hitler in a variety of clownish ways; the dictator's vanity was sufficiently wounded in the mid to late 1930s for him to make this a regular diplomatic issue, and pressure was often brought to bear on Low to water the satire down a little. Low's primary instinct was to refuse. But now, in the midsummer of 1940, and with France fallen, he found a new register. The cartoon featured a solitary soldier, standing on a wave-battered island, fist clenched at a sky blackening with enemy bombers, and the caption 'Very well – alone'. Britain, at last, was completely at war.

17

The Guilt and the Wonder

July 1940

'That night a miracle was born,' wrote a trio of journalists under the pseudonym Cato in early July 1940, just days before the Battle of Britain began and with the nation – and admiring onlookers from America – having had a month to fully take in the story of Dunkirk:

> This land of Britain is rich in heroes. She had brave daring men in her Navy and Air Force as well as in her Army. She had heroes in jerseys and sweaters and old rubber boots in all the fishing ports of Britain. That night the word went round.
>
> In a few hours, the channel was thick with barges, tugs, small coastal vessels, motor boats, lifeboats, private yachts, several hundred ships of all sizes and shapes sailing alongside British destroyers . . . Thus, hungry, bandaged, thirsty, soaked in oil, salt water and blood, the unbeaten Army returned to the shores of England.[1]

This was the first chapter of a polemic called *Guilty Men* written by Peter Howard, Frank Owen and Michael Foot, the latter at the time a journalist for the *Evening Standard* and later to be leader of the Labour Party. The punchy – indeed, furious – thesis was that the gallant soldiers of the BEF had almost been set up to fail by the monstrous moral and intellectual shortcomings of previous governments. Everyone from Neville Chamberlain to Stanley Baldwin, from Ramsay MacDonald to defence minister Sir Thomas Inskip and senior civil servant Sir Horace Wilson was a Guilty Man. What was more, some of these Guilty Men were still in positions of great power – and should be removed forthwith. Not least of them was Chamberlain himself, now Lord President. He was also, by that stage, very seriously ill. Looking back on *Guilty Men* in 1998, Michael Foot wrote:

> I well remember the London of that July: how the sun blazed more brilliantly each day, how the green parks, the whole city indeed, had never looked lovelier. All of us who lived through those times had a special instruction in the meaning of patriotism . . . And one essential element in the exhilaration was the knowledge that the shameful Chamberlain era had at last been brought to an end, and that English people could look into each other's eyes with recovered pride and courage.[2]

'Cato's assertion of 'unbeaten' in that earlier description of the BEF was especially emotive – and especially questionable. The rest of the book is equally purple and unrestrained – twenty-four short chapters filled with cold sarcasm and bitterness. One might have thought such a publication would attract a readership in Westminster, but perhaps not elsewhere. In fact, the public was eager to have the narrative of the war shaped. This furious polemic caught a wave across the country: it ended up selling a colossal 200,000 copies, and very quickly.

Equally, upon publication, there were those – Winston Churchill included – who were appalled at the vilification of their colleagues. Churchill was firm with those who were agitating to force Chamberlain off the government benches and to dispense with the rest of the 'Men of Munich'. 'We don't want to punish anybody,' he said, 'except the enemy.'

Indeed, in the House of Commons, Churchill went to some pains to put out the fires that he thought political colleagues, as well as journalists, were starting. In a speech concerning his regret over the French capitulation – and about how there was simply neither the time nor indeed the moral justification to hold this sorrow against the French people in any way – he referred to internecine conflict: 'They seek to indict those who were responsible for the guidance of our affairs. This would be a foolish and pernicious process . . . I cannot accept the drawing of any distinction between members of the present government . . . We are going to govern the country and fight the war!'

It was the final phrase that garnered the most cheers from the members present. If any further proof were needed that Churchill's ascendancy among the public was complete, the middle of June saw an announcement by one publishing firm that it intended to print his speech of 4 June – 'we shall fight them on the beaches' – as a 'card to hang' or poster, with especial prominence given to the words 'we shall go on until the end'.

At the same time, the legend of Dunkirk had found such traction that the attempted evacuation at St Valery en Caux just a few weeks later, where a number of rearguard Allied troops, notably of the 51st Highland Division, had found themselves trapped, was deliberately painted as an effort in the same vein. This time, however, the venture was largely doomed. Once again, there were 'tiny ships', private motor yachts and lifeboats. The topography was much more difficult though: a prospect of sharp cliffs and narrow beaches, rather than the great white sand dunes. One unnamed civilian volunteer said: 'It was murder. The miracle of Dunkirk was not to be repeated. There was a heavy fog, the sea was rough and the Germans were ready for us this time.' Another volunteer, who had piloted his own boat out, similarly recalled: 'It was like sending toys out to fight tanks. My cabin cruiser got across the Channel without much trouble but there was a fog like a shroud right the way along the French coast – fog reddened by the dull glare of fires ashore and pierced incessantly by flashes of gunfire from coastal batteries.'

If it was bad for the sailors, then it was a moment of utter desolation for the British troops now surrounded and taken prisoner. Their lifeline had snapped. But the point is that 'Dunkirk' – back home – was now firmly established as a by-word for a most momentous achievement; something that other events could be measured against. And the reason primarily was the fantastically attractive image of the gentlemen amateurs, the volunteer civilians with no prior experience of bombs or guns who sailed without blinking into the fiercest fire. Small wonder that naval personnel – the real pivot of those nine days – found such accounts increasingly maddening. But they were invaluable propaganda.

There may not have been a medal (save the later commemorative one) for the retreat; but there were obviously a great many awarded for gallantry and bravery. In mid-June, King George VI travelled to the West Country to make a tour of various regiments, conferring DSOs and other honours as he went. The same was clearly true for both the navy and indeed the air force. The newspapers, daily, made fresh announcements of decorations for men who had shown great bravery in helping to hold off the German advance, or working to shield their fellow men from enemy fire.

So, what might in an unfavourable light be seen as the humiliation of Dunkirk had instead been interpreted by the public as a brave adventure; a couple of weeks after he had exhorted people not to see it as any kind of victory, Churchill himself came round to the idea of invoking it as a means of preparing everyone for battles to come. In Parliament, he made a terrific speech on 18 June, again seemingly designed as much for the consumption of German High

Command as for the domestic population: 'During the last few days, we have successfully brought off the great majority of troops we had on the lines of communication in France . . . we have also brought back a great mass of stores, rifles, munitions of all kinds which have been accumulating in France over the last nine months.' This much was – at best – a giant lie, one calculated to reassure the domestic audience: the German forces would have seen with their own eyes the massive quantities of weaponry and vehicles that the soldiers had been obliged to leave behind. 'We have therefore in this island today a very large and powerful military force. The force includes all our best trained and finest troops and includes scores of thousands of those who have already measured their quality against the Germans and found themselves at no disadvantage.' There were at this point 'great cheers' in the House.

The German invasion of Great Britain, he declared, would require the mass transportation by sea of huge numbers of forces, great quantities of materiel and supplies. 'Here we come to the Navy,' he said. 'After all, we have a Navy. Some people seem to forget that.' In the Commons chamber, this garnered a huge laugh. And, the Prime Minister went on, despite the enemy being full of 'novel treacheries and stratagems' (again, Churchill's language belongs more to the eighteenth century than to 1940), the navy had been built up to such a point as to be capable of repelling a mass invasion in whatever form it came, and that coastal vigilance was never ending. And of course this was the air force which, Churchill said, had actually demonstrated its mastery during the days of Dunkirk. Anyone, he said, who had looked at photographs of the embarkation, and of the trailing lines of men waiting on the sand, would have understood that they were 'an ideal target for hours at a time', and that the only thing that prevented them all from being wiped out was the Luftwaffe's wariness of the RAF.

Moreover, this was now a People's War, though Churchill phrased it differently. 'Every man and woman,' he said, 'will have the chance of showing the finest qualities of the race . . . what General Weygand called the Battle of France is over. I expect the Battle of Britain is about to begin.' And it was here that he declared that in a thousand years' time, men of Britain would be looking back and saying that 'this was their finest hour'.

So, just two weeks after the disaster, Churchill was able to weave a rather more golden narrative; one that placed great emphasis on the RAF and on the groundswell of enthusiasm from all civilians on the Home Front. It was a continuation of the Dunkirk spirit. Perhaps if the speech had been reported in the normal way – relayed by BBC presenters in the form of edited highlights – it might not have had quite the same impact. But for the first time, the Prime Minister later that day made his way to the BBC in order to give largely the same speech before a microphone to some 40 million listeners. The impact was immediate. The reviewers were impressed. 'How much more stirring and reassuring it was to hear [Churchill's] own voice rather than a read summary,' said one commentator. 'He sounded tired, though not . . . less determined and the quality of that strong personality came to the listeners . . . more encouragingly than ever before.'

The war correspondent E.A. Montague, commenting on the speech, was also very much of the view that Dunkirk was an occasion for great national pride. While Churchill used the phrase 'their finest hour', Montague wrote,

> it may stand as the judgement which history will pass on what the British soldiers and sailors and airmen have done already. A war correspondent who has seen the last month of the war in France and the weeks which preceded Dunkirk must be forgiven if he feels a little heated . . . They have fought under handicaps which were not their fault . . . In the circumstances, our forces fought gloriously and withdrew from France with all honour.

For those who had been on the beaches, and who had sailed over, the respite was short. And there were frustrations; a great many soldiers, having been through the storm, now found themselves returning to repetitive training routines on English heathland. Even Lord Gort, the Commander-in-Chief, found himself in a position of stasis, having been moved sideways to become Inspector General of Training. (Happily, later in the war, his talents were rediscovered and found their fullest flowering; as Governor of Malta in 1942, he worked magnificently throughout the gruelling siege to ensure not only military success but also that everyone on that island was fed. After this, he was made a field marshal and Commander-in-Chief, Palestine.)

In the aftermath of Dunkirk, levels of criticism of the army – more specifically, the officer class – did begin to rise sharply. Originating from within the ranks, such criticisms grew so intense that later in 1940, Chief of the Imperial General Staff Sir John Dill told senior officers that they should look into the complaints. David Low – the cartoonist who had so wounded Hitler's pride – was also a source of terrific anger within the military hierarchy. His image of elderly, walrus-mustachioed reactionary Colonel Blimp, conflating all perceptions of senior military figures, found an echo in the diaries of Mass Observation, with many members of the public sharing this view of the military as lethally old-fashioned and anachronistically class-bound.

In actual fact, as noted by historian David French, the sorts of exams that trainee officers had to sit at military colleges in the 1930s were full of up-to-the-minute questions ranging from geography to industrialisation to physics. And in class terms, after Dunkirk, there was a slight decrease in the numbers of college-taught officers, simply because with the sheer weight of numbers now being conscripted and joining up, fresh new talent was being spotted and sent off for training. War was giving them the chance to learn on the job. For every Evelyn Waugh, pestering influential friends for an officer position, there were also sharp young men drawn from marginally less glamorous spheres who had now had some experience in the field.

*

And for many young men – at sea, in the air, or dispatched to the Middle East as members of the infantry – the war was now very much under way. Teddington sea cadet Reg Vine had come back and found the river-based activities of his fellow cadets understandably a little staid. Bumping up his age, he applied at that point to join the navy proper. 'Within two weeks, I got a call to join,' Mr Vine says.

'So I joined the Navy. Done my training. We were down at HMS *Collingwood*.' This was a 'stone frigate' – an onshore naval base – in Fareham, Hampshire, which had opened only in 1940 and was intended specifically for new recruits. 'One night, we were there listening to the radio. Lord Haw-Haw came on and told us: "We've now sunk HMS *Collingwood*." We said: "Eh?"' The puzzled lads looked at each other and laughed, while the broadcast was interrupted by an officer coming over the internal loudspeakers and saying: 'Don't take notice if you're listening to him – we're still here!' It is good to hear, incidentally, that Haw-Haw's traditionally unsettling omniscience when it came to the particulars of British life was on this occasion so spectacularly wrong.

'So,' continues Mr Vine, 'I went from *Collingwood* to Whale Island' – another naval establishment, an island close to Portsmouth – 'to learn guns. Came back to *Collingwood* and this time they put us in a hut on the other side rather than the trainee side. Lucky they did – because this bomber came over one night and dropped a stick of bombs. Two hit the sheds where the blokes were sleeping.' These were young trainees, in the very quarters that Mr Vine had occupied. 'They hadn't been in the navy twenty-four hours. That raid killed forty and wounded a lot. People don't believe me now,' he adds, 'but we helped to get the bodies out. As I was a Dunkirk bloke, I picked up bits and pieces and it didn't frighten me any more.'

As the theatres of war now started to open up right the way across the globe, Mr Vine was to find himself sailing into yet greater dangers, first in the Mediterranean and then in the Pacific. He describes them now with almost apologetic brevity: perhaps a result, he says, of the post-war years when people neither wanted to discuss nor hear about it. 'I was on HMS *Eagle*. We lost 230. We got torpedoed by bloody Italians. Three torpedoes. We went down in twenty-seven minutes. We were 200 miles out of Malta. We were rescued by fishermen and HMS *Indomitable*. Luckily it was warm – and you also won't find many sharks in the Med.'

Then, he says, 'I was in Mountbatten's crowd.' This meant sailing to the Far East for manoeuvres against the Japanese. There was one abiding phobia that stuck with young Vine: 'It always frightened me, the idea of getting sunk. We lost a hell of a lot of men out there, and the thing that always used to worry me – it wasn't just the sinking, but the sharks.'

For Arthur Taylor, who had managed to negotiate the dual hazards of Dunkirk and being a member of air force personnel among thousands of angry soldiers, there was very little time upon his return to take stock. Having been dispatched with other RAF signalsmen to Uxbridge in west London, then Liverpool, the next few days in June were a haze. This was partly to do with getting back into normal sleep patterns after the non-stop wakefulness of Dunkirk, but a new battle was coming; and, as Mr Taylor says, 'I think we were well prepared for it.

'I was sent down to RAF Lympne, near Folkestone. Our job was to sit in the control room, like air traffic control. We had VHF transmitters. Their range wasn't very far. We had to look after those signals.' In effect, Mr Taylor and his colleagues were operating early warning systems, waiting for the anticipated Luftwaffe onslaught that was to become known as the Battle of Britain. 'And we also had binoculars, checking out all the hills around to see if anyone was signalling in Morse.' Fears of fifth column spies were running very high in those post-Dunkirk days; there were many reports and rumours of the most incongruous agents being discovered. One of the more colourful was a popular rural vicar who would not allow anyone into his bell tower; the reason, as supposedly discovered, was that at the top, he had concealed some sophisticated radio equipment with which he was signalling directly back to Berlin. Mr Taylor recalls other practical restrictions: 'Civilians were not allowed on beaches. But those of us in uniform could walk along them – and that meant walking along with a girlfriend too!'

The banning of access to the beaches was symptomatic of a nation that was bracing itself. All along the coast of southern England, defences – barbed wire, gun emplacements – were materialising on sand and pebbles. RAF Lympne was at the heart of what was termed 'Hellfire Corner'; that point of southern England which, up until and throughout the Battle of Britain, attracted the most attention from German bomber pilots. Eventually, in July 1940, says Mr Taylor, RAF Lympne came under sustained attack; it received about 400 bombs, and these, tragically, killed a great number of WAAFs who were working there. At this stage, Mr Taylor was still only nineteen; as his war went on, his expertise with radio and mechanics was to take him to defensive positions all around the British coast and then out to a specialised training establishment in South Africa. He even found the time, in 1941, to get married, making best use of four days' leave to do so. There was no time for tarrying.

Just a few miles away from RAF Lympne, Admiral Bertram Ramsay, back in Dover, had been appointed Knight Commander of the Bath. In the immediate aftermath of the Dunkirk evacuation, he had found a chance once more to write one of his expressive letters to 'darling Mag':

> All is now done and the task is behind. The relief is stupendous and the results beyond belief . . . My staff worked like a perfect machine. On leaving, all alike, sailors, soldiers and airmen, said that they had enjoyed it and felt so much the better for the experience . . . I wish I could have some time with you to tell you of the many sides to the last four weeks and the many wonderful deeds and events. I don't suppose there has ever been anything like it before . . .

And his acceptance of the honour prompted a high-spirited telegram, addressed to 'Lady Ramsay' as she now was. 'I am proud to be the first to congratulate you on your new title,' he wrote. 'Love, Bert.' But he himself was consistent in his modesty; in a later letter, he told his wife his thoughts on the KCB award:

> Actually I feel an awful fraud as the success of the evacuation was brought about by the combined efforts of a great number of persons. So it is not to be expected that I would be blown out with self-esteem or anything like that, but I console myself with the knowledge that if things had not gone well, I alone would have borne the responsibility and the blame . . .

The awful responsibility had not disappeared; every day, in his igloo, Ramsay was facing directly out towards a potential invasion fleet sitting twenty-five miles away. He accepted any boosts to his own morale with intense gratitude. Later in June, he received a letter from Winston Churchill: 'My dear Admiral Ramsay, I am so glad to offer you my congratulations on your promotion to Knight Commander of the Bath . . . The energy and foresight called for in so formidable an undertaking and the courage required to carry it through in the teeth of the loss gave you full opportunity to display your qualities.' A few days afterwards, Churchill paid a personal visit to the igloo. 'Yesterday's jaunt with the PM,' wrote Ramsay to his wife, 'was a welcome interlude.'

'Darling Mag' had complained of the filthy weather up in the Borders; Ramsay saw the bright side of the summer storms. 'Bad weather means less enemy air and motorboat action and is unsuitable for the launching of the invasion armada,' he told her. 'If the weather really has broken up after the prolonged fine spell, it may well spoil Hitler's carefully worked out plans and as time is on our side, it is a pleasant thought.'

That thought would have dissolved away in the weeks that followed; first, with the increasing numbers of bomber raids, and then, during the midst of the Battle of Britain, the bombardment of Dover and Folkestone by German long-range guns. Yet Ramsay contrived throughout all of this to maintain a lively Dover social life; and local aristocrats and minor royals found the time to visit him even among the pandemonium of air-raid sirens and falling bombs. The architect of the Dunkirk evacuation also seemed to embody that spirit which was now being so frequently invoked; tough and practical, and yet with a whimsical side that could lead him to moon over the 'loveliness' of the countryside or fret about the difficulty of getting hold of decent brandy.

Like everyone else, this was just the start of Admiral Ramsay's war: there were many harrowing days to come. But his remarkable achievement was somehow in resetting the national attitude to it. In the aftermath of Dunkirk, there was neither the over-weening self-confidence of a country that had beaten the Germans once before; nor, at this moment of existential crisis, was there much apparent appetite for making terms. Everyone knew that the fight would go on. And the tone that we hear in Admiral Ramsay's letters to his wife are echoed in various diaries and Mass Observation entries. Perhaps the leitmotif of getting on with life – having guests round for tea, keeping the garden in good order – might have erred slightly towards the self-conscious; but no matter. Hitler's forces had paused before, in May, whether intentionally or not, allowing the BEF to reach Dunkirk. During this longer pause over the weeks of summer before the onslaught of the Luftwaffe a miserable failure had been neatly turned around; not by the Prime Minister, or his government ministers, or the denizens of the Ministry of Information, but from the very start by all those women who rushed out to greet the trains.

Days before the people of Kent watched, mesmerised, as the battle for England unfolded in white lines on blue above their heads, slight adjustments were made to the normal British routines. The Derby was run, for instance, just a week after Dunkirk; but it was renamed 'The War Derby' and the atmosphere was reported as being 'sober' (though we might assume that this was meant in a relative sense). The FA Cup final also went ahead, on 10 June, though for this day it was renamed 'The War Cup'. West Ham met Blackburn Rovers at Wembley and beat them 1–0. 'The audience insisted on colour despite the official decision to reduce pomp and circumstance to a minimum,' went the match report. 'All [they] did was replace the trappings of royalty by the striped shirtings and brightly coloured braces of the happy cockney.'

Meanwhile, was Herbert Morrison, the Minister for Supply, first to coin the 'spirit' phrase? Certainly he was among the first; on 13 June 1940, in a radio broadcast, he declared: 'Millions of men and women in Britain are working harder than they have ever worked in their lives before. They have caught the spirit of Dunkirk.'

On 30 June, Air Marshal Goering ordered the Luftwaffe to draw the RAF into battle. That weekend, even without knowing of such orders, British civilians and soldiers alike seemed prepared. With young pilots on the knife-edge of standby, and with the entire east coast – 'from the Wash to the Tweed' – declared a defence area, the spirit was active. It was even to be seen in a newspaper advertisement for 'Marshall and Snellgrove's ladies fashions', featuring an illustration of a fancy hat which was in fact 'steel-lined millinery . . . this becoming hat has a "stelmet" – steel-lining giving protection. No one knows you are wearing it.' Churchill's oratory is widely credited as having steeled the British people for the conflict to come; but there is every sign that the British people had reached the same conclusions quite spontaneously, and without his prompting. And it seemed, via some morphic resonance, that 'the spirit of Dunkirk' was transferable; that combination of endurance, bravery and mad good humour in the face of an almighty onslaught had spread fast from the bloody French beaches to the whole of Britain.

18
The Moment of Dunkirk

The phrase lodged in everyday language, and it has been there ever since. Just a few weeks after the Battle of Britain, and while the infernos of the Blitz were roaring, in November 1940 a special ceremony was held in Brighton to award brass plaques to the sailors who had crewed the little ships. Admiral Beamish spoke of the way that the nation had been defined: 'We rose to the occasion in the old way with our good humour and good nature . . . the world looked on, the world marvelled.' And this was thanks not just to the navy and the army, but also to 'our sea-faring islanders' with their 'skill and spirit'.

The 1940 success of *Guilty Men*, with all its florid finger-waggling, perhaps was the prompt for similarly speedy literary efforts. At the end of that extraordinary summer of Spitfires, two new books materialised on the bookstalls, giving concise accounts of the Dunkirk retreat. *Dunkirk and After* was by Gordon Beckles – 'one of Europe's highest paid journalists', as the curious advertisement ran. 'There is much evidence of hurried judgement,' sniffed one reviewer, who disliked the prose but liked the '64 pages of excellent photographs'. There was also James Lansdale Hodson's *Gentlemen of Dunkirk.* A journalist who had been with the BEF all the way through the retreat, Hodson depicted in his account men fighting with valour in the midst of failure and betrayal; those themes were now set in concrete. As far as the reading public was concerned, there were none to match the Tommies in terms of moral courage, and if they had not been so terribly let down by Belgium, as well as by insufficient preparation, then the day would not have been lost.

Against the predictions of government psychologists who had warned of mass psychosis, the British public absorbed the Blitz against London and other industrial cities in September and throughout that autumn and winter. They had at last fully awoken from the odd torpor of the 'Bore War'. The evacuated soldiers, who had by now been returned to their barracks to receive fresh training and fresh equipment, received all sorts of new orders. Some were sent out very quickly to Cairo and Alexandria in Egypt, in readiness for conflict with Mussolini's forces in the sands of North Africa. Others found themselves posted to defensive duties around the country. And Churchill's fresh government of unity now began in earnest the business of controlling production, output, consumption and – as far as it could – morale. The days of Dunkirk had produced not just an electric shock, but also a sort of national burst of energy.

And throughout those days and weeks and months of bomber raids and constant, exhausting alert – from ARP wardens to civilians crouching in their corrugated iron Anderson shelters – the story of Dunkirk was further burnished. A few months after the event, in 1941, the Poet Laureate John Masefield (a sailing man himself) published *The Nine Days Wonder,* a blend of reportage and poetry devoted entirely to the evacuation. Reflecting on the logistics of the little ships and 'knowing some of the difficulties', he wrote, 'I should say that the Operation was the greatest thing this nation has ever done.' Having offered admiring descriptions of captains, of silent soldiers, of airmen forced to bail out and fired upon mistakenly by

Belgian soldiers, and of naval ratings, Masefield rhetorically asked why it was that the Germans – so overwhelming in numbers and power – did not prevail. The answer: 'He came up against the spirit of this Nation,' which, 'when roused, will do great things.' Masefield continued:

> The Nation rose to the lifting of the Armies as to no other event in recent times. It was an inspiration to all, to feel that will to save running through the land. The event was as swift as Life; no possible preparation could be made; the thing fell suddenly, and had to be met on the instant. Instantly, in reply to the threat, came the will to help from the whole marine population of these islands . . . Hope and Help came together in their power into the minds of thousands of simple men, who went out into the Operation Dynamo and plucked them from ruin.[1]

There were also several poems, among them 'To the Seamen', which contained the lines:

> Through the long time the story will be told;
> Long centuries of praise on English lips,
> Of courage godlike and of hearts of gold
> Off Dunkerque beaches in the little ships.

The short book was a tremendous success. It was also adapted into a BBC radio programme blending readings and music; very much now a part of what was becoming known to some as 'The People's War'. Dunkirk had quickly come to seem a symbol for that war.

This phrase, 'The People's War', had actually been around for a while, even during the days of Chamberlain and appeasement. It took a hard-edged satirist to express a comic (and right-wing) distaste for the term. *Put Out More Flags*, Evelyn Waugh's 'Phoney

War' comic novel – which piercingly lampooned the Ministry of Information among other targets – was published in 1942. And yet even in the satire, the subject of Dunkirk itself received a different emphasis of treatment:

> Finally, when it was plain . . . that in the space of a few days England had lost both the entire stores and equipment of her regular army and her only ally; that the enemy were less than 25 miles from her shores; that there were only a few battalions of fully armed, fully trained troops in the country; that she was committed to a war in the Mediterranean with a numerically superior enemy; that her cities lay open to air attack from fields closer to home than the extremities of her own islands; that her sea routes were threatened from a dozen new bases, Sir Joseph said: 'Seen in the proper perspective I regard this as a great and tangible success. Germany set out to destroy our army and failed; we have demonstrated our invincibility to the world.'[2]

The comedy seemed to suggest that the English – and their upper classes in particular – were hopeless, and either fools or mad. But actually, strangely, there is a sense of proud invincibility there too. If the phrase had once had Trotskyist overtones, as Waugh suggested, 'The People's War' was now a mainstream term, a commonplace sentiment.

Sentiment of a different kind was found in a hugely popular 1940 short story, later lengthened to a novella, called 'The Snow Goose: A Story of Dunkirk' by American author Paul Gallico. A love story set on the bleak Essex marshes, the story sees the romantic (and hunchbacked) artist hero sail out from his lighthouse in his small boat to help at Dunkirk; the doom of war closes in on him and the girl who loves him. It is still in print, a quiet favourite of many.

But Dunkirk, for some, had political reverberations too; seen as a catalyst for which the vast majority of people had been waiting.

In his essay 'The Lion and the Unicorn', written in 1941, George Orwell stated baldly:

> The English Revolution started several years ago and it began to gather momentum when the troops came back from Dunkirk. Like all else in England, it happens in a sleepy unwilling way but it is happening . . . The war and the revolution are inseparable. We cannot establish anything that a western nation would regard as socialism without defeating Hitler; on the other hand, we cannot defeat Hitler while we remain economically and socially in the nineteenth century. The past is fighting the future.[3]

Orwell had identified the groundswell of thought that was to result in the following year's Beveridge Report and, after the war, in the inception of the welfare state; and he had identified this strong desire for change, for modernity, in the men who trooped wearily off the boats. This was a time when the graffito 'Uncle Joe for King' was seen in naval barracks. There were numbers of young working men who – knowing nothing of the truth of 1930s Soviet Russia – had fixed on it as the ideal society. Meanwhile, middle-class Britain in the 1930s – especially in the south-east and the expanding Home Counties towns – had enjoyed growing wealth. Yet it was these middle managers in the new modern industries who also saw the need for a social earthquake – the cutting of the old school tie. Dunkirk might be identified as a point when the country was catapulted fully into the modern world.

But posterity had to be attended to. Winston Churchill, ousted as Prime Minister and Leader of the Opposition in chilly 1949, was persuaded to make recordings of his finest wartime speeches; so, once again, those beaches were invoked. They were also frequently invoked by other politicians. Dunkirk became synonymous with another attractive idea that the English had about themselves; that they would leave everything until the last possible moment but then suddenly pull triumph from the most hopeless situation.

One of the very last films made at Ealing Studios was *Dunkirk*, which opened in 1958; the cast list now is almost a parody of that period of British cinema, ranging from John Mills to Bernard Lee and every other familiar face from that time. But the film itself was sober, and to an extent, realistic. There were no 'phoney heroics', as one reviewer approvingly noted; and, indeed, an unusual amount of bleakness. There were uncomfortable scenes involving Belgian refugees, along with a not entirely flattering portrait of the army's command structure. Another reviewer adroitly described the film's appeal as lying in the fact that the story was now a 'national religious experience'.

Since then, that 'religious experience' has lost little of its potency. And as one would expect from a religion, it has phrases that here are offered as secular prayers or mantras. In 1964, one of the most shameless invocations – and by no means the last – came from Prime Minister Harold Wilson. His incoming Labour government had been hit by an attack on sterling almost as soon as it came into power, and at the party conference he declared: 'They misjudged our temper after Dunkirk but we so mobilised our talent and untapped strength that apparent defeat was turned into a great victory. I believe that the spirit of Dunkirk will once more carry us through to success.'

He was laughed at for this comparison; but the phrase was ingrained in the national consciousness. Wimbledon commentators used it; everyone facing power cuts during the three-day week of 1973 used it. The phrase was mostly used in a semi-jocular fashion, with a hint of black humour about it. No matter how awful things got, the Dunkirk spirit would somehow see us through. The phrase was even picked up – with quite staggering nerve – by Argentina's General Galtieri in 1982 when he suggested that with some Dunkirk spirit, his country could soon reclaim the Falkland Islands from the British soldiers who had fought back the original incursion.

It has had a more powerful artistic afterlife; in his 2001 novel *Atonement*, later successfully adapted for the screen, Ian McEwan gave a searing account of the beaches, the backdrop to the violent and horribly unjust misfortunes of the novel's protagonist. C.J. Sansom's recent *Dominion* posited a world in which Britain sued for peace after Dunkirk; this parallel-world story is set in the 1950s where Britain has a Vichy-style government and Churchill is leading the resistance movement. Lately, there has been a reprint of Mary Renault's extraordinary 1953 novel *The Charioteer*, set in 1940, which focuses on a corporal recovering in hospital from his experiences at Dunkirk and his burgeoning gay relationship with a conscientious objector – highly unusual subject matter for the 1950s. But it is the fact of Dunkirk that gives the book an even greater frisson of power.

Politicians will never resist invoking those days. During the January floods of 2014, ministers were once again telling us about the need for the spirit of Dunkirk. But this is really not how all those soldiers, all those pilots and sailors and ships, should be remembered. For what we see now in the boats, in the veterans' accounts, touches us all on a deeper level.

The figure most commonly cited is around 68,000; that is, the number of men in the BEF who were killed, wounded or captured. Other figures suggest that of that number, some 3500 were killed in May and June 1940; according to the Dunkirk memorial, set in a dignified garden on the edge of the town, with graves from both wars, the figure was in the region of 4500. Many more deaths were to come a few weeks later when the Germans sank HMS *Lancastria*, creating the most horrific death toll, among whom were around 5000 soldiers. For the summer of 1940, the total figure of those killed in the BEF is something like 11,000. During the retreat and the evacuation, figures also indicate that some 14,000 men were wounded. Those taken prisoner were numbered at around 41,000.

But such bald numbers can only ever be abstractions. No one can really imagine 11,000 dead bodies. The weight and bulk of such statistics is matched against the colour cine footage taken by the triumphant Germans as they entered Dunkirk; the macabre sight of a British corpse in the oily water, the body having been brought back in by the tide. Only then can you start to extrapolate, to envisage the blood in the dunes, the charred remains in the bombed-out Dunkirk basements. No matter how much time Reg Vine had spent in his uncle's abattoir, nothing could have prepared him for any of that. Think also of the young seaman Vic Viner – a lad with a revolver, commanded to keep control of 150 frustrated, angry, frightened men, the sands around them sown with the dead. Many veterans are blithe and light now even about the banshee scream of the German planes, the increasing shortages of food and water on those reddened beaches, under that hot sky; they were not blithe then.

Gareth Wright had enjoyed a brief taste of 'Saturday night soldiering' as a Territorial reserve in 1939. After the nightmarish events of Dunkirk, the soldiering was not only real but also armed him with the experience he needed for what was to come. After a few weeks in Essex bases, he was sent out to North Africa; his first destination was Casablanca. By now he and his friends were acutely aware of what the enemy could do. The same was true of Clydeside apprentice Bob Halliday, who set sail for Alexandria that autumn. One Dunkirk legacy became a serious issue on that voyage; the young man collapsed, bleeding profusely from one ear. They got him off board at the port and whisked him through for expert medical treatment. It was found that Mr Halliday was missing an eardrum. This had been the effect of the bomb blast near the Dunkirk beach which had lifted him off his feet and smashed him into a garage wall. Somehow or other the young man had, since then, put up with the discomfort from his ear. Rather like soldier Harry Malpas, who had a shot-out knee replaced by a German field surgeon, Mr Halliday had his eardrum reconstructed – something of a miracle in 1940. But it was felt that he could not be expected to fight in an environment where the ubiquitous sand might at any point enter that ear and cause more problems. He was to be shipped home; but at the last minute, Mr Halliday made a case for staying and joining the navy in the Mediterranean instead.

Just a year before, these lads had been apprentices, shop delivery boys, trainee tailors. Now they were disciplined fighting men. At Dunkirk and at Dover now, there are memorials to the fallen. The Dunkirk lists of the dead show a striking fact; for all those in their early twenties, there is a surprising number of soldiers who would have termed themselves 'the old sweats' – men well into their forties. One private who fell was forty-eight years old. He was old enough to have fought in the Great War. But for those who escaped – the overwhelming bulk – those days and nights were a rite of passage, a searing initiation. It was an emergency that no number of war games or training exercises could ever have hoped to simulate. It required not just bravery, in the face of a terrifying relentless aerial attack, but also patience and grace. Such qualities are sometimes innate. When they are not, they are all the more admirable.

Medic Charles Searle recalls the summer of 1944, the Normandy landings, the push through France. He was among those who tended to liberated prisoners of war in 1945. He also saw the concentration camps. Mr Searle remembers one man who – having been starved for so long – ate ravenously when a stew was made. The prisoner ate too much, and his shrunken stomach and disgestive system couldn't cope. He died, hideously. In other words, Mr Searle went out and saw much – horror as well as beauty – from Germany to India. But Dunkirk stays with him especially as the time when his eyes were opened to just how dark the world could be; the sight of German pilots following the line of white dusty French roads and aiming their guns not at soldiers, but at scattering women and children attempting to flee.

Young sailor Vic Viner later took part in the most crucial of missions – on a destroyer protecting the merchant convoys, Britain's fragile lifelines, up through the North Sea and to the Arctic, sailing among lethal minefields, being constantly stalked by silent U-boats.

It was not unrelentingly bleak; Mr Viner now particularly recalls the pleasure of catching the freshest fish. He had had many years' experience, starting out as a boy in 1933 and sailing off to corners of the world as yet untouched by the twentieth century. But Dunkirk was the moment when he understood the full, terrible gravity of war. His elder brother had perished in the flames of that noble, heroic, silly paddle steamer the *Crested Eagle.* As Mr Viner patrolled the beaches with a revolver, the soul-shaking thuds of landing bombs sending concentric ripples of shock through the air, it is somehow extraordinary that he survived whereas his brother had not. The result in later life was a continual series of alarmed flashbacks. 'That screaming noise of the Stukas,' he says. 'I've got DVDs, a few of the documentaries, and play them loud, just to hear it – when the dive-bomber comes, my stomach gives a little jerk even after all this time.

'That noise put terror into men. And if you think that that noise would have gone into someone who was already on the end of his rope, that must have been a thing that blew him out.

'Well, it did affect me of course. Twenty years after the war had ended, I was in bed, and I suddenly jumped out of bed and hit my head on the bedroom wall. My wife didn't quite know what had happened. It was only then that I told her what, twenty years back, I had really been through.

'I had nightmares now and again, obviously, but you would do, wouldn't you? I kept them to myself. I didn't tell anybody. And I had a breakdown and I didn't even tell the doctor.' He recovered very quickly, but his doctor was intrigued. 'The doctor said to my wife later: "Vic has had some mental shake-out somewhere. But I've asked him and he says he doesn't know what happened. He's not told me." I didn't tell my first doctor until many years afterwards.' Mr Viner thinks now – and a later doctor agreed with him – that if he had spoken about it, then this breakdown might have been avoided. Certainly, he had no problems after he had opened up about his experiences. But after the war, in wider terms, there was a curious clamming up going on all over. Part of it was self-imposed;

most families will have memories of a grandfather or great-uncle who would always refuse to be drawn on the subject of the war. Reinforcing this, as veterans now recall, was the very strong sense that actually, no one *wanted* them to talk, and no one wanted to hear. Who can say how much damage and suffering was caused in the post-war years by that silence?

Oddly, the legend of Dunkirk was one of those things that helped to fill the strange silence. Veterans might not have spoken of their individual experiences, but there was something about the sheer communality of the evacuation that made it possible to revisit in general terms. For it wasn't just about the soldiers; this was the start of the wider People's War.

Another crucial trigger for affectionate recall: so many of the little ships, in the aftermath of the war, were returned to their old roles. The Thames motor yachts once more glided past the aristocratic splendour of Cliveden; paddle steamers returned to the Isle of Wight, where their defiantly old-fashioned air made them even more charming for pleasure seekers. The cockle boats of Leigh-on-Sea got back to their hard work. And boats such as these are now living history; after invaluable work by the Association of Dunkirk Little Ships to make sure the stories were known, they have the most extraordinary resonance. Many, sadly, could not be preserved. Some of them were already ancient by the time they reached Dunkirk in 1940; some of the pleasure boats ended up rotting away.

But there were still more than enough vessels to take part in the Queen's Jubilee Pageant in 2012. On that unseasonably cold 3 June, there were thirty-nine of the little boats that had taken part in Operation Dynamo. Out at the front of the procession near the Royal Barge was MTB 102 (MTB standing for motor torpedo boat), which not only saw action at Dunkirk but also carried Churchill and Eisenhower in 1944 at the time of D-Day. The rest sailed downriver, through the City of London, under Tower Bridge and past the Queen and the Duke of Edinburgh as they stood at St Katharine's

Dock. The boats ploughed through a chilling silvery mist. The veterans on board, knees wrapped in tartan rugs, were kept well supplied with nips of spirits. The pageant – with its total of 670 vessels – was intended as a celebration of Britain's maritime nature. The little ships of Dunkirk received the most attention; recent history has the greater emotional resonance. The boats evoke an odd mix of fascination and unconditional affection. Moreover, to see them sailing on the river, it was impossible for anyone not to try and picture them out in the Channel, so acutely naked and vulnerable to the enemy above. It was impossible not to imagine these delicate looking craft sailing through shimmering infernos, their unprotected crews simply focusing on keeping their eyes front.

The sight of the boats also offered a seductive line of continuity, all the way back to the seafaring spirit of the first Elizabethan age. Later that day, as the little ships docked in the futuristic mini city state of Canary Wharf – a universe away from the dirty old working river that so many evacuation volunteers saw on those summer's evenings sailing down the estuary to the dark sea – the veterans disembarked. The backdrop may have been sleekly modern but the boats on the water were an unchanging portal to the past. And that was at the heart of the day, for 95-year-old Vic Viner and for others; that the past never really dies. And that a story such as Dunkirk – so bizarre, random and occasionally tragi-comic, as well as heroic and horrifying – will continue to live on. It is not only about crisis, and deliverance, and the defiance of death with good humour. It continues – and will continue – to resonate because underneath all that, it is the glittering thread of a river leading to the open sea, and to an unknowable world beyond; and the desire to make that voyage, no matter what.

Notes

1 'Would You Like to Join the Army?'

1 Mass Observation Diarist 5039, Highams Park. The Mass Observation archives are held at the University of Sussex
2 Mass Observation Diarist 5035
3 Alan Bullock, *Life and Times of Ernest Bevin*, Vol. 1, Heinemann, 1960, cited by Daniel Hucker in 'Franco-British Relations And The Question of Conscription 1938–39', *Contemporary European History*, November 2008
4 Anne Olivier Bell, ed., *The Diary of Virginia Woolf 1936–41*, Hogarth Press, 1984
5 Quoted from Henry Green, *Pack My Bag*, Hogarth Press, 1940

2 'Their Tax in Blood'

1 William Philpott and Martin S. Alexander, 'The French and British Field Force: Moral Support of Material Contribution?', *Journal of Military History*, July 2007
2 Talbot Charles Imlay, 'A Reassessment of Anglo-French Strategy During

the Phony War 1939–40', *English Historical Review*, April 2004
3 Philpott and Alexander, 'The French and British Field Force'
4 Cited in Madeleine Mayhew, 'The 1930s Nutrition Controversy', *Journal of Contemporary History*, July 1988
5 Mayhew, 'The 1930s Nutrition Controversy'
6 As quoted on the BBC's *The People's War* webpage, 2003, www.bbc.co.uk/history/ww2peopleswar
7 Philpott and Alexander, 'The French and British Field Force'
8 BBC, *The People's War*, 2004

3 'They Threw Us In'

1 Jeffrey Legro, 'Military Culture and Inadvertent Escalation in World War II', *International Security*, Spring 1994
2 Bell, ed., *The Diary of Virginia Woolf 1936–41*
3 BBC, *The People's War*, 2003
4 Moir's account can be found at www.harry-tates.org.uk, along with other veterans' stories
5 Brian P. Farrell, 'Admiral Bertram Ramsay', *Oxford Dictionary of National Biography*
6 Letter from Admiral Whitworth, Ramsay Collection, Churchill College, Cambridge
7 This and all subsequent quotations from Admiral Bertram Ramsay's correspondence are from the Ramsay Collection, held at Churchill College, Cambridge
8 Samuel Hynes, 'War Stories: Myths of World War II', Johns Hopkins University Press, Winter 1992
9 Frances Partridge, *A Pacifist's War*, Hogarth Press, 1978
10 Professor David Dilks, 'The Twilight War and the Fall of France: Chamberlain and Churchill in 1940', Royal Historical Society, 1978
11 As quoted in John D. Fair, 'The Norwegian Campaign and Winston Churchill's Rise to Power in 1940', *International History Review*, July 1987

4 Blitzkrieg

1 Colonel J. Lee's full account is held in the National Archives, Kew
2 Roy Jenkins, *Churchill*, Pan, 2001
3 Norman Longmate, ed., *The Home Front: An Anthology of Personal Experience*, Chatto and Windus, 1981
4 Colonel J. Lee, National Archives, Kew
5 Bell, ed., *The Diary of Virginia Woolf 1936–41*
6 David K. Yelton, 'British Public Opinion, the Home Guard and the Defence of Britain, 1940–44', *The Journal of Military History*, July 1994
7 Angus Calder, *The People's War: Britain 1939–45*, Jonathan Cape, 1969
8 Joel Blatt, 'The French Defeat of 1940: Reassessments', *Reflexions Historiques*, Winter 1996
9 Martin Alexander, 'Fighting to the Last Frenchman? Reflections on the BEF Deployment to France and the Strains in the Franco-British Alliance 1930–40', *Reflexions Historiques*, Winter 1996

5 'They Just Kept Marching Us'

1 Paul Addison and Jeremy A. Crang, eds, *Listening to Britain: Home Intelligence Reports on Britain's Finest Hour*, Random House, 2011
2 Brian Foss, 'Message and Medium: Government Patronage, National Identity and National Culture in Britain', *Oxford Art Journal*, 1991
3 Mass Observation diarist 5032 (male, young Londoner)
4 Bell, ed., *The Diary of Virginia Woolf 1936–41*
5 David Woodward, *Ramsay at War: The Fighting of Admiral Sir Bertram Ramsay*, William Kimber, 1957
6 Quoted in John C. Cairns, 'De Gaulle Confronts the British: The Legacy of 1940', *International Journal*, Spring 1968
7 Cairns, 'De Gaulle Confronts the British: The Legacy of 1940'

6 'A Ring of Steel and Fire'

1 Diary entry of Evelyn Waugh, as quoted in John Lukacs, *Five Days in London*, Yale University Press, 2001
2 BBC, *The People's War*, 2003

7 Dynamo

1 Quoted in Walter Lord, *The Miracle of Dunkirk*, Allen Lane, 1983

2 BBC, *The People's War*, 2004

3 Quoted in Woodward, *Ramsay at War*

4 As recounted in Lord, *The Miracle of Dunkirk*

5 BBC, *The People's War*, 2004

6 Douglas Gough's account held by Shropshire Libraries, and quoted in BBC, *The People's War*, 2004

7 Geoffrey Nickholds's account contributed by his son Peter to BBC, *The People's War*, 2005

8 'Just Follow the Ferries'

1 Quoted in Lord, *The Miracle of Dunkirk*

2 Quoted in 'Dunkirk Logs' on the website www.thamestugs.co.uk

3 Christian Brann, *The Little Ships of Dunkirk*, Collectors' Books, 1989

9 'Blood All Over Your Hands'

1 Quoted in David J. Knowles, *Escape from Catastrophe*, Knowles Publishing, 2000

2 Quoted in Knowles, *Escape from Catastrophe*

3 Quoted in Knowles, *Escape from Catastrophe*

10 'The Hour Is Too Solemn'

1 Ben Pimlott, ed., *The Second World War Diary of Hugh Dalton*, Cape, 1986

2 BBC, *The People's War*, 2004

3 Quoted on www.qaranc.co.uk, which also contains a fuller account of the Queen Alexandra Royal Naval Nursing Service, and in particular the hospital ships

4 Quoted in Robert Kershaw, *Never Surrender: Lost Voices of a Generation at War*, Hodder and Stoughton, 2009

11 'What Have We Let Ourselves In For?'

1 Quoted in Knowles, *Escape from Catastrophe*

2 Mass Observation diarist 5422 (female, London)

3 Quoted in Knowles, *Escape from Catastrophe*

12 'I'll Come Looking for You!'

1 Mass Observation diarist 5039 (male, London)

2 Private D. Warren, 2nd Battalion Hampshire Regiment, National Archives, Kew

3 From Peter Davison, ed., *The Complete Works of George Orwell*, Vol. 12, *A Patriot After All*, Secker and Warburg, 1998

4 Davison, ed., *The Complete Works of George Orwell*, Vol. 12

13 Remote in Some Dream of Pain

1 Charles Graves, *Women In Green – The Story of the Women's Voluntary Service*, Heinemann, 1948

2 Graves, *Women In Green*

14 'Beyond the Limits of Endurance'

1 An interesting analysis of the impact of French collapse in 1940 is David Reynolds, 'Fulcrum of the 20th Century?', *International Affairs*, April 1990

2 Davison, ed., *The Complete Works of George Orwell*, Vol. 12

3 John Thornton's account, held by Warwickshire Libraries, and given to BBC, *The People's War*, 2005

4 Quoted in Woodward, *Ramsay at War*

15 The Spontaneous Legend

1 Quoted in Nigel West, ed., *The Guy Liddell Diaries*, Frank Cass, 2009

2 Psychiatrists' essays held in the Ramsay Collection, Churchill College, Cambridge

3 Mass Observation diarist 5420 (female, Birmingham)

16 'Very Well – Alone'

1 Professor Winifred Cullis of the British Information Service went on to write wartime essays such as 'Impact of War Upon British Home Life' (1942)

2 Mass Observation diarist 5039, Highams Park

3 Francis Williams, ed., *A Prime Minister Remembers: The War and Post-War Memoirs of the Rt Hon Earl Attlee*, Heinemann, 1961

17 The Guilt and the Wonder

1 Quoted from 'Cato', *Guilty Men*, Victor Gollancz, 1940

2 From Foreword to Penguin 1998 reissue of *Guilty Men* by Michael Foot, one of the original authors behind 'Cato'

18 The Moment of Dunkirk

1 John Masefield, *The Nine Days Wonder*, William Heinemann, 1941

2 Evelyn Waugh, *Put Out More Flags*, Chapman and Hall, 1942

3 George Orwell, *The Lion and the Unicorn*, Secker and Warburg, 1941

Acknowledgements

First, an enormous debt of gratitude to Ian Gilbert, Commodore of the Association of Dunkirk Little Ships. Thanks to him, and the Association, I was privileged to meet and interview an array of distinguished and fascinating veterans. For further information on the work and activities of the ADLS, visit the website www.adls.org.uk. There you will also find beguiling pictures and details of the wide range of little ships and their varied careers. Obviously, a huge debt of gratitude as well to all the veterans and their families who were so generous with their time, among whom were Arthur Taylor, Nic and Stephen Taylor, Jean Malpas, Reg Vine, Vic Viner, Bob Halliday, Gareth Wright, Charles Searle, and also to Jean Valentine and Patricia Clark, whose memories prompted further enquiries. Many thanks also to Andrew Riley of the Churchill College Archives Centre, custodians of the papers of Admiral Ramsay, and also to David Ramsay, son of the above, who pointed me in the direction of this limitlessly absorbing collection of letters, memos and documents. Thanks also to Sarah Sinclair at the Naval and Military Club, and

Victoria Thompson at the Imperial War Museum. Extra gratitude to Graham Coster and Iain MacGregor; thanks also to Steve Gove for such fine, patient editing, Lucy Warburton for pulling the whole thing together so skilfully and brilliant Jessica Axe for so ingeniously letting the world know.

Selected Further Reading

Addison, Paul and Crang, Jeremy, eds, *Listening to Britain: Home Intelligence Reports on Britain's Finest Hour*, Bodley Head, 2010

Bell, Anne Olivier, ed., *The Diary of Virginia Woolf*, vol 5, Hogarth Press, 1984

Brann, Christian, *The Little Ships of Dunkirk* , Collectors Books, 1989

Briggs, Asa, *Go To It! Working For Victory on the Home Front* Mitchell Beazley, 2000

Broad, Richard, and Fleming, Suzie, eds, *Nella Last's War: A Mother's Diary 1939–45*, Profile, 2006

Calder, Angus, *The Peoples War*, Pimlico, 1992

'Cato', *Guilty Men*, Victor Gollancz, 1940

Chalmers, Rear Admiral W.S., *Full Cycle: Ramsay*, Hodder, 1959

Colville, John, *The Fringes of Power – the Downing Street Diaries 1939–55*, Weidenfeld and Nicolson, 2004

Davison, Peter, ed., *The Complete Works of George Orwell*, vol 12: *A Patriot After All*, Secker and Warburg, 1988

Divine, A. D., *Nine Days of Dunkirk*, Faber and Faber, 1959

Gallico, Paul, *The Snow Goose*, Michael Joseph, 1941

Garfield, Simon, ed., *We Are At War*, Ebury, 2005

Gates, Eleanor, *End of the Affair: Collapse of the Anglo French Alliance 1939–40*, Allen and Unwin, 1981

Goddard, Victor, *Skies to Dunkirk – A Personal Memoir*, Kimber, 1982

Harrisson, Tom, and Madge, Charles, *Britain by Mass Observation*, Cresset Library, 1986

Jenkins, Roy, *Churchill*, Macmillan, 2001

Knowles, David J., *Escape From Catastrophe – 1940 Dunkirk*, Knowles Publishing, 2000

Lord, Walter, *The Miracle of Dunkirk*, Allen Lane, 1982

Lukacs, John, *Five Days In London: May 1940*, Yale University Press, 1999

Masefield, John, *The Nine Days Wonder*, Heinemann, 1941

Montefiore, Hugh Sebag, *Dunkirk: Fight To The Last Man*, Viking, 2006

Neave, Airey, *The Flames of Calais: A Soldier's Battle*, Hodder, 1972

Renault, Mary, *The Charioteer*, Virago, 2013

Tebutt, Melanie, *Being Boys: Youth, Leisure and Identity in the Inter-War Years*, Manchester University Press, 2013

Thompson, Julian, *Dunkirk: Retreat to Victory*, Sidgwick and Jackson, 2008

West, Nigle, ed., *The Guy Liddell Diaries*, Vol 1, Routledge, 2005

Woodward, David, *Ramsay At War: The Fighting of Admiral Bertram Ramsay* Kimber, 1957

Index